Renewing Gender

Renewing Gender

An Orthodox Perspective

Jean-Claude Larchet

Translated from the French
by Archibald Andrew Torrance

Holy Trinity Publications
Holy Trinity Seminary Press
Holy Trinity Monastery
Jordanville, New York
2025

Printed with the blessing of His Grace,
Bishop Luke of Syracuse
and Abbot of Holy Trinity Monastery

HTSP
HOLY TRINITY
SEMINARY PRESS

An imprint of:
Holy Trinity Publications
Holy Trinity Monastery
1407 Robinson Road, Jordanville, NY, 13361
holytrinitypublications.com

ISBN: 978-1-942699-57-6 (paperback)
ISBN: 978-1-942699-61-3 (ePub)

Library of Congress Control Number: 2025939814

Cover: Digital illustration: "Hands reaching" by Rrose Selavy; Adobe Stock No. 507470044. "Texture-background," freepik.com; No.1137413

Printed in the United States of America
by Versa Press Inc. 1465 Spring Bay Road, East Peoria, IL, 61611
versapress.com

Contents

Introduction

Over the last twenty years, three schools of thought have come from the United States and have imposed themselves on Western Society. First, there is gender theory which lies at the root of every kind of "gender study". Secondly, there is radical feminism, and thirdly "woke thought" closely linked to it.

The strength of their impact may be gauged by the enormous number of studies, both for and against, devoted to them, by the way they have been introduced into educational institutions and by the way they have been backed by legislation in almost all the societies of the world.

Their success arises from their active promotion by a small number of unrepresentative groups from the LGBTQI+ movement. These, using militant tactics, try to justify all manner of sexual orientation and behavior differing from heterosexuality. They are supported by most of the media in the West, which are themselves pressured by international institutions. This all fits into an ultra-liberal worldwide political movement which seeks systematically to support minorities. This has gradually so impressed itself on our minds that men and women are no longer conscious of their identities of sex and gender, and this undermines their relationships. A world which has lost all its bearings has been a fertile field for these ideas. The ethics of the past are ignored, and mankind has adopted an individualistic and promethean idea of freedom, under the illusion that an individual can self-define independently of any natural fact.

These ideas have provoked a strong reaction since they are being imposed by a tiny minority on the majority of mankind. They propose, as did the totalitarians of the twentieth century, to create a new man in a new world with new morals. They enforce their ideas with a repressive legal apparatus designed to stifle all criticism. In this, they imitate the methods of totalitarian regimes, but less visibly: "soft totalitarianism" as some say.

Christianity is targeted by these thought systems. It is seen as responsible for the relationships that have pertained between man and woman for 2000 years and for their character acknowledged by Western civilization. It is blamed for this. Its basic ethical and anthropological teachings are rejected and deliberately deconstructed, decomposed by design. Christian ideals are opposed under a cloak of tolerance and inclusion and the result is hatred and division at every level of society: married couples, families, and communities.

The present work is based on the vast literature that concerns gender theory and the radical feminism which is akin to it. It also draws from writings on the nature of mankind and the relations between man and woman as seen by Christianity, enlightened by the Bible's teaching and the anthropology developed by the Church Fathers. It aims to bring clarity to the present confusion, examining what lies beneath modern trends of thought, what they provoke in society, and how they ascribe to Christianity positions which it does not truly hold.

As regards this last point, we do not intend simply to oppose one concept by another. We show that certain Fathers of the Church developed a most subtle exegesis of the text of Genesis which can throw light on the ideas of gender theoreticians. Some of the criticisms they level against the social positions of man and woman and their "gender roles"[1] can be acceptable, since sin and the passions of fallen human nature have distorted the identity of each sex and their mutual relationships. Our aim is also to show how Christian spirituality teaches a transfiguration of gender which rises above the limits of fallen nature and the confusion, deviations, and dead ends found in gender theory and radical feminism.

The first part of the book describes the historical and ideological roots of gender theory, of radical feminism and of that part of woke theory linked to it. The reasons for the current flourishing of such ideas are exposed and their weaknesses are identified.

The second part presents the Christian teaching on these ideas. Various common misinterpretations are corrected, of the Bible, of the doctrine of the Church Fathers, and of Christian life. Emphasis is placed on the difference between fallen nature and man's original nature, which is also his nature when perfectly restored in Christ; and also on the difference between gendering and sexuality. The ideal relationship between man and woman is complementary and blossoms in harmony. It should be founded on spiritual love, tempered by the struggle against the passions and the practice of virtue. Monasticism too transfigures gender in its own way. Christian spirituality can bring about, spiritually, a degree of fluidity of genders without, for all that, denying them. The word of St Paul the Apostle: In Christ "there is neither male nor female" (Gal 3:28), understood correctly, is the theme of this second part.

PART ONE:

GENDER THEORY AND ASSOCIATED IDEAS IN THE MODERN WORLD —A CRITICAL ANALYSIS

Chapter 1

The Definition and Roots of Gender Theory

Definition

Over the last ten years gender has become one of the main preoccupations of our age. The philosophical developments it requires have led to much debate, but, more importantly, it has consequences for society in modern mentalities and institutions, especially in medicine, law, and education.

Gender theory has been widely criticized, but those who promote and defend it have rarely faced up to these objections. Instead, they simply say that such a theory does not exist and never has. This bald denial and refusal to engage with criticism are signs of laziness and bad faith. Doubtless it also reveals unease at the pertinence of certain objections. Moreover, it seeks to avoid the connotations of a "theory": a hypothetical intellectual construct which is both fragile and uncertain, falsifiable, and replaceable.[2]

The partisans of gender theory prefer to speak of "gender studies." The word "studies" sounds serious and learned and suggests roots in the universities. Using the plural rightly shows that a unified theory of gender does not exist, just many ideas. They are inspired by different sources and sometimes clash. However, they are all the same at the root, and differ only in secondary matters. It is unreasonable to deny the existence of a gender theory since over the last few years so many books and articles have appeared which promote its principles. It is noteworthy that one of the founders of gender theory, Judith Butler, who is probably its main promoter, regularly uses the term "gender theory." So, there are many reasons to consider that it is legitimate to speak of gender theory, provided due weight is given to the various nuances adopted by its various promoters.

Throughout the history of humanity up till now, in every civilization and society, humanity has been seen as divided into two genders, masculine and feminine, with their special characters, as are most of the animals. These two genders are based on the biological difference between the male and female sexes, naturally linked to them and continuous with them. Gender theory affirms that there is no essential or natural relation between sex and gender apart from what is subjectively imposed by society as a whole or by individuals: the relation established between them is, at the root, purely social or cultural and has nothing to do with the body and its objective sexual attributes. It is artificial, contrived, and so relative, like all other cultural constructs.

From this foundation, gender theoreticians start by saying that these relationships should be undone or deconstructed[3] by destroying the social "stereotypes" on which they are based, for these lead to inequality and discrimination: such inequality is always in favor of men and their victims are women. They base this idea on a system, the patriarchy, which they seek to destroy.

At another level, gender theoreticians have differing views. Some of them state that between masculine and feminine there is a spectrum of genders.[4] Others affirm that there is a third gender: neutral, where those who feel themselves neither man nor woman can be placed along with those who feel they are both at once, either a mixture of the two, or alternating between the two. Others preach purely and simply the abolition of gender to avoid the duality that results from referring one to the other. For them, sex has no objective reality. It is simply a representation which is completely dependent on the representation of gender. Some of them[5] use a formula which recalls the existentialist formula: "existence precedes essence" and affirm that gender precedes sex, or the representation of gender precedes the representation of sex. Then, if one were to destroy the representation of gender, the representation of sex would vanish along with sex itself.

As a result, all of them believe that individuals, once freed from all sexual social conditioning, can freely, as they wish, determine their gender independently of their biological sex and its physiological characteristics, to suit their desires, their preferences, and their phantasms. Someone endowed with the masculine sex, both biologically and physiologically, is free to see himself as being feminine and to live accordingly. Someone of the feminine sex is free to see herself as masculine and to live accordingly. Both may also choose to see themselves as embodying two genders at once, or alternatively as having no gender at all. This is not a question of nature but of individual choice; not of the body's biological and physiological constitution and its appearance, but of self-consciousness and self-representation. Biological sex is of no significance or importance and nor is the body. The important thing is the gender which one chooses for oneself, or which one refuses to choose in one's own individual consciousness.

Some gender theorists accept the different genders, recognizing two or more, but consider that they can be changed at will. Since gender has no root in nature, each individual may enjoy any identity, any sex, and every sexual orientation. Eric Fassin, who translated Judith Butler and introduced gender theory to France writes thus: "The transvestite is everyone's true self."[6] Society assigns a gender to each of its members as a function of each one's biological sex and assigns the role that goes with it. This is replaced by the roles of one or more genders independent of biological sex, defined and chosen by each individual.

Other gender theorists deny that there is any variety in gender and preach a humanity without gender, identifying with "the universal."[7]

One can see that gender theory takes many forms, but all start from the same hard core: the theory that there is no continuity or natural relationship between gender and sex. They are disconnected; so are culture and nature; so are the free orientation of the individual and cultural conditioning. On the practical level this is expressed in the project of deconstructing the social "archetypes" of masculine and feminine through political and social militancy. The aim is to reform society so as to set up, under the cloak of equality, a blurring at every level of the differences between man and woman. Their sexual identity is to be suppressed to allow their attributes to be completely interchangeable.

The diversity of gender theory and its inner unity are explained by its history.

Origins and Development of Gender Theory

Four main stages can be distinguished in the development of gender theory.

A. The Analysis of Pathologies During the Years 1950–1960

The first distinction between sex and gender dates from 1955. It is due to the American psychologist John Money (1921–2006). He studied the clinical case histories of subjects presenting biological characteristics from both sexes. At that time, they were called hermaphrodites, but today they are called intersexuals. He distinguished sexual identity, which is biological, from "gender identity" and the "gender role" through which it is expressed. This corresponds to each individual's subjective perception and to their social experience of masculinity and femininity. According to Money, this perception and the experience that goes with it are determined by society through education and the cultural environment. He saw a confirmation of his theory in the clinical study conducted by the psychiatrists Joan and John Hampton of five hundred hermaphrodites, and went on to apply it to help children, whose birth sex was indeterminate, to extract themselves from this sexual ambiguity. It was a social handicap which he sought to overcome by asking the parents to decide which sex the child should have. He would then prescribe appropriate surgical and hormonal treatments whilst the parents were to bring up the child in accord with what was normal for the chosen sex. By emphasizing the second part, he affirmed that social conditioning was determinant of "gender identity" and the "gender role" assumed by individuals.[8]

Another pioneer in this field is the American psychiatrist Robert Stoller (1924–1991) who founded the Gender Identity Research Clinic. Its purpose was to research human sexuality, and it paid special attention to transgender people those who felt they belonged to the other sex. Stoller used the idea of *gender* to indicate the sentiment of sexual identity, as opposed to sex, which biologically determines the difference between masculine and feminine.[9]

B. The Philosophical Developments of the Years 1960–1970

During the years 1960–1970, a philosophy of gender was developed on three levels.

1) Existentialism affirms that the free subject is prior to his nature or essence: man is not defined *a priori* by an essence, or a nature imposed on him by necessity. Instead, he defines himself during the course of his life, an idea summed up by the famous formula of Sartre: "Existence precedes essence."[10] When applied to sex and gender, this idea implies that anyone may choose a gender independent of sex, which comes from biological nature.

Simone de Beauvoir, Sartre's partner, shared his existentialist philosophy. She was a pioneer of feminism and defended this idea. Her famous formula, which may also be applied to men: "One is not born a woman. One becomes one"[11] is nonetheless ambiguous. Denying the natural property by which gender may be defined implies that it may be determined by individual choice; but it also implies that it may often arise from the influences of life in society, especially education in the family and in schools. This should be seen as relative and should be challenged so as to arrive at some other choice, which brings us back to the original meaning.

2) Marxism was very fashionable at that time in intellectual circles, and several leading feminists, such as Monique Wittig and Christiane Delphy adopted its ideas. They thought of the relationships between man and woman in terms of class struggle: the revolt of the oppressed (women) against the oppressors (men). The final victory of women would lead to a classless society.
3) "French Theory,"[12] the name given in the United States to so-called postmodern philosophy, was developed by Derrida,[13] Foucault,[14] Deleuze and Guattari,[15] Bourdieu,[16] and Baudrillard. The movement was very successful in the United States. Its main founder was Derrida, strongly influenced by Sartre who also had a great influence on Judith Butler, the main pioneer and promoter of gender theory. "French Theory" is not the unified and coherent system that its name would imply. However, the philosophers who represent it have two points in common which, from the start, influenced gender theory and radical feminism (see below).
   i) They give pride of place to the rejection of norms, values, and universal principles in every domain.
   ii) They believe that everything in society has a binary structure arising from the language and thought which underpins it. It reflects and justifies the couple and relationships of dominants and dominated. To put an end to the rule of the dominant this binary structure must be deconstructed and eliminated: for instance, man and woman; heterosexual and allosexual. They refer to their own thought as "postmodern" which is fundamentally characterized by deconstructivism.

C. Radical Feminism

Radical feminism, as opposed to moderate feminism,[17] is without doubt the movement which has done most to impose gender theory.

Both kinds of feminism agree that most societies are inegalitarian, placing men over women as regards power, status, and their social role. The women are in a state of inferiority and submission.

Moderate feminism, the earliest to develop, seeks to bring the social conditions of men and women closer. It aims to grant women the same rights in society as men (political and economic), the same status, and the same treatment. It also seeks to alter private life so that tasks that were once the preserve of women—housework and raising children—should be shared; but though it did question the way certain attributes could be assigned to a particular sex, it did not question the duality of gender. Nor did it question the link of gender to biological sex, which led to it being called *inclusive feminism*.

Radical or extremist feminism appeared later to challenge the link between gender and sex. It also aimed at equality, but of a different kind. Genders had to be interchangeable as regards sexual identity. The duality of genders is abolished for it is seen as having no natural reason, but as resting instead on a purely cultural or social construct which systematically seeks the advantage of men over women. This construct is called the "patriarchy."

This concept draws on two ideas. There is "French Theory" which considers that the relations between men and women are of domination. This is seen as systematic and systemic: a whole social system where males dominate females. There is also Marxism which was so fashionable amongst intellectuals at that time. It provided the concepts from which several important feminists developed their thought. Monique Wittig and Christine Delphy are examples. They viewed the relations between man and woman in terms of a class struggle. The oppressed class (woman) rebelled against the oppressors (men) and the final victory of this rebellion would lead to a classless society. The two influences are linked, since some of the proponents of "French Theory," especially Bourdieu, were themselves strongly influenced by Marxism.

Based on this analysis, radical feminism seeks the destruction of all social structures, marriage, the family, education etc., which establish and perpetuate a difference between man and woman and preserve this duality. It sees both sides of the duality as a source of inequality. In its most extreme form, it excludes men with hatred (misandry) and violence (verbal at least). This is why it is called exclusive feminism (one which excludes).

Radical feminism arose in the English-speaking world around the end of the 1960s and was then imported into France. Amongst its notable theoreticians are Judith Butler,[18] Anne Fausto-Stirling,[19] Monique Wittig,[20] Catherine A. MacKinnon,[21] and Christine Delphy.[22] They show quite a variety of approaches both in their ideological roots and in their particular aims and commitments. Nonetheless they all agree on the content of the hard core of gender theory.

D. The LGBTQIA+ Movement

Gender theory went on to be exploited by the LGBT movement, now known as the LGBTQIA+ movement, a title which includes all the main sexual orientations apart from heterosexuality: lesbians (female homosexuals), gays (male homosexuals), bisexuals (those who have a double sexual orientation), transexuals (those who have changed sex by surgery or hormone treatment), transgenders (those who believe that they have a gender which does not correspond to their sex), queers (or genderqueers: those who feel that they do not belong to any sex or gender: they are also called nonbinary), intersexuals (those who are born with neither masculine nor feminine sex[23]), asexuals (those who feel no need to engage in sexual relations; some of them are represented in France by "l'Association pour la visibilité asexuelle" (Association for Asexual Visibility). The sign + means that other categories may be added to allow for other sexual orientations. In the United States, the title is longer: LGBTTQQIAAPO+. It signifies Lesbian, Gay, Bisexual, Transgender, Transexual, Queer, Questioning (those who are not sure about their gender), Intersex, Asexual, Allies (heterosexual allies of one or more of these groups), Pansexuals (those who are attracted sexually to every gender), Other (all the rest). But around fifty other denominations may be added. Since 2014 they have been offered as options, alternative to masculine and feminine, to those registered on Facebook. We present them here in English for they are almost exclusively used in the English-speaking world:[24]

—Agender: those who identify themselves as genderless
—Androgyne, Androgynous: those who claim a gender identity in between masculine and feminine, neither man nor woman

—Bigender: those who claim two genders or more (trigender)

—Cis or Cisgender: those who live by the gender corresponding to their birth sex. They largely correspond to heteronormative genders. Cis is opposed to transexual and Cis gender to Transgender.

—Cis Male, Cis Man, Cisgender Male, Cisgender Man: a man with a masculine gender identity.

—Cis Female, Cis Woman, Cisgender Female, Cisgender Woman: a woman with a feminine gender identity.

—Female to Male: a trans individual, trans in the sense girl to boy or woman to man, but who may be part way between the two genders and not necessarily entirely male gender.

—FTM: an abbreviation of the above which has the advantage of not naming the two genders, masculine and feminine.

—Genderfluid: someone with fluid or multiple genders which crosses the frontier between masculine and feminine.

—Gender Nonconforming: those who refuse to conform to the gender given them at birth and to the norms of sex and gender imposed by their social and cultural environment.

—Gender Questioning: the undecided who question their relationship with sex and gender.

—Gender Variant: those who express their gender in different ways, perhaps as Gender Nonconforming, but not necessarily,

—Genderqueer: gender identities that lie outside and in reaction to the heterosexual duality man/woman and to gender stereotypes or those that combine several gender identities. This term combines all willingly dissident gender identities which may or may not be related to volatile sexual orientation. Some Genderqueers may identify as Transgender.

—Intersex: Those whose sex cannot be assigned according to the biological criteria for identifying men and women—chromosomes, appearance of genital flesh, reproductive organs: an identity chosen for those who refuse early sexual assignation through hormones and surgery (intersex children).

—Male to Female: a trans individual in the sense boy to girl, man to woman.

—MTF: as above, but without mentioning gender.

—Neither: those who identify neither as man nor as woman.

—Neutrois: those who identify as genderless (see Agender).

—Other: those whose gender identity(ies) do(es) not lie within the binary system of sex and gender, or within a third or any other gender.
—O: an alternative to M(an) or W(oman) on administrative documents.
—Pangender: those who refuse heteronormative binary gender which corresponds to the difference in sexuality, because they practice several or all genders. Close to Genderqueer.
—Trans: a generic term which describes transsexual and transgender individuals, and those who identify as such.
—Trans*: a portmanteau term which allows trans people of different kinds to be grouped together. The star, sometimes replaced by an apostrophe, indicates that transsexuals and transgenders are not distinguished. Close to trans.
—Trans* Female: someone not of the feminine sex who claims to be both trans and female.
—Trans* Male: someone not of the masculine sex who claims to be trans and masculine.
—Trans* Man: someone not of the masculine sex who claims to be trans and man.
—Trans* Person: someone who claims a trans identity and a gender other than his/her birth sex.
—Trans* Woman: someone not of the feminine sex who claims to be both trans and a woman.
—Transgender: a term which includes those who do not wish to identify as transsexual because of the medical and pathological connotations of this term, or those who claim other gender identities which may or may not be linked to the construction of alternative sexes.
—Trans Female: a trans feminine individual identifying as a woman.
—Trans Male: a trans masculine individual identifying as masculine.
—Trans Man: a transsexual or transgender individual, assigned as a female at birth but who identifies as a man.
—Trans Person: any trans individual, or a trans individual who claims a trans identity as much as a gender identity.
—Trans Woman: a transsexual or transgender individual, assigned as a man at birth but who identifies as a woman.
—Transgender Female: Someone with feminine gender identity who, unlike transsexuals, has not undergone surgery or hormone therapy to match sex to chosen gender, or had recourse to either.

—Transgender Male: Someone with masculine gender identity who, unlike transsexuals, has not undergone surgery or hormone therapy to match sex to chosen gender, or had recourse to either.
—Transgender Man: someone who identifies as a trans man, but not transsexual.
—Transgender Person: someone who identifies as transgender; a broader term than transsexual or transgender indicating disconnection from birth sex or biological sex.
—Transgender Woman: someone who identifies as a trans woman but not transsexual.
—Transsexual: Someone identifying as medically transsexual, who usually is treated with hormones and surgery to bring sex, gender, and self-presentation into harmony.
—Transsexual Female: Transsexual Woman.
—Transsexual Male: Transsexual Man.
—Transsexual Person: a transsexual individual.
—Two Spirit: a generic term indicating men who take on a feminine identity and gender and women who take on a masculine identity and gender amongst the Native Americans.

This list has a surreal quality which has not been missed.[25] It was doubtless prepared as an exhaustive list (for now) including cases which are extremely rare, imaginary, or conceived in the abstract. However, one may remark that many descriptions are of the same category: 26 for those who say they are trans, 8 for those who do not wish to be assimilated to any gender, 3 for those who claim several genders, and 3 for those who claim the gender of their biological sex.

The various representatives of the LGBTQIA+ movement have found in gender theory a theoretical justification for their sexual orientations. Once the natural and essential link between gender and biological sex is denied, the duality of gender and its normal heterosexual form in society as the basis of the couple is no longer absolute. Any freely chosen form of subjective sexuality becomes legitimate in every way and with all its consequences.

E. Woke Thought

Gender theory has also been taken up by woke thought (wokeism). It was developed recently in the United States before being brought to Europe. The term "woke" comes from the verb "to wake" to describe a state of wakefulness in the face of injustice and discrimination toward certain minorities. It was first used to react to discrimination against black people by white people and then applied to the area of gender to call for a fight against the domination of women by men. Then it was applied to the domination and exploitation of animals by mankind. In woke thought, this domination and exploitation are systematic. All the members of every group concerned, be they whites, blacks, males, females, or human beings, are taken together and tarred with the same brush as forming a system. The alleged systematic domination by men is called the "patriarchy."

It is interesting to observe that this train of thought has its theoretical roots in "French Theory," or postmodern thought as expressed in France. It has the same roots as gender theory. They arise from the combination of five of its main ideas:

1) The idea, developed especially by Derrida, that modern language and the thought it expresses are founded upon pairs of opposed concepts, each of which draws its meaning from its difference from the other. Examples are good–evil, true–false, beautiful–ugly, man–woman, heterosexual–homosexual, man–animal.
2) According to Bourdieu, these pairs are engraved in our minds and create a social hierarchy. This leads to a domination of the first over the second. The first gains privileges, whilst against the second there is discrimination.
3) The idea that language, and the thought it expresses, is in fact set up by the dominant and is at their service.
4) From this arises the idea that knowledge comes from power, so that rationality and science are repudiated. They are seen as social constructs prepared by the dominant with no relation to reality. So woke thought rejects the findings of science, and also reason and common sense, concerning the biological and physiological differences between races, between men and women, and between mankind and the animals. Once this is done, woke thought becomes an ideology. It is a closed system of thought, fortified to resist all objections which are all seen as deriving from the dominant.

5) The idea that to be dominant or dominated is a systematic attribute of all those in a group.

There is the imperative to end the discrimination which some suffer at the hands of others: blacks at the hands of whites; women at the hands of men; allosexuals at the hands of heterosexuals; animals at the hands of men. This supposes the end of all dualities by canceling in each the dominant party. At a deeper level, dominant thought and its linguistic tools must be supplanted by a new mindset and language. The institutions (especially educational) and media are to be mobilized to this end. Woke thought seeks to push through this program, not only in the present and the future, but also in the past. Collective memory is to be blotted out. Literary references and monuments to those supposed to have helped to create a group which dominates another are to be effaced. This attempt to "purify culture" is called *cancel culture*. Woke thought is thus a militant movement which practices the exclusion of those it sees as dominant.[26] Socially, it takes the form of intolerance and violence, replacing supposed inequalities and discrimination with the inversion of the same and with new forms of discrimination.

Woke thought has been examined by many critical studies[27] which we will not examine in detail in this work. From the start, it has been mainly about race, but where it has been applied to gender, the critical assessment of gender theory will apply to it as well.

Chapter 2

The Promotion of Gender Theory in Modern Western Societies: Its Supports, Its Rationale, Its Forms

Over the last twenty or thirty years, gender theory has gained great influence in society. It has been introduced into several levels of the education system so as to mold the minds of the young from the earliest age. In France, for example, it is disseminated in primary schools where ministerial decrees have given rise to new methods of education which align with it. It has appeared, since 2010, in the schoolbooks used in Première and Terminale by young people from 16 to 18 years of age. It is a compulsory course in the Institût des Sciences Politiques which trains young people for the elites of politics and the Civil Service and in various other institutions of advanced study. Teaching these ideas at all educational levels has long been practiced in the English-speaking world, where it is more highly developed. Indeed, acceptance of gender theory is often a prerequisite for employment as a teacher.

Moreover, in most societies institutions and laws have been reformed to reflect these ideas, and a whole system of legal repression has been directed against those who may criticize such things.

Gender theory has gained the power to mold the minds of a great number of citizens, even those whose education, ideas, and habits are totally foreign to it.

Why is it that gender theory has become so widely accepted and how did this come about? Its "scientific" foundation rests on the study of rare and marginal pathologies: hermaphrodites and transexuals. Its philosophical development involved the speculations of certain thinkers presented to a very limited audience of intellectuals, mostly American. Sociologically it affects directly sexual minorities who make up a tiny percentage of the population.[28]

First, it has had widespread support from the media. This support comes from several roots.

Gender theory belongs to "mainstream thought" which is "politically correct". This is an exclusive thought form which seeks to be universally accepted and which begins by capturing the minds of those who are to propagate it.[29] No one who does not think this way[30] can be recruited to a job in the mainstream media, be it the press, the television, or the radio. Question the thought, and you're fired. Media controlled by the State can be especially strict in this regard and apply all sorts of pressure on their employees. As a result, the majority of journalists will hasten to show how correctly they think and behave at the slightest prompt. They do not simply take on the ideas and behavior recommended by gender theory, promoting various examples of its application. They also criticize all those who do not accept it. Moreover, most of those invited to take part in television shows about it are intellectuals from the world of the arts and the media who support gender theory and seek to spread it.

Another important factor nowadays is the work of associations and lobbies,[31] in this case associations of radical feminist and LGBTQIA+ lobbies. They can exert powerful influence through their connections to leaders of the media, of the cultural world, and of politics. This benefits the associations by making them appear representative so that through activism in the media they can apply pressure on the politics of the State.

Another strength of the movement, linked to the above, is the support given to gender theory by States themselves and by international organizations. Many States have helped to impose gender theory through their educational and legislative systems.

Often States apply the directives of international organizations. The Council of Europe and the UN adopt gender theory[32] officially and then apply heavy pressure on unwilling States. In this, they are helped by militant NGOs.[33] They require gender theory and its applications[34] to be adopted as a condition for receiving their grants, and those who drag their feet are threatened with legal action, exclusion, or economic sanctions.

The postmodern States of our time have devoted a remarkable amount of energy to organizing society. This is mainly due to the weakening of their political and economic power. As the sociologist Zygmunt Bauman has shown, they no longer have the power of States from the preceding, modern,[35] era since powerful multinational corporations have reduced their influence in the political and economic domains.[36]

All this makes it clear that, in recent times, politics at the State level has been defined by three pressure groups: international institutions,[37] feminist and LGBTQIA+ lobbies, and political parties which use policies for the reform of society as a means of getting votes.

But there are other factors of a more general nature, present in societies and civilizations, which help to explain the flourishing of gender theory and the concepts linked to it.

One factor is the excessive importance given to minorities in modern Western societies. The sociologist Christopher Lasch had already noticed this thirty years ago.[38] This leads the media to give them the same attention as that given to the majority. Often, quotas are imposed, even when the minority represents as little as 1 percent of the whole. They are also favored by institutions that practice "positive discrimination" to their advantage, allowing them privileges denied to the majority. This naturally creates new unfairness and new inequalities which, paradoxically, become tolerated and enshrined in the law.

A second factor is the arrival of worldwide ultraliberalism whose roots and aims are economic. To achieve its ends, it seeks to abolish borders, limits, and regulations in every domain. It aims to abolish moral values which may impede free markets and to extend market principles to every area of existence.[39] The field of morals and ethics[40] suffers from the fluidity which marks postmodern societies. Their structures and values have become blurred, inconsistent, unstable, and interchangeable as the sociologist Zygmunt Bauman has shown in his remarkable analysis.[41]

A third factor, implied by the first two, is globalization. This favors the rapid development and diffusion of emerging ideas, and the general adoption of originally marginal thought forms. Online media and the social networks which they enable are factors that favor this expansion.[42]

A fourth factor is the ideology of progress. Modern man is driven to go beyond traditional structures and ways of life to seek change and novelty in every domain. Novelty is systematically viewed as improvement.

A fifth factor is the growth of individualism in modern societies and their emphasis on individual freedom. This is seen as the power to dispense with any framework, to reject all rules and, unconstrained, to enjoy everything without limit. It is important to realize that this freedom rejects nature itself, accused of being a predefined framework which determines existence. Although few may realize it, this is an application of the principles of existentialism which claims that individuals have absolute power to define themselves.[43] God is also rejected as the creator of this nature and its laws.

A sixth factor is the assertion that society and culture are more important for the education of man than his nature, and that they determine what he becomes. This idea can be found in the works of Jean-Jacques Rousseau,[44] but it was developed in the anthropology and ethnology which flourished around the middle of the twentieth century. The relativity of cultures was emphasized, including Western culture.[45]

A seventh factor is the weakening and destruction of the married couple and traditional family in modern Western societies. There is a disenchantment with marriage and a huge rise in unmarried couples which break and remake at will because of their unwillingness to face the difficulties of life together and to overcome them. There are more and more divorced couples, reconstituted families, single-parent families, and homosexual couples. Thanks to the biological techniques of medically assisted procreation, it is possible for children to be born without father or mother. The child is conceived from sperm from a donor and/or an egg from anonymous donors and may be born from the womb of a surrogate mother. These developments, especially the last two, lead to the weakening or elimination of traditional parents. This makes it difficult or impossible to bring up children with a normal psychology, boys modeling themselves on their fathers, and girls on their mothers. The huge increase in "free-love" or promiscuity "free unions" is linked to various factors: (1) the sexual liberty which flourished in the 1960s and rebelled against all social norms, the hippy movement and the French revolt of May 1968; (2) the pride of place given to physical pleasure in a society which is ever more materialist, consumerist, and hedonist; (3) putting desire before will; (4) the rejection of all inner asceticism and of every sacrifice and effort which could stabilize relationships; (5) a reluctance to commit to anyone long term in an unstable and deliquescent society whose future is uncertain.

An eighth factor is the disenchantment of intellectuals with Communism. Up until the 1980s this was an ideal which could guide and power their activity. They aimed at a new society where all inequalities would disappear. Then, in every area of life where they had been found, the oppressed class would throw off the yoke of its oppressors. These ideas were then recycled into "woke thought" keeping the general categories of Marxist theory, especially class struggle. Its promoters, like those of gender theory, affirm that it doesn't exist except as an invention of their opponents. However, it is clearly marked by common elements which unite its different expressions.

A ninth factor is the decline and loss of influence of Christianity[46] in the modern West which has taken place over the last fifty years. For two millennia it had an enormous influence on the structure of the traditional family. It justified the durability of the traditional couple of man and wife and provided the ethical and anthropological framework for sexual relationships.

Into the vacuum left by the decline of Christianity came a new anthropology and new ethics with an obvious pseudo-religious, and even sectarian character. "The morals of *gender studies*," wrote Raoul Weiss, "are clearly designed as a religion and a political theology."[47] Like religious preachers, the theoreticians and militants of gender theory aim to create a new world for a new man. Elizabeth Montfort writes: "What is at stake with *gender ideology* is not so much the fate of homosexuals or women, but the dawning of a new world based on new ideas of the individual, a new relationship to reality, to nature and to oneself and a new logic—nothing less! … Homophobia may exist and inequalities between men and women persist; but these are simply pretexts to allow the construction of a new humanity, free of any standards of behavior and any sort of order. In this society everyone is a new god through willpower, since he defines himself in a denial of reality."[48] Pierre-Olivier Arduin writes: "The objective of this anthropological heresy [which is gender theory] is to build a new humanity unchained from sexual differences."[49] Bringing about this new world and its new man requires methods that belong to those of the sects.

Eric Fassin follows American gender theorists and has done much to make known Judith Butler in France. In his writings and discourses on this subject, his main idea is that the question of gender is not a matter of private choice. It is a collective work, which the State has the duty to set up, guarantee, and impose through all the force of law and the courts. For him, sexuality is not a matter of intimate relationships but of State intervention and control. This is typical of totalitarianism. It closely resembles what Orwell imagined in his novel *1984*. Things are given names contrary to what they really are. Like the "Minister of Truth" in the novel, they call this "democratic." So, starting from the promotion of free will and individual choice, as we have seen above, these gender theoreticians end up denying them from another angle. They end up, paradoxically, by imposing their own choice.

The gender theoreticians bombard people with their propaganda which is backed up by the mainstream media, the police, and the courts: a thought police. Dissuaded from opposition by this repressive system, our postmodern societies strongly resemble the totalitarian societies, of the left or of the right, which dominated much of the world in the twentieth century, though it still remains a "soft totalitarianism."[50]

For the gender theoreticians and those who fight for it, what is important is to alter minds.[51] This is why they seek so strongly to introduce their theories into the education system at the earliest age. Young minds are more receptive and more easily molded. They can easily be changed.

The method used is a veritable brainwashing. It starts with a systematic criticism of all ways of thought considered as "old fashioned." They are presented as "archaic" and "out of date" since what is new must be better than the old. This ideology of progress may be challenged ever more strongly, but it is still widely believed. It preaches that anything that upsets established order is "progress." Their aim is to "deconstruct archetypes," both masculine and feminine, and to replace them with a "deconstructed human being" with no reference to natural sex. This being is self-defining by individual choice, the principle of gender theory. It pretends that gender is a choice which has nothing to do with the body, but which must be "enlightened" by the promotion of a multiplicity of genders and even nongenders.

It also seeks to impart to children a new *ethos*—a new way of life—by teaching them new forms of behavior. The education system, outside the family, is used as a lever to crush or outflank the upbringing received in the family.[52] This is made easier by the fact that children spend more time at school with their teachers than at home in a close relationship with their parents.

This change of mentalities in schools and in the whole of society is brought about by using a new vocabulary, the "newspeak" of which Orwell wrote. It allows a new form of thought to be expressed.[53] Thus, the word "sex" and its derivatives are eliminated from our vocabulary and "gender" is substituted. "Heterosexuality" is used to indicate the sexuality which has been normal for humanity since its origins and in every civilization. This suggests that it is simply an alternative to "homosexuality" and equivalent to it. The word "transformism" is also used to mean transsexuality or transvestitism. The sex of the newborn is no longer mentioned. It is the "sex assigned at birth."[54] This suggests that sex is not a natural property but an arbitrary attribution which may be changed in the future. One speaks of "parentality" to blot out the terms "maternity" and "paternity." "Parent" is used to designate both "father" and "mother," eliminating their difference and even their sexual existence. Gender theory lobbyists have even managed to get these words imposed in official documents, eliminating "man" and "woman" as well as "Sir" and "Madam."[55] They may no longer be used in administrative documents or official acts.[56] The Roman Catholic Church has even modified its baptismal certificates to accommodate this trend.[57] In the English-speaking world, medical professors and personnel have been obliged to refrain from any expressions that might trouble transgender individuals, those who change their gender without modifying their sexual organs. Since transgender women (men who have adopted feminine gender) may have a penis and prostate cancer, and transgender men (women who have adopted masculine gender) may be pregnant or have cancer of the uterus, they must now be described as "individuals with a penis, "individuals with prostate cancer," "pregnant individuals" or "individuals with uterine cancer." The campaigns against cancer must be directed toward "those with a prostate" or "those with a uterus." A trans man giving birth is described as "an individual giving birth," and thereafter as a "parent who gave birth." The same expressions are used for genuine women who bear children. A person breast-feeding a child is described as "giving milk from the chest."[58]

Those who promote gender theory in education, in the media, and in politics are so militant and forceful that they resemble a religious sect. They are like missionaries with their catechism which they hide beneath the intellectual cloak of "agency."[59]

The moralizing nature of this scheme is obvious. It is also paradoxical and contradictory. Those who promote it allow themselves unlimited permissiveness in their ideas and behavior. Yet they apply hyper-moral strictures to others and can be violently intolerant of those who do not share their views.

This scheme of imposing new ethics is promoted by various kinds of psychological pressure. One method is to put forth various mixtures of ideas to targets for conversion with the aim of making them feel guilty. These mixtures give the procedure an intellectual cloak of "intersectionality,"[60] so dear to "woke thought."[61] For example, any criticism of the theoretical justifications put forth by members of the LGBTQIA+ is treated as homophobia, and more recently as genderphobia. These are seen as being on the same level as racism, which is seen as a crime against humanity. The ideas of homophobia, transphobia, discrimination, and racism are often knowingly and willingly used abusively so as to silence any kind of criticism.

Another means of giving potential converts a guilty conscience is to speak of the systematic victimization of minorities, with deliberate exaggeration[62] of the kinds of oppression and discrimination which are denounced.[63]

Chapter 3

Criticisms of Gender Theory

At the end of this book there is an abundant bibliography which shows how gender theory leaves itself open to criticism on many grounds: biological, physiological, psychological, sociological, ethnological, anthropological, and philosophical.

The First Reason for Criticism: Gender Theory's Desire to Dominate

Gender theory was put together by a few intellectuals employed by universities, some famous. However, their audience was limited to minorities and fringe groups.[64] It was militant associations of these minorities who popularized it. They lobbied the media and those in politics, who then broadcast and applied their principles as we have already seen above.

These ideas were then absorbed by these institutions through which their promoters sought to impose them on everyone through social reforms designed to make them seem normal and ordinary. This aroused much criticism from all sides which showed their weakness: insubstantial foundations, self-contradictions, and damaging effects on society and those who make it up.

It is true that gender theory is right to underline the cultural dimension in the definition of masculine and feminine. This concept has indeed a certain relativity, but this had already been noted in the past. The modern debate as to the relative importance of the innate and the acquired in man is nothing new. It started long ago.[65]

In our time, feminism has led to a better recognition of woman's dignity and of the respect which is due to her. She is now seen as fundamentally equal to man in status and law, recognized in society, in the family, and in the couple.

This was all achieved by moderate feminism which continues to improve matters. There was no need for recourse to gender theory, far less to its more radical and exclusive forms.

Another positive contribution is a greater respect for minorities who may have been mocked, ostracized, or even persecuted.

However, the main interest of the theory for these minorities was to give them a means of appearing normal, or even normative. Those sexual, or even anti-sexual, behaviors which had formerly been seen as abnormal and deviant could now be presented as options in an "inclusive" society. They would be included in its essential structures and normal behavior. The aim is to build a new man in a new world which fits in with the ideals of its promoters. The inspiration may be Marxist or neoliberal, but radical feminism almost always sees itself as a "political feminism."

Whilst these ideas were restricted to such minorities, they aroused little opposition. It was when the project went global that criticism arose. For it started to take the form of social reforms which challenged the traditional structures of society itself. The relationships between man and woman were affected exactly where they had been, in general, most harmonious and satisfactory: marriage, the family, fatherhood, motherhood, and ways of procreation. When the school system began to be used to disseminate it both in the abstract and in practice, it aroused a vast and hostile opposition. Of course, criticisms of gender theory had already been developed, especially in the United States where it was born by intellectuals who disagreed with those who promoted it in universities. Its promoters also criticized each other. Although they all agreed on the core of the theory—that gender is purely artificial and cultural, and that all are free to choose their gender, or an absence of gender—they do not always agree on its roots, expressions, and applications.

An Intellectual Construct Divorced from Reality

The first objection we may address to gender theory is that it is an abstract intellectual construct. It is hypothetical, uncertain, and relative as are all theories. Yet it claims to apply to the whole human being, the body, the mind, and the spirit. It seeks to regulate mankind's individual and social existence. Without any scientific foundations which might validate it, it is simply one ideology amongst many: one which, with its universal claims, tries to create a new man and a new world. The best-known example of such an ideology in the twentieth century is Marxism, which was also an inspiration for many of those who promoted gender theory.

As an intellectual construct, gender theory shows itself to be disconnected from reality. It does this deliberately. It sees gender as a subjective or cultural construct unrelated to objective reality of sexes. Moreover, it believes that sexes themselves do not truly exist. They are determined by cultural or individual ideas about them, or by what is said of them. These ideas arise from a combination of immaterialism, nominalism, and solipsism which claim that nothing exists apart from what the individual perceives, or that the being of a thing is just the way it is perceived. This is summed up in the dictum "esse est percipi aut percipere."[66] It is also inspired by philosophical idealism which holds that all reality comes back to what the spirit determines.[67] These two stances are the opposite of realism. They reduce knowledge to a set of subjective views, individual or collective. They are relative, without realizing that this means that they are themselves relativized.[68] So, it is not surprising that some gender theoreticians have a very fluid perception of their own gender. It fluctuates according to their moods and the time of day. This is recognized by Judith Butler who thinks of each day as a voyage between genders,[69] each of them identified with different representations, acts or roles.[70]

To speak of an "intellectual construct" is perhaps too generous. This is the world of imagination and phantasm.[71] It is purely irrational. The facts of biology[72] are set aside and reality[73] itself is denied.

Reality has been so far supplanted by phantasm that for many transgenders or nonbinaries the physical characteristics of their bodies count for nothing. Moreover, they believe that others, who recognize these characteristics, are in error.[74]

The Basic Error: Uniquely Cultural with Nature Excluded

The basic idea of gender theory, that gender is entirely constructed with no natural foundation, is clearly false. Its supporters are surely correct in saying that cultural and subjective factors are important. Where they go wrong is when they consider them to be exclusive. That is, they deny the existence of a natural foundation or even a natural component. Men are different from animals which are completely dependent on their instincts[75] which arise from their nature. Men always combine natural elements (innate) and cultural elements (acquired) in their behavior. It is true that natural elements blossom and express themselves in relation to a setting. For man, this is cultural in a broad sense. Moreover, a person has some influence over the properties of nature, to develop or restrain them, to inhibit or direct them. It is nonetheless true that these changes must be brought about the basis of natural potential,[76] and that man's free will acts on both culture and nature.

Natural and cultural factors coexist and combine in various proportions. It is not always possible to measure them, but they are never abolished, though in human life, education, social pressure, and personal will power may all, to some extent, modulate and control natural factors, even instincts. There is a long-standing debate between those who give first place to natural factors and those who give it to culture, but both fall into error if they claim exclusivity.

The Denial of the Body as a Concrete Fact so as to Change or Deny It

Gender theorists are the sworn enemies of natural order and nature itself as they never tire of saying. Like true existentialists, they see it as a predefined essence, established rules to which man must submit. It would limit, or even deny, his freedom. They aim for absolute freedom, even over their own bodies. They reject all external constraints and every orientation defined by nature through genetic, organic, or physiological constitution. They even reject the body's structure and shape.

This idea shows itself at its most radical in attempts to remodel the sexuality of the body. We see this in transexuals. It shows itself also in the attitude of the transgenders. Without modifying their bodies, they deny its sex or reject its spontaneous natural tendencies. They even deny the body itself, but in a way which, in truth, is only possible as a representation. This leads to psychological unease and trouble since the body and its instincts are undeniably real and material and resist such attempts.

The desire for total mastery of the body is not the sole preserve of transexuals,[77] but is characteristic of our civilization. We see it in plastic surgery and all other means of changing the appearance of the body: piercings, implants, and tattoos. It is also present in the mutilations seen in contemporary art "performances" which are so spectacular and unhealthy.

This unease of man about his body is seen throughout the history of philosophy, from Plato[78] to Foucault.[79] His lack of mastery over either its constitution or its form disturbs him and hinders his ambitions, be they spiritual, psychological, or physical. It troubles him spiritually too. The gnostic sects bear striking witness to this, as do, more subtly, the writings and practices of the ascetics of every religion. Here is a deep problem. It affects the human condition in this world at its limits, which are finite. The spirit finds this hard to accept since it has no limits to what it can conceive or imagine. It also affects mankind's hope of reaching the ideal, or at least a better condition, where its limits would be ontologically surpassed. This, in its way, is the aim of the trans movement in all its facets,[80] but in fact, this denial of limits is an unrealistic, childish, and even pathological[81] utopia. Man may regret his lack of wings to fly, not having ten arms like Shiva or many eyes like the cherubim. He may regret that he is not like the mythical man in Plato's *Banquet,* who had two faces pointing in opposite directions so that he could see and hear from all sides; and four arms, four hands, and four legs which allowed him to move easily in all directions; and two sexes, male and female, so that he could self-reproduce.[82] Yet, like every being in this world, man is defined by his characteristics which he must accept. Only in this way can he find inner peace and happiness. Refusing them places him in a permanent state of frustration and failure. Plato's mythical man was punished by Zeus for having wished to reach the god's measure. Similarly, Adam fell from his original bliss for having tried "to become a god," believing the serpent's promise. Whoever goes against nature condemns himself to "unnatural hell" as Eric Fassin put it, in the illusion that he himself might escape it. Even without invoking divine punishment, we can indeed recognize that nature always avenges herself on those who deny her and act against her.

The Refusal to See That Natural Factors Are at the Root of the Reality of Sexes and Their Difference

A. The Denial of the Facts of Nature, and Their Knowledge Through Science

We have seen how for some gender theorists the sexes, and not just genders, are a construct of collective or individual psychological culture and not at all a natural fact. For Judith Butler, the body is fundamentally "neutral material" which can be molded and oriented as desired. It is a kind of tabula rasa on which one may construct, at will, a girl or a boy, or any other imaginable sexual identity.[83] This is the principle of the transgender movement. For most gender theoreticians it is gender which determines sex, which otherwise does not exist.

This denial of the reality of the two sexes, masculine and feminine and their properties and qualities can be classed as delirium. In psychiatry this is defined as denying reality and seeing in its place a pseudo-reality created by the imagination, which is often the object reached through a rational construct designed to support it. Gender theorists are not content to reject what the senses and common sense perceive: the spontaneous perception of two sexes and the differences that go with them. They also reject all scientific facts which support this perception since for them, science is a servant of the "patriarchy."[84] This is a huge regression into the irrational, comparable to that found in fundamentalist movements of certain evangelical movements in the United States or in radical Islam where it is maintained that the earth is flat and its roundness a creation of atheist Western science.[85]

B. A Reminder of the Scientific Facts

Some American researchers, led by Lee Ellis, have summarized 18,000 scientific studies conducted over more than 100 years. These reveal a long list of differences between the two sexes which are described in a work of nearly 1000 pages.[86]

Current scientific understanding of the differences between the sexes starts with the basic difference in the chromosomes of woman (XX) and man (XY). Consequently, their primary sexual characteristics are different: the genital organs of sexual reproduction.[87] Secondary sexual characteristics are also different, which, for the most part, appear at puberty when hormone production is activated.[88] These differences also affect psychology and behavior, though in a way less well defined and more fluid. There are, of course, a few ambiguous cases: hermaphroditism, or those who have certain features of the other sex. These are rare cases, a tiny minority which can hardly be used to set the standard but are the "exceptions which prove the rule."

The most basic scientific fact is that the two sexes are distinguished by different sex chromosomes: XX for the female; XY for the male. This applies to most mammals and to certain insects and plants. There's no cultural influence or subjective choice here!

The determination of sex by the chromosomes takes place when the male sperm fertilizes the female egg. The sex is completely determined between the sixth and eighth week of pregnancy by a fragment of the Y chromosome: SRY (Sex Determining region Y). It codes for a protein: TDF (Testis Determining Factor) which causes the growth of testicles. In its absence, the embryo grows ovaries. The genital organs are fully developed after fifteen weeks of pregnancy.

The nature and growth of the genital organs are the second factor which confirms the reality of the sexes and their duality. They are both different and complementary, integrated into an ordered system for the reproduction of the species.

A third factor, related to the above, is the secretion of hormones, linked to each sex, and their roles. They are already at work after six weeks of pregnancy. They act on the hypothalamus to program reproductive functions. In a girl, they activate the neurons which will set in train her cyclical ovulation when she grows to puberty. In a boy, the testicles secrete testosterone which progressively activates the masculine features of his body.

From the start of pregnancy, boys develop faster than girls and usually weigh more than them at birth. After birth, boys grow more quickly than girls, but puberty usually comes two years earlier in girls. Another well-established fact is that women live longer than men, about five to seven years more which scientific studies attribute to genetic differences linked to sex. Another important point is that the brain itself has sexual characteristics as testifies an abundant scientific literature.[89]

Physical sexuation, and the existence of just two sexes, is what is observed from the moment a human being is conceived. It is confirmed as the embryo develops, is born, and grows to adulthood. There is a vast scientific literature on this subject too.[90] There are some cases, very few, where the sexes may be confused. Hermaphroditism is an example. Certain differences between them may be partly effaced, or specific characteristics of one sex may be found in the other. This can be explained by genetic or hormonal factors which affect the development and growth of the child. They are extremely rare.

The main question for us is this: how far do these physical factors affect psychological and behavioral factors? Does the physical differentiation of the sexes (male and female) determine the formation of two corresponding genders (masculine and feminine)?

Scientific research shows that the differences between male and female bodies have an impact on psychology, sensorial, affective, and cognitive, and on the behavior of men and women. Jean-Paul Mialet, a neuropsychiatrist writes: "The spirit has a sex like the body and is equally affected. The spirit is incarnate: it has a sex. In the vast majority of cases, the sex of the spirit is that of the body."[91] This sexuation of psychology and behavior can be observed before any social or cultural influence could affect it.[92] This is most important.

Scientific studies have revealed a greater empathy in girls than in boys. From the very first days of their life, boys tend to prefer to observe the movement of objects, whilst girls seek visual contact with a human face.[93] Just a few hours after birth, a girl responds to the crying of another baby whilst a boy pays no attention. During the first three months of life visual contact, seeking to communicate, rises 400 percent with girls, but only 20 percent with boys. At each stage of their development, girls are more sensitive to the emotions of others than are boys.

When language is acquired, girls speak more freely than boys and with more fluidity. From the age of two, boys become more aggressive than girls. Thus, when a solution to problems of relationship is sought, boys tend to resort to physical methods whilst girls employ verbal strategies. These differences persist into adulthood: women are more talkative than men, which gives them the reputation of being "chatty"; they take more interest in other people than do men, which gives them the reputation of being curious; they relate more easily to others than do men which seems to influence their choice of career, which is often in human relations.

Intellectually, women have greater intuitive intelligence than men, who have a more rational mentality. So, women tend to approach matters in a more concrete and synthetic way, whilst men have a more analytical and abstract approach. So, in his relationships with things and people, man appears more thoughtful and hesitant whilst women are more spontaneous. Neither approach is better than the other; they are just different. According to Simon Baron-Cohen, a researcher at the University of Cambridge, who has specialized in these studies, the feminine brain is mainly wired for "empathy" whilst the masculine brain is wired for "systematization." Empathy identifies emotions and thoughts in another person and replies with an appropriate emotion, whilst systematization analyses, explores, and constructs systems.[94]

It is virtually certain that the very strong empathy of women is linked to their role as principals in the procreation and raising of children. Empathy and language are essential for the raising of children from the very first weeks after conception and in the early years of life, even before language is acquired.

On the whole, women have a more psychological approach to sexual relations and relations between the sexes. They are more emotional and more progressive. Men, however, are more physical, impulsive, and immediate. The powerful way the hormonal system influences these matters has been the subject of much scientific research.[95]

Scientific studies often report that men are more gifted, on average, than women as regards spatial representation in three dimensions and the orientation, and rotation of objects. However, women have a wider field of vision than men which gives them a richer perception. They notice better than men when objects are substituted for others: changes which occur in their field of vision. Women also move their hands more precisely and have better control of these movements than men.

Mental illness also varies between the sexes. For example, Asperger's syndrome (a form of autism) affects 8 to 9 men for every 1 to 2 women;[96] Tourette's syndrome affects nine times as many men as women; but depression affects women two to three times as much as men, and anorexia five to six times as much.

The differences listed above, apart from the frequency of mental illnesses, are based on the average for men and women. There may be considerable dispersion around the average, so there may be many individual exceptions to the rule; this does not mean that the results are wrong: they apply to the average of the population.

Men and women are distinguished by their roles in childbirth. The woman's role is well defined by her physiology, better than the factors that define the role of the man. "Maternity," writes Sylvaine Agacinski, "is perhaps what reveals a feminine characteristic which has no masculine equivalent."[97]

Nonetheless, certain feminists rejected early on the idea that maternity and what goes with it are essential to the nature of woman.

In the thought of Simone de Beauvoir, maternity is seen as an enslavement to natural determinism, the opposite of freedom.[98] This has led some feminist theorists to deny the idea of a maternal instinct which makes women wish to bear children and care for them as they grow.[99]

Many women who belong to the more radical strands of the feminist movement exclude motherhood from their lives. They see it as an intolerable form of dependence. It makes them beholden to their biological nature and all the social and family obligations which arise from childbearing. Worse, they become dependent on a man who is seen as using motherhood as a way of dominating the woman. This starts with the sexual relations which lead to conception and carries through into the family unit where the care and raising of children are largely, or entirely, the preserve of the woman.

More recently, the gender theorists of feminism have helped to improve the image of motherhood.[100] Rather than seeing it as a handicap and an alienation, they value it as a way for a woman to blossom, and in this way, as intimately linked to feminine nature;[101] or, at least, as an essential component of her potential; but they do not deny what can be added to modulate the natural gifts of a human being. This movement shows how an aspect of the nature of women, which was denied by abstract theories, has resurfaced.

It can hardly be denied that the biological, physiological, and psychological natures of women predispose them to motherhood. Nor can one doubt that in the sexual dimensions of the natures of man and women there is an instinct to reproduce. In this, they are like all mammals. As in all mammals too, the woman has an instinct which encourages her to care for her children. Her genes, her hormones,[102] and the wiring of her brain give her the physiological potential to do this.[103] On top of this are the qualities linked to her human psychology: empathy, as noted above, and her special gift of language. These natural gifts are adapted to the psychological, emotional, and intellectual needs of an infant. Man has also his own natural gifts which allow him to provide what is needed for the life and growth of the child. This can be seen in the males of the various species of mammal, but in mankind, they have an extra psychological dimension.

Some feminists deny the link between femininity and motherhood. They try to show that there is no such thing as a maternal instinct. They base their case on the fact that at certain times in the past, mothers of a certain social status have confided their babies to wet nurses unrelated to them, and later to governesses.[104] Indeed, it is not rare to find women who have felt little interest in their child during pregnancy or after birth. They say that they had to force themselves to provide the care needed by the child. There are also cases of ill-treatment of young children and even infanticide. However, in the main, taking all societies at every historical epoch, these kinds of behavior are rare. They occur because in the human being, instinct, or behavior arising from biological and physiological causes, may be modulated, consciously and unconsciously. Self-will and personal choice may be factors as may be personal values or their absence and pressure from the social milieu. But here again, the influence of culture and personal choice can in no way deny the existence of natural inclinations,[105] which may not predetermine behavior, but which guide it.

The special qualities of women linked to her potential maternity reach beyond biological childbirth. A sterile woman of any age still has these qualities which can be expressed socially. In the case of nuns, they are expressed through Christianity as spiritual motherhood. This is treated more fully below. As Sylvaine Agacinski writes: "What is traditionally seen as 'maternal' behavior is not closed in on itself but can be a universal model of openness to the other in general."[106]

Cultural Factors and Individual Choice Do Not Destroy Sexuation Though They May Modulate in Some Cases

The above remarks show that there is a clear biological difference between the sexes which affects their psychology and behavior, both of men and of women. However, this does not lead to behavior set in stone, but orients it strongly.

What is absolutely true in animals is only relatively true in mankind. We have our instincts, but these can be modified by cultural and psychological factors, conscious and unconscious, which interact with them. Human persons have some freedom of choice over the leanings of their individual natures. They may be pushed and directed by biological factors, but through will power they can resist this pressure more or less easily. However, this does not justify gender theory. The result is not just the pure product of social conditioning or individual choice amongst several equal possibilities.

Culture, which depends on the social setting which varies with time, can modify the directions of biological nature. It influences human behavior, first through imitation. Later, there is peer pressure from the group and close acquaintances. A person's behavior is also molded by culture acquired through reading and watching audiovisual media, and by his or her moral, philosophical, and religious values.

These different influences are often seen as masculine or feminine and may be taken as archetypes or reference points. Powerful social influencers systematize them so that they serve for the young as models for constructing their identities and personalities. Clearly this is a strong influence which contributes to individual and collective gender identity.

These ways of seeing male and female can be challenged for different reasons. Ethics may indicate that they do not respect the dignity of man and woman and demean their basic equality. However, this does not undermine the natural continuity between sex and gender found in almost all cases.

This continuity is seen in every society, in every age, and in every place. Men and women are distinguished by their specific qualities which cannot be exchanged. In both patriarchal and matriarchal societies men are men and women are women and this is recognized by everyone.[107]

What the feminist movement challenges, and sometimes rightly, are "gender roles." These depend entirely on society and its culture. They set the relationships between men and women, and their respective functions within society and within the couple and the family. However, these gender roles do not formally correspond to genders. They are not to be fundamentally identified with them. This is a mistake of gender theory: it mixes them up. Throwing out gender along with gender roles is like throwing the baby out with the bath water.

Unchanging Facts

Gender theory and its applications are now taught in primary schools[108] with the aim of "deconstructing stereotypes." This seeks to persuade the children that to be a boy or a girl is a matter of choice: gender is in every way interchangeable. The theoretical section of this program is generally taught using illustrated books and videos. There is also a practical section. Usually, boys are made to wear girl's clothing and girls to wear boy's clothing. Each are then made to play with the toys of the other gender. This attempt at inversion appears to be a total failure which is confirmed by similar experiments in other areas. This failure simply confirms that each sex has its own basic interests. These cannot be attributed solely to social conditioning—since they occur at the youngest age.

Experiments have shown, for example, that boys tend to play with moving objects (balls and vehicles for instance) whilst girls prefer soft toys and dolls. One finds similar tendencies amongst young monkeys. Before they were exposed to them, they had never seen such toys, so it is impossible to imagine that they were socially influenced.[109]

Girls and boys show the same kind of difference in what they choose to draw. Most boys draw mobile objects, cars, trucks, and trains. Girls, in contrast, prefer people, flowers, and butterflies.[110] However, these matters are rather superficial. At a deeper level, the failure of an attempted inversion and the existence of resistant invariants are seen in most children who are medically assigned a gender not in accord with their sex.

The Physiological and Psychological Dangers of Gender Confusion: Another Kind of "Gender Troubles"

A. The Dangers of Assigning to a Child a Gender Which Is Not His(her) Own

The way magazines and documentaries have promoted gender theory has unfortunately already damaged society. It is quite common for small girls to think that boys are better and wish to resemble them and even wish to change their sex. Boys may have the same attitude to girls. In recent years the influence of social media has led to such an increase in these cases that they have become a veritable epidemic in the United States.[111] Virtually all these desires disappear naturally after a time which means that it is best to wait.[112] However, their families, influenced by the propaganda of gender theory, may go along with their "personal project." They may encourage their child in his or her wish to undergo medical treatment. Puberty blockers may be prescribed, the injection of hormones and even surgery, all designed to change sex.

Many experiments of this kind have proved disastrous after several years[113] when the reality of nature pushes aside former desires and fantasies. Young adults realize that their gender corresponds after all to their biological sex. At the same time, the puberty blockers and injections of the hormones of the opposite sex may cause severe bodily illness in the short term: infertility, cardiovascular problems, thromboses, osteoporosis, and cancers. They also cause psychological problems: depression, sometimes accompanied by suicidal tendencies which are often put into effect; and the surgical treatments prescribed take forms which can be classed as mutilations.[114]

In the United States there are now many legal cases taken by transgender people against their parents, accusing them of having encouraged what is now seen as a mutilation of the body.

We must note that in the previous cases relating to children or adolescents, under the influence of and support of a certain social environment, who manifest the desire to have a gender and a sex that does not correspond to their biological sex, who experience gender dysphoria in relation to psychological disorders of a psychotic nature—autism (mostly), schizophrenia, bipolarity, and so forth—a large number of recent scientific studies show that among these young people experiencing difficulties in identifying their gender, the proportion of autistic and schizophrenics far exceeds that observed in the ordinary population.[115] The first, according to certain studies, can go up to almost 50 percent, and the second up to 30 percent. This conversely means that among young people experiencing gender dysphoria, a high proportion are autistic and schizophrenic.[116] This leads to the *a priori* suggestion of the possibility of a psychological disorder in any young person experiencing gender dysphoria. It invites the medical profession to adopt a reserved and at the very least a wait-and-see attitude toward requests for medical treatment with a view to a change of sex from people whose judgment is disturbed and whose will is weakened or destroyed by underlying conditions.

B. The Psychological Dangers of Limitless Indistinction or Fluidity of Gender

Gender theory proposes that genders are indistinct and fluid without limit. Judith Butler even suggests passing from one to another at will during the same day! This has a very negative effect upon the relations between man and woman. The roots of identity are blurred so that no one knows who anyone is: man, woman, both at once or neither; and no one knows who he or she is. A Swiss psychiatrist has recently reported that in recent years many patients have come to consult him about their identity. They are troubled about it, especially men who have a relationship with a masculinized woman, a point to which we shall return. They ask him: "Can you teach me what is a man?" And since all strains of feminism promote the model of a virile woman, many women wonder what femininity is. *Gender Trouble* is the title Judith Butler chose for her best-known book. It is not what she thought, but instead is a psychological pathology which leaves some men and women disturbed and unhappy at the loss of their bearings.

Children of homosexual couples also lose their bearings since they do not know who is their mother and who is their father, The parent may be absent, or they may be confused between social and biological parents, deprived of any means of establishing their own identity.[117]

Extrapolating from Pathological or Deviant Cases to Generalize and Normalize Them

As we have shown, gender theory is based on pathological or deviant cases. To begin with, these were hermaphrodite children, or those whose sexual organs were damaged. John Money worked on these cases with Joan and John Hampton. With the consent of the parents, they assigned a gender and attempted to produce its physical characteristics with hormones and surgery whilst the parents tried to raise the child in the assigned gender. This was followed by Robert Stoller's studies of transsexuals. Then came the promoters of gender theory who belong to the LGBTQI+ group who refer to these previous studies. Most of these people, radical feminists, and gender theoreticians alike, are lesbians.[118]

If one works methodically in any area, science, philosophy, or sociology, one does not extrapolate from a tiny number of special cases to arrive at general principles. This is even more the case with gender theory where gender is disconnected from its root in biological sex which is seen as irrelevant.

Behind all this is a wish to make pathological cases seem normal and deviations from the general rule as acceptable. This could be seen as a way of avoiding discrimination, but in no way can it justify making what is normal relative and what is deviant normal.

The problem becomes worse when masculine and feminine genders are presented as minor constituents of a whole spectrum of genders. Facebook does this with the fifty-two gender options it offers its clients.[119] Heterosexuality is relativized in this list, by calling it cisgender with cis males and cis females. The aim seems to be to convey the idea that true heterosexuals are strange and marginal cases just like all the other cases cited.

This becomes utterly intolerable when homosexuality is set up as the standard and heterosexuality is seen as an anomaly. Some even see heterosexuals as repressed homosexuals. Michel Schneider[120] has denounced, as a new dictatorship, this idea where the heterosexual model is seen as a false model, and deep down, everyone is believed to be homosexual whether (s)he knows and accepts it or not. "Heterosexuals are homosexuals who are ashamed." They say: "We must move from the heterosexual norm to another, that everyone is homosexual or should be."[121]

Ambiguous Cases Confirm the Reality of Two Different Sexes

A few cases, such as hermaphroditism, are ambiguous, but their ambiguity confirms the existence of the two sexes which allow them to be defined. It is clear that these are anomalous in nature. Gender theorists have abused us by placing hermaphroditism on the same plane as the two sexes so as to allow them to create other equivalent sexes. Even John Money, who inspired gender theory, did not go that far. For hermaphrodites he prescribed hormone treatment, surgery, and education so that the child could be raised as one sex or the other: one of just two.

Transsexuals also confirm the reality of the two sexes and their corresponding genders. They feel unable to identify their gender with their sex. Then they try to make their sex correspond to their chosen gender with hormone treatment and surgery. The different kinds of homosexuality confirm the existence of two sexes and genders as well, for most homosexuals seek out a virile partner or an effeminate partner.

It is striking to see how virile the main female promoters of gender theory appear. This may well be due partly to genetic or hormonal factors. There is probably also an identification with certain archetypes of virility. They may denounce them, but they also adopt them as a means of gaining social worth.[122]

The Schizophrenic Character of Gender Theory

Gender theory presents certain symptoms which indicate schizophrenia: a dissociation of the psyche from the body; perceiving the body, or some of its organs, to be a reality external to oneself; rejecting the organs which represent one's own body; and ambivalence in the presentation of oneself.

A. The Separation of the Psyche from the Body

Although gender theory aims to reduce conflict between sexes and eliminate their disunion, it simply creates further disunion. The first is the separation of the psyche from the body. The natural continuity between biological sex and gender is rejected. Most of those who embody gender theory represent themselves psychologically in a way that is at odds with what they really are physically: their psyche is discontinuous with their physical reality. This is true even for transsexuals. The new sex of a transsexual is an artificial construct which can never correspond to the basic natural reality of the equivalent biological sex.[123]

B. The Rejection of the Body

As we have seen, many of those who embody gender theory reject the body. The body is experienced as foreign to oneself, like a garment decreed by biological nature which is often seen with disgust. Living as if one's body, or some of one's organs, are foreign and external to oneself is a typical symptom of schizophrenia.

Rejection of the Difference and Narcissism

Here is a paradox: gender theorists present themselves as those who respect the difference (or differences). Yet gender theory itself is a denial of difference, or at best, an indifference to it. For as we have seen, gender theory has been introduced to primary schools in order to persuade girls and boys that they are interchangeable and that there is no difference between them. The radical feminist movement also denies the difference, for it totally and utterly rejects the masculine, one of the two poles of the basic difference. Nonbinarism is another example of this. It denies the duality of gender by refusing to identify with either.

Denying the difference makes you a loser. For a human person blossoms through recognizing a difference with the other and accepting it so that a complementary relationship can grow through an exchange which builds up the human person.

In this denial of the difference lies a form of narcissism which is expressed by a desire for self-reproduction and is enabled by medically assisted reproduction and surrogacy. These were originally developed to help sterile couples of man and woman. Now they have been permitted by law, without any medical reason, for homosexual couples and single women. The aim is to reproduce without the other. Of course, another person is needed to give the sperm or the egg, and a surrogate mother may be required; but these people are all unseen and impersonal, far off and/or anonymous. The woman desires to give birth without a man, without a father for her child. The man desires a child without a woman, with no one to be the child's mother. He wants to be the only begetter and to raise his child as an image of himself. He will be the sole image of his gender for the psychological development of the child.

We had the contraceptive revolution which broke the link between the sexual act and reproduction. And now we have assisted reproduction and surrogacy which break the link between reproduction and the sexual act.

The psychoanalyst Michel Schneider writes: "Failing to take account of the difference between sexes leads to an indifference to sex. When there are not two sexes, there is no sex. Many people may wish to be relieved of the need to meet another and to make love to have children. In time this need may disappear. It may become possible to clone human beings so that we may reproduce, like amoebas, by scission and cellular mitosis. This would avoid all the pain of desiring and winning the heart and body of another. It would be 'the brave new world.'[124] … At last humanity would be delivered from the yoke of seeking a woman to reproduce if one is a man, or the reverse if one is a woman."[125]

Hatred of the Male in the Radical Feminism Which Promotes Gender Theory

In our times, feminism in general has had the positive effect of restoring dignity to women who face a widespread masochistic mentality. This puts women down and sees them as objects of desire, subject to the phantasms and sexual impulses of men who dominate them by physical and psychological violence. This has been somewhat checked by the way the rape, bullying, and violence suffered by some women has been denounced by feminist associations on social media. The #MeToo[126] movement has allowed many women to emerge from behind a wall of silence to salve the wounds which they have borne in their unconscious for many years, wrecking their lives. Nonetheless, within radical feminism these acts of violence, though rightly denounced, have been generalized most improperly.

A typical attitude of radical feminism, the movement mainly responsible for the promotion of gender theory, is to detest the male (misandry) or to hate him[127] (androphobia[128]). It is no longer only the misdeeds of individual men which are condemned, but the male in general. He is belittled and treated as negligible, as one with whom no harmonious, balanced, and equal relationship is possible. He is considered to be a representative of the patriarchy,[129] as a dominator and an oppressor. He is supposed to be violent by nature and whoever he is, to be a potential or actual sexual aggressor.[130] In all cases he is thought to be systematically and solely to blame for any violence in his relationship with women.[131] He is stigmatized and victimized, expelled from the couple and the family and even from social relationships. His castration and elimination are advocated, and any form of violence against him is justified, even murder.[132] A well-tried system of propaganda has persuaded public opinion that the male is the one who solely and systematically discriminates against women and oppresses them, whilst women are always the innocent victims.[133] This gives birth to new ethics: the sex seen as dominant is evil, whilst the other is good.

These ideas have an effect which goes beyond the domain of radical feminism. They help to make all relationships between men and women very difficult, strained, confrontational, or even impossible. The aggression of certain women, members of associations, and published authors who promote aggression have so frightened certain men that they avoid women altogether.[134]

The Consequences for Feminine Sexuality and Procreation of Rejecting Heterosexuality, Seen as a Means of Masculine Domination

Radical feminism almost always assumes that relations between men and women are always colored by sex. Sexuality is supposed to be the main means of masculine domination, both within the couple and in society at large. Society is seen as a "patriarchal system." This leads to the rejection of all sexual relations between women and men. Some feminists recommend abstinence, a new form of otherworldliness and puritanism.[135] Others recommend feminine homosexuality as a means of pleasure without men.[136] Another result of the evolution of feminism is that motherhood[137] is once more accepted. With this goes social pressure for the legal recognition of medically assisted procreation for single women and lesbians living together. They take sperm from a masculine donor, distant and anonymous so that he can be ignored. Conception is then an impersonal technique which takes place in the laboratory with no sexual relations. So, children are born without fathers, and both girls and boys are raised to reject and even hate the masculine sex.

Confusing Difference with Inequality and Discrimination, and Equality with Sameness and Lack of Difference

Gender theory has a problem: it confuses the difference between man and woman with inequality. So, it refuses to accept the difference, systematically seeing it as an inequality. Any recognition of the difference is treated as discrimination. Intersectionality, which is now so fashionable in sociology, places sexes and genders on the same plane as races.[138] To affirm that there is a difference between races is seen as racist. This is plainly ridiculous since there are biologically observable differences such as genetics, shape of the face, skin color, and hair type. In reality, to be racist is to affirm that one race is superior to another.[139]

Confusing equality and sameness is linked to the idea of getting to one through the other. This confusion arises partly from the inequality of power, linked to sex, in almost all societies, which corresponds to the distinction between men and women.[140] However, the campaigns of moderate feminists show that this inequality may be reduced without denying distinctions and differences. In physics it is obvious that objects which are quite different may weigh the same. In the same way, two different people may have the same value through their respective qualities. This is true whatever their gender.

A False Idea of Freedom

Gender theorists have the idea that freedom means to be able to do as one pleases without any constraint. It is seen as absolute power, able to deny the reality of the body and to pass over all natural limits and laws. It also means that one may ignore all social laws and values whatever they may be. This is like the thought of a young spoilt child who knows no rule or limit but believes himself to be at the center of a world which will obey his every wish. It is also close to existentialism which believes that all which exists is built up independently of any prior fact: from nothing. The individual sets himself up as the creator of himself and of the world. He pays no attention to anyone or anything but sets himself up as the Creator in his work of creation *ex nihilo*. An example is the creation, noted above, of more than fifty new genders, or lack of gender, apart from "masculine" and "feminine." This aims to give the idea of a great range of choice, or almost limitless freedom. It also shows how each individual who chooses one of these genders wishes to set him(her)self apart from others. The desire to escape the common condition of mankind is combined with inflated individualism.

Another aspect of this idea of freedom in gender theory is that one can change gender at will, several times per day according to Judith Butler, One can change sex, alter nature, and change social norms. This idea supposes that each individual has an all-powerful will which allows him(her) to mold him(her) self as he(she) wishes, and to change the world about him(her) to suit.

This reveals another root of gender theory apart from those examined in Chapter 1: Renaissance humanism and its promotion of individualism. This humanism rejected God and set up mankind as the center and origin of everything, and individualism went on to place the individual at the center. Cartesian philosophy illustrates this. It considers individual consciousness (*cogito*) as the basis of existence, first of the subject himself, then of the whole world, thus determining what he (she) is. For Descartes, what the mind conceives is more important than the fact itself, which echoes down the ages in the philosophies of idealism and rationalism. Mankind's struggle to possess and master nature is also Cartesian. The technology developed in the nineteenth century was to this end. In the twentieth century mankind went even further to develop techniques for fabricating human beings without sexual interaction.

Liberalism made individualism worse. An example is the promotion of minorities which is a kind of social individualism. This breaks up society into many tiny independent entities which are often at odds with each other. There is also progress, that ideology of the Enlightenment, which has become an engine of capitalist development. It drives individuals to change and to reject all stable values, norms, and institutions. It makes people believe that any change is for the better. It is progress.

PART TWO:

GENDER AND ITS TRANSFIGURATION IN CHRISTIAN ANTHROPOLOGY AND SPIRITUALITY

Chapter 4

Christianity and Gender Theory

Faced with Chaos, Preserve the Basic Values of Christianity

Gender theory dreams its world and partly manages to bring it about in the tiny group of its promoters. This world is chaotic, broken up, and divided. Its main aim and its primary effect are "deconstruction," which basically means destruction. The struggle of gender activists leads first to ruin. No new archetypes are provided to replace those destroyed. The new man who is to replace the former man defines himself "on the basis of nothing" as Sartre said. The definition is purely subjective, driven by the desires and phantasms of each individual, or group. There is no model to guide and inspire their behavior and development.

Gender theory struggles against discrimination linked to sex or gender, but this serves to create new discriminations.[139] In its struggle against violence, it creates new forms of violence.[140] By idolizing individualism, it fragments human nature into many tiny pieces, all irreconcilably at odds with each other.[141] Rejecting every ethical norm means rejecting what is normal.

Freedom of choice and the right to be different are promoted as absolute values; but to those who wish to live by traditional norms and values, they are no such thing. These people are constantly criticized and pressed to change. Gender theorists preach great tolerance, but only for those who share their ways and views.

In the United States, where the theory pervades everything, there are Christians who feel threatened, and try to protect their children, often at great sacrifice, by placing them in private schools or giving them home-schooling. Some Christians even attempt to create a parallel society, based on Christian values and able to preserve them.[142]

However, Christianity has never sought to create a separate society, even in the most unfavorable conditions. Historically it has applied the words of Christ: "My kingdom is not of this world" (John 18:36). Spiritually, the Christian receives in baptism a new birth. He no longer depends on the biological or social worlds but on the Church, the image and expectation of the Kingdom of Heaven. There he lives as a new creation who strives to conform to the Will of God and the ethics of the life in Christ. He gave us the precepts and, by the example of His life amongst us, showed how they should be lived. In their turn, the saints have followed His path, showing forth His bright image in their lives.

In every age, Christians have the duty to hold fast to their idea of man, his beginning, his nature and his end. They must keep to their ethics and way of life. They must discern the new ways of thought and behavior which arise and evaluate them in the light of their own values. When we see the trouble caused by gender theory, intellectually, ethically, and in society, we must reaffirm the true Christian view of the nature of man, woman and their relationship. This is the main aim of this book.

The Misconceptions of Christian Teachings

Those who promote gender theory often criticize Christianity on four main grounds:

—Its anthropology recognizes just two genders, masculine and feminine, out of the spectrum proposed by gender theory.
—It is attached to the notion of nature seeing it as given by God, normative and intangible.
—As a couple, it only recognizes man and woman, in a monogamous and indissoluble union.
— Its ethics exclude, even within this couple, all deviant forms of sexual relations.

In the context of "gender studies" the Christian concept of genders is most often understood incorrectly. The teaching of St Paul and the Church Fathers on the nature of man and woman, and their relationship is seen in a negative light: woman devalued before man. Yet it may also be interpreted in a way which enhances the worth of woman. Christianity is often blamed for the inferior position of women over the last two thousand years. However, there is much evidence that the anthropological and social status of women was better under Christianity than it was in the society of Antiquity. There are also many historical studies that show how this degradation of women was brought about by the political and social reforms of the last three hundred years, which were unrelated to Christianity.

This is the main purpose of this book: to address these misunderstandings and errors about how Christianity sees the sexes, the genders, and their relationships. It adopts an objective approach enlightened by a re-reading of the Scriptures, the writings of the Church Fathers, and historical facts.

The Legitimate Aims of Gender Theory

Some of the basic concepts and aims of gender theory may be seen as worthy, though the direction they take and the way they are applied are unfortunate. The freedom of the person is emphasized. The person is seen as being able to stand back from the tendencies of nature and the models and requirements of society. The limits that the duality of gender and sex places upon mankind are perceived as something to be surpassed.

The movement aims to put an end to the discrimination that some people suffer on account of their personality, their ideas, their behavior, and their choices in life. It also aims to achieve a perfect equality between men and women at every level. It struggles against all forms of inequality and discrimination. Absolute respect is sought for woman from man. All forms of violence are condemned including sexual relations without consent, and gestures or words which refer to sex and denigrate those to whom they are addressed.

Points of Contact between Christianity and Gender Theory and Their Limits

Some of those who have studied gender theory, both favorable and unfavorable, have found points where Christianity and gender theory coincide. Indeed, some gender theorists believe that there are patristic texts, related to Christian anthropology and spirituality, which confirm and justify some of their views.

First of all, there is the first account in Genesis of the creation of mankind which can be seen as prior to a distinction of the genders.

Secondly, there is the famous passage of St Paul in the Epistle to the Galatians: In Christ "there is neither male nor female" (Gal 3:28).

Thirdly, in Christian spirituality, women acquire qualities that are traditionally seen as masculine, and men acquire qualities that are traditionally feminine. The two genders are both spiritually and psychologically permeable to each other. They are no longer opposed or separated.

Fourthly, in both masculine and feminine monasticism, sexuality, marriage, maternity, and paternity are renounced.[143]

The fifth point is how Christian ascetics set the body at a distance and strive to master natural instincts and inclinations.

The sixth point, linked to the fifth, is the value given to the virtue of chastity. Anything with a sexual connotation directed to another is excluded, be it word deed or gesture. Nothing is imposed but instead, another person is given perfect respect.

The seventh point, linked to the two previous points, is that human nature can be partly overcome and transcended through an effort of the will.

The eighth point is that mankind gains freedom by rising above the limitations of nature.

The ninth point is faith in the world to come, where according to the word of Christ, people will live without husband or wife. (cf. Luke 20:34–36)

To this list may be added certain social elements.

The first is how Christianity was at the root of the liberation of women from the inferior status which was theirs in Greek and Roman Antiquity.

The second is the way the Gospels place great value on women,[144] as do the Church Fathers[145] and St Paul despite the apparent contradiction with some of his epistles.

The third is the power exercised by women in the Christian societies of Antiquity and the Middle Ages. They were influencers (to use a modern term) and heads of large social institutions such as monasteries, hospitals, orphanages, and schools.[146]

It is interesting to see that these elements echo some of the preoccupations and positions of those who promote gender theory; but they are analogies not identities. The points of view and contexts are different. So are the points of reference and the aims. Thus, various points of Christian teaching are accepted or rejected for the wrong reasons by gender theorists. They do not grasp the overall context of Christian anthropology and spirituality.

The texts of the Old and New Testaments are often complex and ambiguous. They have to be viewed in this light to be correctly interpreted. The same goes for the fundamental patristic texts which deal with this subject. Understanding them correctly requires deep knowledge of their authors. This is particularly the case for St Gregory of Nyssa and St Maximus the Confessor who are the two main sources underpinning our reasoning. Their history has to be viewed by a mind free of all the prejudices of modern mentalities.

Christianity preaches freedom but understands it quite differently to gender theorists. Its point of reference is the nature of man: his original nature not his fallen nature which it opposes by fighting the passions which are part of it. This is a most important distinction for the study of our subject, since different groups either exalt or denigrate human nature, completely confusing its two states.

Christianity's own concepts allow the development of its own gender theory. This can include certain positive aims of the gender theorists of our time. This allows them to reach what they seek, which otherwise would be beyond their reach, hence the title of this book.

This does not mean that institutional Christianity, as embodied in different societies over the ages, has achieved this. It is an ideal that is reached only by a few of the best, who get there through a long and difficult inner struggle. On the whole, it has been hindered by hostile social structures, often longlasting and well entrenched; and even more by the passions which strongly affect fallen human nature. For these passions often inspire the social structures themselves and make them resistant to change.

The aim is to "transfigure gender." This requires a long and hard struggle against the passions which divide men and women in couples, families, and society. They divide first each person against him(her)self and on a larger scale, they divide social classes, different nations, and different races. Some gender theorists have been attracted by parts of Christian teaching, but others find them too limited. Some of these limits can be overcome, but others cannot.

Christianity teaches that, rather than abolishing them, we can rise above the inequality and opposition of gender spiritually. Removing inequality cannot remove differences since these do not necessarily lead to inequality.

Instead, the basic differences between genders are seen as a richness. Man and woman are complementary beings who enrich one another in their harmonious loving union. Each is enriched and fulfilled by their differences.

Moreover, Christianity teaches that the heterosexual couple and the traditional family are the true reality, rooted in nature and instituted by God. The parents are a father, of the male sex and gender, and a mother of the female sex and gender. The idea that sexual orientation can be varied and multiple, resting solely on individual choice, is unacceptable. The various forms of altersexuality or allosexuality are deviations or anomalies which those who wish to be full members of the community must correct.[147] Nonetheless, Christianity respects those persons themselves who belong to sexual and gender minorities.[148] The person is not judged but approached with love for these are the basic commands of Christ.

Chapter 5

The Creation of Man and Woman in the Image of God

So God made man: in the image
of God He made him;
male and female He made them.
(Gen 1:27)

Christian anthropology and its idea of gender are based, primarily, on Scripture and, first of all, on three passages from the book of Genesis 1:26–27; 2:18–25; and 5:1–2. In this presentation of the Christian anthropology of the Orthodox Tradition, we will also refer to the Greek Fathers, especially St Gregory of Nyssa and St Maximus the Confessor. Their thought on gender is subtle and profound and has given rise to many recent studies of the subject. We will also refer to the text of the Septuagint which the Greek Fathers took as their reference. It is the text still used today by the Orthodox Church. For the subject of our study, it differs from the Hebrew (Masoretic) text in several interesting ways.

In the Septuagint, the first text (Gen 1:26–27) reads thus: "Then God said, 'Let Us make man in Our image, according to Our likeness. Let them have dominion over the fish of the sea, over the birds of the heaven, and over the cattle, over all the earth, and over every creeping thing that moves on the earth.' So God made man; in the image of God He made him; male and female He made them."

In verse 26, there is no definite article which gives "a man" a general value, independent of any reference to gender. This is confirmed in the Greek text of the Septuagint by the word used: *anthropos* to translate *adam* in the Hebrew text. It generally means a human being, without specifying the sex. In verse 27 the definite article precedes the noun, and the distinction of sex appears through the use of "male" (ἄρσεν) and "female" (θῆλυ). These adjectives are used later in Genesis 5:2 and also apply to the animals entering Noah's Ark in Genesis 6:19.

There are two parts to the text describing man's creation: "in the image of God He made him;" and "male and female He made them." For some Fathers these two parts should be dissociated. The second part does not explain the first but describes a second phase. The basic primordial message is that the value of the human being comes from being created in the image of God. This precedes the distinction of the sexes and applies to each equally.

St Basil of Caesarea writes: "No one, through ignorance, should take 'man' to refer simply to the masculine sex." He continues: "The woman, just like her husband, has the privilege of being created in the image of God."[149]

For St Gregory of Nyssa, when it is written, "God made man," it means the whole of humanity without distinction of sex: "When the Scripture says: 'God made man,' this indeterminate turn of phrase means all humanity. For in this creation, Adam is not named as he is later in the story. The name given here to man is not this man or that man but the name of universal man. So, this universal appellation of nature leads us to a conclusion like this: by divine foreknowledge and power the whole of humanity is included in this first institution."[150]

St Gregory also explains that the phrase: "male and female made He them," refers to a second level of humanity. The first level is what makes man a being in the image of God, according to the model which is Christ. "Male and female" indicates "a division not related to the divine."[151] He writes:

"'God made man,' says Scripture. 'He made him in the image of God.' From this moment the creation of the being in the image of God attains its perfection. Then Scripture continues the story of the creation and says: 'God made them male and female.' I think that all must realize that this aspect is not found in the prototype. As the Apostle writes: 'In Christ Jesus there is neither male nor female.' Yet Scripture states that man was divided according to sex. So, the creation of our nature is, in a certain sense, double. There is that which makes us like the divinity and that which divides us into sexes. This is the interpretation suggested by the order of Scripture itself. First it is said: 'God made man; in the image of God made He him.' Only afterwards is it said: 'Male and female made He them.' This division is foreign to the divine."[152]

A little later he suggests that the image of God in man lies in the rational, the intellect, and the reason. Sex corresponds to the irrational element.

"As can easily be seen, the human being exists on two levels. There is the Divine level where reason and intelligence do not admit a division into male and female. Then there is the irrational level, bodily and divided into sexes. Every being enjoying human life possesses both levels completely."[153]

It has often been said that Gregory taught a double creation; but the above text shows that he did not teach two successive creations, but creation on two levels. In fact, "creation" is not the most appropriate word. There is a duality, but it is logical rather than chronological. The sexes are added to the image without being divine attributes. God foresees that sexuality will be needed after the fall to allow mankind to reproduce. Before he had sinned, man was to increase as the angels do[154], not biologically or sexually; but *sexuation* exists from the beginning in the division into male and female.[155] Not all commentators make this distinction. Some of them assimilate sexuation and sexuality, placing them after the fall. As I. Floeri writes, "Gregory always applies the phrase 'division into male and female' uniquely to the time before Adam had sinned.[156] After he had sinned the word 'marriage' is used.[157] This phraseology shows that the division into sexes did not of itself lead to the attraction required for marriage. This agrees with what Gregory said of the 'tunics of skins' with which Adam and Eve were clothed after their sin (cf. Gen 3:21). They bring to mankind death, the passions and the sexual instinct.[158] The division into sexes is never mentioned since Adam and Eve were already thus, even before they received the tunics of skins."[159]

The image of God assimilates man to God, whilst the division into sexes tends to assimilate him to the animals.[160] But at this stage St Gregory does not view this negatively since sin and its consequences have not yet occurred. The biblical text itself has a positive meaning since it continues: "Then God saw everything He had made, and indeed, it was very good" (Gen 1:31).

St Maximus the Confessor also expresses profound ideas on this subject. Some parts of his thought accord with the thought of St Gregory of Nyssa, but others go further. In chapter 67 of the *Ambigua to John* St Maximus raises the distinction between male (ἄρσεν) and female (θῆλυ). He distinguished three phases: two *extremes* (concerning respectively the beginning and the end) and a median. The first phase is raised in other texts, but the first two are only raised here as relating to an important point: the sexuation of man at his creation. The text is as follows:

"[The first] extreme is: 'Let Us make a man in Our image, according to Our likeness; (ποιήσωμεν ἄνθρωπον κατ' εἰκόνα ἡμετέραν καὶ καθ' ὁμοίωσιν)' [Gen 1:26]; the median: 'So God made man ... male and female He made them. (καὶ ἐποίησεν ὁ θεὸς τὸν ἄνθρωπον, ἄρσεν καὶ θῆλυ ἐποίησεν αὐτούς)' [Gen 1:27]; [the second] extreme: 'In Jesus Christ ... there is neither male nor female (οὐκ ἔστιν οὔτε ἄρσεν οὔτε θῆλυ)' [Gal 3:28]. The extremes and the median differ for the latter has notions of male and female (τό ἄῤῥεν καί τό θῆλυ), whilst the former do not."[161]

Although St Maximus uses the idea of extremes for the first and the third phases, this is still one of his customary triads, with a beginning (or principle, ἀρχή)—middle (μεσότης)—end (τέλος).[162] Looking at the way he presents his second and third terms, it is like the triad of genesis (or coming into existence) (γένεσις)—movement (κίνησις)—stability (στάσις).[163]

1. When he refers to the passage from Genesis as the beginning or principle: "Let Us make a man in Our image, according to Our likeness" St Maximus is not thinking of the concrete creation of man, but of God's plan. In the terms he uses elsewhere, this is the *logos* of human nature, conceived by and contained in the divine Word before coming into existence at the right time by an act of creation.[164] The plural, used in the text of the Septuagint indicates the Great Divine Counsel (the Trinity) which St Maximus mentions in other contexts. The fact that it is a plan is indicated by the verb ποιήσωμεν which may be translated as "we will make" or "let us make" in the sense of something to be accomplished not as something actually being done.[165] "Let us make a man" (or, as in some translations: "Let us make man") signify man in general. This is human nature at a more general level than the nature specified by the sexes, "male" and "female," which is a divided nature, spread amongst humans of masculine and feminine sex. This higher and more general level is basically defined by the image and likeness of God. In this perspective, the division of humanity by gender does not exist. Fundamentally, both men and woman are created in the image and likeness of God. St Maximus considered that the image is defined above all by the higher faculties of the human

spirit: the mind or intellect, the reason, and the power of self-determination and hence freedom. The likeness lies in the virtues whose seeds are placed in human nature at its creation; but each person, through free will, must cultivate them so that they bear fruit.[166]

2. The second phase treated by St Maximus is the median, expressed by the passage: "So God made man in His own image; in the image of God He made him; male and female He made them." This verse refers to the actual creation which follows from the plan set forth in the first phase. St Maximus omits here "in the image of God He created him." In this way he underlines that there was not a double creation, first of a sexless nature then of a nature specified by two sexes and two genders, male and female. This is different from the concept often attributed to St Gregory of Nyssa, but which, as we have seen, is not truly his. He upholds original sexuation in this way leaving aside the chronology of the second account of the creation of man (Gen 2:7, 18–23) which he never mentions. There, the human being is first created as male and then, starting from there, as female. It is important to remember that in the thought of Gregory of Nyssa sexuation is not the same as sexuality, which is just one way in which sexuation can be expressed, psychologically and physiologically.

For both St Maximus and for St Gregory sexuality is a result of ancestral sin and the fall.[167] Physiologically it implies sexual relations.[168] It is linked to desire and pleasure, so spiritually it is linked to sin and joined to the passions.[169] For him, sexuality did not exist for man in Paradise. He considers that man could then reproduce without sexual[170] or material[171] relations. He does not develop his thought on this matter. He most likely borrowed the idea from St Gregory of Nyssa.[172]

However, sexuation was given to man when he was created. He received all its attributes, both psychological and physical,[173] so sexuality existed as a potentiality from the beginning. St Maximus does not explain this paradox; but St Gregory suggests that God foresaw that man would sin, and so would die. Man would lose the life of Paradise but would still need to reproduce so that humanity might last. After the fall, this could only come to pass sexually, through the body and matter.[174] St Maximus wrote little about sexuality and never gave a complete and coherent analysis of the question. Nothing proves that he got this idea from St Gregory, but nothing proves that he did not.[175] It is the only way of providing a satisfactory solution to the problem of a sexuality which exists but is *a priori* inactive.

3. The third phase considered by St Maximus is the other "extreme" going beyond the "median." It is summed up by the formula: "In Jesus Christ there is neither male nor female," which comes from St Paul's epistle to the Galatians (3:28): "There is neither Jew nor Greek, there is neither slave nor free, there is neither male nor female; for you are all one in Christ Jesus."

This third phase in the thought of St Maximus brings us back to the first, aligning with his principle that the beginning coincides with the end.[176] As we will see in other texts, St Maximus does not envisage here the abolition of sexuation. He has in mind a state where man and woman are seen in the unity of their common nature which is logically prior to a view of their sexual characteristics. We will not treat this matter here, but later in a special analysis.

Before concluding this chapter, it must be emphasized that none of the Fathers suppose that man was initially created *both* male and female, that is to say, androgyne or hermaphrodite. This comes from certain rabbinic commentaries[177] which base themselves on the use of the singular in the Hebrew text: "male and female He made him" not "male and female He made them." The same idea can be found in the Gnostics.[178] All the Fathers teach that spiritually, the nature of the human being is primordial since it is created in the image and likeness of God. The gender is secondary, as St Paul forcefully reminds us in Galations 3:28 where he refers to Christ and Christian spiritual life.

Chapter 6

The Divine Plan for the Harmonious Synergy of Man and Woman

And the Lord God said:
"It is not good for man to be alone;
I will make him a helper comparable to him."
(Gen 2:18)

Chapter 2 of the book of Genesis presents a more detailed and chronological version of the creation of man and woman.

Then God formed man (τὸν ἄνθρωπον) out of dust from the ground, and breathed in his face the breath of life; and man (ὁ ἄνθρωπος) became a living soul. Then the LORD God planted a garden eastward in Eden, and there He put the man (τὸν ἄνθρωπον) He formed. . . . Then the LORD God took the man (τὸν ἄνθρωπον) He formed and put him in the garden of Eden to tend and keep it. . . .
And the LORD God said, "It is not good for man to be alone; I will make him a helper comparable to him (Οὐ καλὸν εἶναι τὸν ἄνθρωπον μόνον ποιήσωμεν αὐτῷ βοηθὸν κατ αὐτόν)." Also, God formed out of the ground all of the wild animals of the field and all the birds of heaven, and brought them to Adam to see what he would call them. Thus whatever Adam called each living creature, that was its name. So Adam gave names to all cattle, to the all the birds of heaven, and to all the wild animals of the field. But for Adam there was not found a helper comparable to him (τῷ δὲ Αδαμ οὐχ εὑρέθη βοηθὸς ὅμοιος αὐτῷ). Thus God brought a trance upon Adam, and he slept; and He took one of his ribs, and filled up the flesh in its place. Then the LORD God built the rib He took from Adam into a woman (εἰς γυναῖκα), and brought her to him. So Adam said: "This is now bone of my bones and flesh of my flesh. She shall be called Woman, because she was taken out of Man (αὕτη κληθήσεται γυνή, ὅτι ἐκ τοῦ ἀνδρὸς αὐτῆς ἐλήμφθη αὕτη). For this reason a man shall leave his father

and mother and be joined to his wife (προσκολληθήσεται πρὸς τὴν γυναῖκα αὐτοῦ); and the two shall become one flesh." Now the two were naked, both Adam and his wife (ὅ τε Αδαμ καὶ ἡ γυνὴ αὐτοῦ), and were not ashamed.

The first account of the creation of the human being in chapter 2 sets forth the Divine plan. Both male and female are created equally in the image of God, yet with sex. However, the second account appears to suggest that God had at first thought to create a single human being, called in the Septuagint *Anthropos,* a sexless word. Then God says that "it is not good that man should be alone." This phrase is extremely important since it shows that the human person is not sufficient unto him(her)self. Alone, the person cannot be fulfilled and cannot lead a good life except in a permanent relationship with another.

What follows shows that no other created being is an adequate partner. Only another human can fill this need, and this human must be of the other sex. So God creates the woman from the rib of the man, showing that she shares his human nature. She has the same nature and essence. But with what God takes from man, He makes a woman, a human being of the other sex.

A feminist reading of this passage emphasizes that woman is posterior to man. She is taken from him and is presented as his helper. This is seen as depicting the inferiority of the woman and her dependence on man. However, it is easy to interpret the text differently. It shows that when man is alone, he is unfulfilled. Without the woman he is weak, and incapable of leading a good life without her and so to fulfill himself. "Help" does not mean "slave," but support. Though the reverse is also true, that woman needs man to become fulfilled, it is striking that the passage does not state this clearly but emphasizes the weakness and dependence of the man. This is then confirmed, where it is written, "For this reason a man shall leave his father and mother and be joined to his wife," rather than the opposite. This seems to set the adult male in a relationship with his wife resembling the relationship of children to their parents.

God could have made a clone of Adam, but instead He chose to create a being like him, yet different. They shared the same human nature; so they were at the same level and could enjoy perfect communication and unity, which is not possible with any animal in creation. With different sexes, they are complementary which allows them to go beyond themselves to true fulfillment.

They are not bound to stay enclosed in self-reproduction, or contemplation and love of another identical self, in other words, in a form of narcissism.

Since woman is taken from the flesh of man, she is one flesh with him and he with her (bone of his bones and flesh of his flesh as the text puts it). But the sex given by God to this woman taken from man makes them both become one flesh ("and they shall become one flesh.") in two other ways.

The first way is in a union of sexes which is not sexual. St Irenaeus of Lyon explains this as follows: "Adam and Eve were naked and were not ashamed, for they still had the innocent minds of children. It was impossible for them to imagine any of those thoughts which, perversely, arouse desires of shameful pleasure. They still preserved the integrity of their nature, … and [their soul] could not conceive that which is evil. So they had no shame in kissing and caressing each other chastely as children do."[179]

The second way is psychological and spiritual. The word "to become" used in the biblical text is especially important. It signifies a task to be accomplished and not simply the expression of the instinct which drives man and woman to come together in fleshly union. The task is first a psychological task: the fulfillment of each in relation to the other; but it is also a spiritual task.

St Maximus the Confessor sees in the division into male and female a polarity which Adam and Eve were called to bring to perfect unity in Paradise. They were to unite also four other polarities found in creation: created and uncreated, sensible and intelligible, heaven and earth, and paradise and the rest of the world.[180]

These five divisions are present in the world from its creation. They imply no conflict, separation, or opposition, but rather distances to be removed and polarities to be reunited. The first man was called to abolish these distances and to unite these polarities. He was quite able to do this. It was his duty. St Maximus explains that he was to be a mediator. For this he was equipped as "the last being to be introduced amongst the creatures, like a link," and "a laboratory where everything was concentrated." Man was not called to unify the realities of creation in a single entity by assimilating them to each other or melting them all together in one. For it is clear, for example, that the created and the uncreated, the sensible and the intelligible are different essences and cannot be fused into one single essence. Man's true task is to bring about this unification of different realities through what St Maximus called their *logoi*, their deepest spiritual reality, their beginning and end in God. Man's intellect may achieve this through contemplation.[181] This process brings the realization and knowledge of the relationships between things which apparently have none and appear totally separate. St Maximus gives as an example the idea that the creation is separate from God which he attributes to ignorance. Contemplation moves upward. St Maximus explains that in the Divine plan, man is called "to bring about in harmony the reciprocal unification of the extremes of beings, working from those which are closest to each other to those which are furthest separated, from those which are least to those which are most excellent, through a tension which ends in God." He also writes: "He is to unite in himself beings whose nature keeps them at a great distance from each other. Union with God, the cause of all, brings all things to one. Man begins this unification with his own division into male and female, and goes on, step by step, in order, through all creation to reach God, the limit of his sublime ascension: God in Whom there is no division."[182]

The division into male and female is engraved in human nature. The spiritual task of man is to unite these two *logoi* which define the two sides into the single *logos* which surpasses them: human nature as a whole. Concretely, the spirit must perceive in both man and woman the human being in each of them: the identical nature, or essence, which each of them possesses and which is the image of God. This *logos* is the *logos* which was God's pattern for creating man, before the creation and division into male and female.

St Maximus explains here: "[Man was to begin] this unification starting from his own division, completely shaking off from nature, by means of a supremely dispassionate relation to the divine virtue, the property of male and female, which in no way was linked to the original *logos* of the divine plan concerning human generation, so that he might be shown forth as, and become solely a human being according to the divine plan, not divided by the designation of male and female (according to the *logos* by which he formerly came into being), nor divided into the parts that now appear around him, thanks to the perfect union, as I said, with his own *logos*, according to which he exists."[183]

The expression "by means of a supremely dispassionate relation to the divine virtue" is important for the whole of this work. As we shall see, the relationship between male and female hardens and changes to conflicts and antagonism through the influence of sin and the passions. So, it is obvious that the process of unification envisaged by St Maximus presupposes a man pure of all passions. He must be in a state of impassibility, full of virtue like the first man before his sin. The process of contemplation, through which the unification desired by God is to be brought about, has the same requirements. In the spiritual thought of St Maximus as, especially in Evagrius of Pontus, and all the Greek Fathers, contemplation is impossible without impassibility.

St Maximus does not see sex or gender as being abolished. It would be absurd to imagine that God should order man to abolish what He had just created. The duty of humankind, male and female, is to prevent this difference turning into concrete division: separation, opposition, and conflict. He must clearly perceive what unites man and woman at the deepest level, so that their relationship should be truly human, between two human beings. In this union there is no tension between the polarities of sex and gender, but positive collaboration.

When he refers to sin and the fall, St Maximus writes of how the first man and woman failed in this task. The relation between the sexes, by becoming also a sexual relation, was much changed for the worse through the effects of sin and passion.

Chapter 7

Sin and the Fall

> Then the eyes of the two were opened, and they knew they were naked.
> (Gen 3:7)

The biblical account of the original sin has consequences for the relations between man and woman. These can be broken down into three stages. The first relates to the respective roles of the man and the woman in the process and act of sinning. The second concerns the effects of the sin on sexuality. The third concerns how the relations between man and woman were affected.

The Respective Roles of Man and Woman in the Process and Act of Sin

Chapter 3 of the book of Genesis describes the process of ancestral sin in this way:

> Now the serpent was more cunning than all the wild animals the Lord God made on the earth. And he said to the woman, "Has God indeed said, 'You shall not eat of every tree of the garden'?" And the woman said to the serpent, "We may eat the fruit from the trees of the garden; but from the fruit of the tree in the middle of the garden, God has said, 'You shall not eat it, nor shall you touch it, lest you die.'" Then the serpent said to the woman, "You shall not die by death. For God knows in the day you eat from it your eyes will be opened, and you will be like gods, knowing good and evil." So when the woman saw the tree was good for food, was pleasant to the eyes, and a tree beautiful to contemplate, she took its fruit and ate. She also gave it to her husband with her, and he ate.
> (Gen 3:1–6)

Many commentators have interpreted this text in a way which is unfavorable to the woman. The serpent, that is, the devil, spoke to her rather than to

Adam since she was weaker, more open to suggestion, and dependent on her senses. For Adam she would then be the seductress, the temptress, and so fundamentally responsible for the fact that he sinned. Yet none of this can be found or even suggested in the text itself, nor can it be deduced from it.

As regards the first point, the serpent could have tempted Adam as he did Eve. That he chose to tempt Eve may suggest that he targeted her since he saw that she was the more important and valuable of the two.

As regards the second point, Eve's actions show her desire to share: seeing that the tree was good for food, that it was pleasant to the eyes, and a tree desirable to make one wise, she gave to her husband and he spontaneously accepted. She clearly did wrong. She did not realize that she had been cheated and that the quality of the fruit was an illusion, but Adam was just as much in the wrong. What would feminist commentators have said if Adam had been the first to take the fruit and then given it to Eve? They would have said that this showed how man dominates woman, bossing her about, and forcing her to do his will. She would be seen as passive, enclosed in a role of submission.

In the next part of the text God asks Adam what has happened. He relates the facts, not judging or blaming Eve:

> So the LORD God called Adam and said to him, "Adam, where are you?" He replied, "I heard Your voice as You were walking in the garden, and I was afraid because I was naked; so I hid myself." Thus He said, "Who said you were naked? Have you eaten from the one tree which I commanded you not to eat?" Then Adam said, "The woman whom You gave me,[184] gave me of the tree, and I ate."
>
> (Gen 3:9–12)

In the same way, God does not judge Eve morally. He simply asks her what caused her to act in this way. She replies factually, placing the responsibility for what took place on the devil who deceived her:

"So the LORD said to the woman, 'What is this you have done?' The woman said, 'The serpent deceived me, and I ate' (Gen 3:13).

God Himself lays the blame on the serpent and punishes him for his sin:

"Thus the LORD God said to the serpent: 'Because you have done this, You are cursed more than all cattle, and more than all the wild animals of the earth. On your breast and belly you shall go, and you shall eat dust all the days of your life"[185] (Gen 3:14).

Afterward, God says to Adam:

"Because you heeded the voice of your wife, and ate from the one tree of which I commanded you, saying, 'You shall not eat from it, cursed is the ground in your labors'"[186] (Gen 3:17).

These words do not mark out the woman as guilty, nor as a seductress: "the voice of the wife," means simply her words. It is also significant that God does not say to Adam, as to the devil, "you are cursed," but "cursed is the ground in your labors."[187]

God seems to have been indulgent toward the first woman and the first man.[188] What followed their common sin is not presented as a Divine punishment, but more as a consequence of what they did: suffering will enter the life of the man and the woman. For the woman, sufferings will come with childbirth, and for the man, through tilling the ground.[189] Death also appeared as a consequence of sin:

> To the woman He [the Lord] said: "I will greatly multiply your pain and your groaning, and in pain you shall bring forth children. Your recourse will be to your husband, and he shall rule over you." Then to Adam He said, "Because yo heeded the voice of your wife, and ate from the one tree of which I commanded you, saying, 'You shall not eat of it', cursed is the ground in your labors. In toil[190] you shall eat from it all the days of your life. Both thorns and thistles it shall bring forth for you, and you shall eat the herb of the field. In the sweat of your face you shall eat bread till you return to the ground from which were taken. Earth you are and to earth you shall return."
>
> (Gen 3:16–19)

The Effects of Sin on Sexuality

The text makes almost no reference to sexuality being aroused by original sin. This is indicated indirectly by the reference to childbirth which is one of its effects. Then it is indicated again where she who has been referred to as "the woman" is given the name of "Eve" to mark her childbearing. "And Adam called his wife's name Life [Eve] because she was the mother of all living" (Gen

3:20). Sexual union and childbirth are clearly mentioned in chapter 4 after the account of the expulsion from Paradise: "Now Adam knew Eve his wife, and she conceived and bore Cain" (Gen 4:1).

We must remember that biological childbirth through sexual intercourse did not exist before the fall. St Gregory of Nyssa and St Maximus the Confessor thought it inconceivable that if Adam and Eve had remained eternally in Paradise they would have remained alone with no one else. They suggest that in Paradise men would have reproduced non-biologically, without sex.

St Gregory of Nyssa has left a long passage on this subject in *The Creation of Man*. "Before the fall," he writes, "the text makes no mention of childbirth, nor of the pain which it brings, nor of the instinct of procreation. When God expels Adam and Eve from Paradise after their sin and the woman is condemned to the pains of childbirth, it is only then that Adam knows his wife in marriage[191] and the first child is born.

Is it then possible to say that 'if, in Paradise, there were no marriage or pains of childbirth, ... the multiplication of human life would not have occurred'? As Christ says to the Sadducees: 'But those who are counted worthy to attain that age, and the resurrection from the dead, neither marry nor are given in marriage;[192] nor can they die anymore, for they are equal to the angels and are sons of God, being sons of the resurrection' (Luke 20: 35–36) where 'the grace of the Resurrection is shown to us as the return to their former state [that of Paradise] of those who fell.'" So, St Gregory concludes that "the life before the fall was, in its way, angelic." He goes on to explain: "As we know, there is no marriage amongst the angels, yet their host is infinitely great ... So we, like them, if sin had not changed us and made us fall from the equality we once enjoyed with them, would not have needed marriage to multiply.

How angelic nature multiplies is beyond telling and beyond the reach of man's conjectures: but it is certain that this takes place. This way of multiplication would also have been man's, for his nature is close to the angelic. It would have raised humanity to the level fixed by the Will of God. Some may find it hard to conceive of such a way of procreation for mankind, where marriage is not needed. We ask these to tell us how the angels exist and how their hosts make up a unique race which can still be numbered. To those who believe that it is impossible for man to be without marriage, we have grounds to give this reply: man would be without marriage as the angels themselves, for our likeness to the angels before our fall is proved by the restoration of all things to their former state."

St Gregory goes on to explain that God foresaw that man's angelic state would not last, and that he would need to procreate in a different way. So, he gave to man and woman the organs of sexual union to allow them to bear children biologically, like animals, but only after their sin and fall: "He Who brings all things into being, and Who, through His own Will, made every man in the divine image, was averse to seeing the whole multitude of human souls brought into being through the addition of successive generations. His powerful foreknowledge conceived, overall, in its fullness all human nature and raised it to be equal to the angels. Yet His all-seeing power foresaw how our freedom would err from the straight way and the fall from angelic life which would follow. To avoid the mutilation of the ranks of human souls, which would lose the means of angelic multiplication, He gave our nature a means of reproduction better adapted to our slide into sin. Instead of the nobility of the angels, He ordained that we should pass on life to others like beasts and creatures without reason [that is, animals]."[193]

Some patristic commentaries also refer to sexuality in the preceding verses: "Then the eyes of both of them were opened, and they knew that they were naked; and they sewed fig leaves together and made themselves coverings. And they heard the sound of the LORD God walking in the garden in the cool of the day, and Adam and his wife hid themselves from the presence of the LORD God among the trees of the garden. Then the LORD God called to Adam and said to him, 'Where are you?' So he said, 'I heard Your voice in the garden, and I was afraid because I was naked; and I hid myself'" (Gen 3:7–10).

The realization of the man and woman that they were naked has often been taken for an awareness of their loss of the divine grace and glory which had clothed humanity from the first. More prosaically, Adam and Eve are seen as ashamed at discovering their sexes, their sexuality, and at the loss of their initial innocence attested several verses previously: "Now the two were naked, both Adam and his wife, and were not ashamed" (Gen 2:25).

St Irenaeus of Lyon is more precise. Here, he sees the arousal of sexual desire. For him, the coverings of fig leaves were like hair shirts. Adam and Eve chose these leaves which "prick and tear the flesh rather than others which would have been more tender." They were a means of penitence and a means of "repressing the nagging flame of the flesh."[194]

Soon afterwards, the coverings of fig leaves were replaced by tunics of skins: "Also for Adam and his wife the LORD God made garments of skin, and clothed them" (Gen 3:21). St Irenaeus sees in this text a gift of God, Who, in His mercy assuaged their pain.[195]

This episode led St Gregory of Nyssa to develop an anthropology which is key for our subject. He explains: "by the term 'skin' [should be understood] the form (*eidos*) of animal nature with which we have been clothed to acquaint us with the passions." He goes on: "What we have taken from the skins of animals are sexual union, conception, childbearing, defilement, suckling, feeding, excretion, slow growth to adulthood, maturity, old age, sickness and death."[196]

This idea was taken up by St Maximus the Confessor. He also considered that God's initial plan was for a spiritual mode of reproduction which would allow men to reproduce in Paradise.[197] Adam's transgression introduced a new mode of reproduction, like that of animals.[198] It took place through sexual union,[199] bodily and material,[200] infused with bodily pleasure and driven by it.[201] It is accompanied by passion,[202] followed by pain,[203] corruption,[204] (change and decay) and finally death.[205]

St Maximus considers that this new mode of reproduction is intimately linked to sin. It goes against God's initial plan and is a consequence of the transgression of God's commandment by the first man and the first woman. They come together driven by the desire of pleasure[206] and it is the same for their descendants.[207] It is in this sense that St Maximus understands the famous verse of Psalm: "For behold, I was conceived in wickedness, and in sins did my mother bear me" (Ps 50:7 LXX [51:7]).

"Since God's initial plan was that we reproduce without marriage[208] or corruption, Adam's unlawful act, transgressing the commandment, brought in marriage through his violation of the law given by God. Thenceforth, all those who spring from Adam's line are brought forth in iniquity (ἀνομία) and fall under the condemnation of their first father. Moreover, 'in sin my mother conceived me,' signifies that our first mother, Eve, conceived in sin, passionately desiring pleasure. So, we too, falling under the condemnation of the mother, are said to be conceived in sin."[209]

Because of the sin of Adam and Eve, men can no longer come into the world without such conception. With no other alternative, human nature is imprisoned and tyrannized by this "law" with its inevitable effects.[210] St Maximus evokes "the laws ... of nature by which sin, through disobedience, condemned men to become like animals without reason in the way one generation follows another."[211] This new law is the law of the flesh which replaces and opposes the spiritual law which formerly held sway.[212] St Maximus also calls it "the law of sin."[213] It becomes inherent to fallen human nature, so he also calls it "the law of nature"[214] which henceforth is in its grip.[215]

So, St Maximus considers that this fleshly mode of procreation, moved by pleasure and linked to passion, is handed down from generation to generation in all men without exception. With it come its effects: the consequences of the ancestral sin,[216] suffering, decay, and death.

The Consequences of Sin on the Relations Between Man and Woman

In Gen 3: 16: "Your recourse [some translations use *desire*] will be to your husband, and he shall rule over you," two consequences of original sin appear which trouble and change the relationships between man and woman: carnal desire of woman for man (but also of man for woman); and the domination of the female by the male.

Of course, all the other passions, which we have described elsewhere in detail,[217] are joined to these. The first of them is *philautia* or egotistical self-love. The others flow from this: all the sexual passions (described by the word *porneia* by the Greek Fathers); all forms of aggression (irritability, bitterness, anger, rancor, and hatred); fear, anxiety and anguish; sadness and depression; vanity; pride (which includes the spirit of superiority and domination, strongly linked to self-love and egoism).

St Maximus the Confessor stresses that sin and the passions have fragmented human nature. They have aroused the opposition and division of all its members which shows itself in the clash of individual wills.[218] Naturally, this opposition and division have also marked the relationships of man and woman, which are the basic relationships of the human community. This subject is treated in the following passage which also evokes the question of domination, of great interest to our contemporaries.

"In the beginning, the deceiving devil used a ruse which wickedly inspired man with egotistical self-love (*philautia*) and tricked him through the love of pleasure. He separated us from God and our fellow men through individual will (*gnômè*). In this way, leaving the straight way, he divided nature, cutting it up into a multitude of opinions and imaginations. Then, over time, he turned into a law the seeking out and discovery of every kind of evil, aided and abetted by our faculties. So that evil should endure, he made use of the irreconcilable preferences of each individual's will (*gnômè*). In this way, once and for all, he convinced man to depart from his natural path: to turn his appetite from what is allowed to what is forbidden. This led to the three great fundamental transgressions which are at the root of all the others: ignorance of God, egotistical self-love (*philautia*) and despotic power. Every sin depends on these and leans on them and each other. For ignorance of God leads to egotistical self-love from whence comes the tyranny with which we oppress those around us."[219]

Original Nature and Fallen Nature

The idea of nature is controversial in modern debates on gender. Gender theorists are strongly opposed to this idea since it affirms that gender is influenced by biology and not just culture. Worse, it establishes that in nature there are just two genders which does not allow an individual any free choice in the matter. They are entrenched in their beliefs by their atheism which cannot admit that there should be a nature/essence defined by God. In philosophy, this debate was started by Existentialism for which "existence precedes essence." This means that man first exists, undefined, and then defines himself through his own choices.[220]

However, those who stick to the traditional concept of gender are strongly attached to the idea of nature. They see in it an untouchable standard. Either they see gender as a biological fact, or they see it as established by the Creator and worthy of absolute respect.

Eastern Christianity, starting from the patristic tradition and its exegesis of the biblical text, has developed a much subtler anthropology and theology. The concept of nature is seen as ambiguous since it may refer to original nature, created by God in accord with His Will, in truth an absolute standard; or it may refer to fallen nature after the ancestral sin, utterly corrupted, and no standard at all. It is just a way of existing which needs to be cleansed and purified until it returns to the original state it has lost.

So, when nature is mentioned, the nature in question must be defined: original nature willed and created by God which fallen man must try to restore; or present fallen nature which a Christian cannot commend. Instead, a Christian must fight it in all its shifts and infamies, and against all the chains which must be broken for true human freedom to be regained.

Chapter 8

The Recapitulation and Reunification of Genders in Christ

In Christ "there is neither male nor female." (Gal 3:28)

The Greek Fathers understood the saving work of Christ in terms of healing and recovery.[221] In their anthropology and spirituality, the passions which afflict the fallen nature of man arise from an unnatural use of his faculties. This is pathological and leads to different sicknesses and forms of slavery as man becomes attached to his ego and the things of this world.

Christ assumed fallen human nature, but without sin, and so restored it to its original state. Going further, He also accomplished what Adam and Eve should have gradually reached before sin broke their progress. If man unites himself to Christ and lives in Him, he receives this grace which Christ has potentially gained for all. The saving work of Christ is a work of reconciliation and reunification. It brings peace to every division, opposition, and conflict.

This theme runs through the Epistle of St Paul to the Ephesians:

"Having made known to us the mystery of His will, according to His good pleasure which He purposed in Himself, that in the dispensation of the fullness of the times He might gather together in one all things in Christ, both which are in heaven and which are on earth—in Him" (Eph 1:9–10).

"But now in Christ Jesus you who once were far off have been brought near by the blood of Christ. For He Himself is our peace, who has made both one, and has broken down the middle wall of separation, having abolished in His flesh the enmity, that is, the law of commandments contained in ordinances, so as to create in Himself one new man from the two, thus making peace, and that He might reconcile them both to God in one body through the cross, thereby putting to death the enmity. And He came and preached peace to you who were afar off and to those who were near" (Eph 2:13–17).

The first passage treats the recapitulation of all things in Christ, a theme discussed in depth by St Irenaeus of Lyon.[222] The second passage concerns the Jews and the gentiles, but it has been interpreted to apply to all humanity. This wider application is confirmed by another passage from St Paul:

"For it pleased the Father … by Him [Christ] to reconcile all things to Himself, by Him, whether things on earth or things in heaven, having made peace through the blood of His cross. And you, who once were alienated and enemies in your mind by wicked works, yet now He has reconciled in the body of His flesh through death, to present you holy, and blameless, and above reproach in His sight" (Col 1:19–22).

We have seen that St Maximus the Confessor considered that God had given to man the work of unification. He was to unite in himself and bring to God all the polarities present in the world since its creation. St Maximus called them divisions; but we have seen that it is not a question of divisions in the strict sense of the word. It is more a question of what is distinct and of differing nature and which may therefore be separate. Man, called to be the mediator, must act to unite them. Adam, however, distanced himself from God through sin and failed in his calling. What were polarities became real divisions: realities which are separated, at a distance, opposed and in conflict. They were not unified in man's contemplation but were abandoned to the passions born in him.

St Maximus shows that Christ took upon Himself this task where man had failed and brought it to fulfillment. He analyzes the different polarities which Christ united in Himself, following the order which Adam was to follow—(1) male-female; (2) the inhabited world-paradise; (3) heaven-earth; (4) sensible and intelligible; (5) created and uncreated; and concludes his analysis thus:

"And with us and for us, [the Incarnate Word] embraces the whole creation. He unites tightly and unbreakably around himself the extremes through the medians insofar as they are parts of Himself: paradise and the inhabited world; heaven and earth; sensible and intelligible realities.[223] For He, like us, has a body with sensitivity, soul, and intellect. To each He attaches the extreme of the universal element which belongs to it in the way described above. He recapitulates all things in Himself in a way befitting God, showing that the whole creation is one. It is as though creation itself is a human being, perfected through the union of all its members together, bowing to Him in the wholeness of its existence."[224]

As regards the difference between male and female, which is the main concern of this work, there are two texts which show us the thought of St Maximus on this subject.

The first text is this:

"God became man to save man who was lost, binding up in Himself the wounds of nature which affected the nature of the whole universe. He showed that the fundamental *logoi* are superior to those of the parts and accomplished the great plan of God by recapitulating everything, what is on earth and what is in heaven, in Himself in Whom all was created.

For sure, He began this unification of all things in Himself by starting with our own separation. He became perfect man, of us, for us and like us, without need of sexual union, leaving out nothing save sin. I believe that by this He shows that there could perhaps be another way for humanity to multiply, conceived by God. [This would have been set in train] if man had kept the commandment and had not fallen into bestiality by improper use of his own faculties. So, Christ drove out from nature the difference and division into male and female, a difference, as I have said, which He in no way needed to become man, and without which existence would perhaps have been possible. There is no need for this division to last perpetually, for, says the divine apostle, in Christ Jesus 'there is neither male nor female' (Gal 3:28)."[225]

St Maximus here evokes the special way in which Christ came into the world. Unlike other men, he was conceived of a virgin without seed, without sex.[226] There was no pleasure, no sin or passion, and no corruption.[227] This way of conception without sex, as we have seen, was the way willed by God for men from the beginning.

This way of coming into the world of Christ was not just a means to complete unfinished business. Sex, sin, and the passions are part of the way fallen man reproduces. So, this new way which the Word chose to come into the world helps to save the humanity which He had assumed.

He opens the way to childbirth without sex: a spiritual rebirth through baptism which sets up a new spiritual relationship of paternity and filiation.[228] He also avoids in Himself the negative sides of sex: sin, the passions, and their consequences. "'In him there is neither male nor female' (Gal 3: 28). There is no trace of the passions of nature enslaved by corruption or of childbirth."[229] To those who are united with Him He gives the grace to avoid the same things.

St Maximus combines these two themes in a passage from his *Commentary on the Lord's Prayer*:

"Christ is forever born, mysteriously and willingly, taking flesh in those who are saved. Of the soul which brings Him forth He makes a virgin mother who, in short, bears no trace of nature subject to corruption and childbirth through the union of male and female. ... He who examines the nature of what comes into being and what follows from that, without passion and with a clear mind, will plainly see that reproduction starts in corruption and ends in corruption. Christ has none of those passions linked to reproduction and corruption ... if he said truly who proclaimed: For in Christ 'there is neither male nor female' (Gal 3:28). For he clearly refers to the characteristics and passions of nature subject to corruption and reproduction."[230]

Though sexuality is transcended, the qualities of the sexes remain. Yet they are no more bound up in the divisions and conflicts which are linked to sex and the passions which go with it. This is confirmed by St Maximus himself in a passage from *Questions to Thalassios* where he mentions "the various unions which exist between separated creatures thanks to Christ." He notes: "He united the human being by mystically suppressing through the Spirit the difference between male and female, freeing for both the *logos* of their nature from its properties linked to the passions."[231] The passions that have the worst effects on relations between man and woman are aggression and carnal desire which were the first to be uprooted by Christ. This is how St Maximus understands the message of Galatians 3:28: "the divine Apostle says '[in Christ] there is neither male nor female', that is, neither aggression nor desire."[232] This idea can also be found in Clement of Alexandria: "The heretics do not understand that 'male' and 'female' refer to aggression and desire ... so that by repenting one may become 'neither male nor female.'"[233]

This brings us back to the beginning, when the Creator conceived and made man as a human being in His own image with no distinction of sex. In other words, as St Maximus proposes, the end comes back to the beginning. In both, the distinction between male and female becomes secondary before the oneness of humanity. Here we may recall the text of St Maximus quoted in Chapter 5 about the inequality of those things which move between extremes:

"[The first] extreme is: 'Let us make a man (ἄνθρωπον) in our image and according to our likeness' [Gen 1:26]; the median is: 'So God created man in His own image; in the image of God He created him; male and female (ἄρσεν καὶ θῆλυ) He created them.' [Gen 1:27]; the other extreme is: 'in Christ Jesus there is neither male nor female (οὔτε ἄρσεν οὔτε θῆλυ)' [Gal 3:28]. The extremes and the median differ. In the latter, there is both male and female (τό ἄῤῥεν καί τό θῆλυ), but in the former they are not present."[234]

The Creator may have conceived and fashioned man as, first of all, a human being with no distinction of the sexes; but this does not mean that man first existed without any sexual nature. Man, considered at first independently of his sex, is a "logical" anteriority not an "ontological" anteriority. Christ englobes in Himself all humanity, independently of the distinction between male and female, but was nonetheless born into the world as a human being of the masculine sex.

As St Maximus explains, Christ, unifying all things in Himself raised beings from the particular which divides them, to the universal which unites them. St Maximus clearly indicates that it is not the distinctions themselves which are abolished, but the sources of division which lie within them and the fragmentation of nature by sin. Christ, he says: "binds up in Himself the wounds" of all nature, especially those of the "man who was lost," that is, fallen human nature.

The second text is this:

"Thus [Christ] first united in Himself ourselves, suppressing the difference between male and female. Instead of men and women, where the mode of division is especially obvious, He showed us to be purely and simply human beings, made after His pattern, bearing his image pure and unsullied, in no way touched by any mark of corruption."[235]

Here St Maximus affirms that man and woman are first and foremost human beings. They have the same quality and value since they are both created in the image of God. They bear this image identically. It is, one may say, their essential character. As we will see in the chapters that follow, this has very important consequences for Christian spirituality and its idea of relationships between man and woman.

Chapter 9

The Transfiguration of Gender in the World to Come

For in the resurrection they neither marry nor are given in marriage.
(Matt 22:30)

We know very little about the state of the human body after the Resurrection and our manner of life in the Kingdom of Heaven[236] especially as concerns gender and sexuality. However, a passage from the Gospel according to St Matthew is an essential point of reference:

"The same day the Sadducees, who say there is no resurrection, came to Him and asked Him, saying: 'Teacher, Moses said that if a man dies, having no children, his brother shall marry his wife and raise up offspring for his brother. Now there were with us seven brothers. The first died after he had married, and having no offspring, left his wife to his brother. Likewise the second also, and the third, even to the seventh. Last of all the woman died also. Therefore, in the resurrection, whose wife of the seven will she be? For they all had her.' Jesus answered and said to them, 'You are mistaken, not knowing the Scriptures nor the power of God. For in the resurrection they neither marry nor are given in marriage, but are like angels of God in heaven'" (Matt 22:23–30).

This text indicates that in the Kingdom of Heaven the possibility of marriage no longer exists ("they neither marry nor are given in marriage"). It also indicates that those who were married in this life will have a new relationship, different from their marriage. For those worthy of the Kingdom of Heaven it may be supposed that they will be like brothers and sisters, as were Adam and Eve in the beginning, and all those in the Kingdom. The comparison with the angels indicates a spiritual existence, dematerialized but not bodiless, and desexualized since the bodily reproduction of humanity exists no longer. It will be chaste since bodily reproduction has no further use, so the desire and the sexual instinct are linked to it become inactive.[237] However, what we wish to emphasize is that there is nothing in the text to indicate that humans have no sex. As regards their physical and bodily constitution men remain men and women remain women. Yet this difference in sex and gender is no longer linked to the passions or to any inequality or conflict whatsoever. Tertullian writes of this:

"There is no promise that Christians who leave the world will be reinstated in the married condition at the day of the Resurrection. Rather, they will be changed and will put on the chaste state of the angels. Thenceforth they will no longer know any of those torments which arise from the envy of the flesh."[238]

The Fathers who reflected on how our bodies will be after the Resurrection thought that each person would be reunited with his own body,[239] the one he had during this earthly life, with his own personal identity.[240] Death is a temporary separation of the soul from body, which, though it decomposes still keeps a link with the person, a link which will be fully restored at the Resurrection.[241] The body will then receive its life and shape, but will enjoy a new mode of existence.[242]

The question remains as to whether the body, in its new mode of existence, still retains the properties and faculties linked to its earthly life when they may be useless and inactive in its heavenly life; for instance reproductive and digestive organs.

Tertullian replies positively.[243] For him the flesh will rise again "the same and in its wholeness."[244] Moreover, the nature of both man and woman after the Resurrection will correspond to their nature at the beginning, when they were created. Their sexes, present at the creation, affecting both their souls and bodies,[245] will remain after the Resurrection. The sexual organs and digestive organs will still be present in the risen bodies; but eating and reproduction will cease, as will the instincts and desires linked to them in the world. They will remain inactive forever just as they become inactive for a time in the world through fasting and abstinence. There will be another use for these organs.[246] For Tertullian it is the disappearance of the passions, linked to sex, which iſ important aſ ſhown by hiſ remark above.[247]

When he speaks of "the angelic substance which awaits [us] on high which will mold the human race into one sex,"[248] Tertullian does not mean to deny the persistence of sexual characteristics which he affirms so strongly elsewhere.

He sees this as a spiritual transcendence of the duality created by the passions and the division and opposition of sexes and genders which are its result.

St Augustine adopts a similar position.[249] He considers that sexual differentiation, the male-female distinction, will remain, but without sexuality which will be unnecessary, since biological reproduction will be no more. Moreover, man and women will no longer relate to each other through marriage but will live chastely together with none of the passions linked to the fallen world, to sexuality and sex. They will be as the angels in heaven:

"I believe that the opinion of those who believe in the resurrection of the one sex and the other is reasonable. For then the desire which confuses us will no longer exist. For before they had sinned, the man and the woman were naked and yet not ashamed. So, the vices will be cut off from these bodies but their nature will remain. For the sex of the women is in no way her vice, but her nature, which will then be freed from carnal relations and childbearing. However, the members of the woman will no longer function as before but will be adorned with a new beauty which will no longer attract the desire of the one who sees her. Desire will no longer exist. Instead, her beauty will glorify the wisdom and goodness of God Who has created from nothing and delivered what He has made from corruption."[250]

These texts confirm the Christian idea of a general transfiguration of gender. The sexes and genders are not abolished. Instead, they can coexist and work harmoniously together. Human passions are transcended along with all inequalities: domination of one over the other, oppositions and conflicts. Man and woman return to a state like that of Adam and Eve in Paradise before their sin and fall.

Chapter 10

The Transfiguration of Gender in Christian Spirituality

Again: In Christ "there is neither male nor female."
(Gal 3: 28)

The Work of Reunification

Christ is a model for the Christian, but He is also the One Who, through His saving work, gives man the possibility of reaching the human ideal which God intended for us when we were created. Those who unite themselves to Him through the sacramental life of the Church and their personal spiritual lives may reach what Adam failed to achieve. For He, the Son of God, has accomplished this Himself in the human nature which He assumed.

Recall that St Maximus considered that the divine plan for man was for him "[to start] the general unification from his own division. He was, through a most impassible relationship with Divine virtue, to reject completely from his nature the male-female division. For this in no way arose from the Divine plan for man's constitution through his original *logos*. For God's intention was that man [that is, the human being] should appear and become simply man, not divided by the names of male and female, according to the *logos* which governed his creation. He should be without these segments which currently divide him, and this thanks to the perfect union of his own *logos* by which he is."

As we have seen, Christ fulfilled this work in Himself. He gave back to mankind the power to achieve this ideal life in the relationships of men and women.

As we have already explained, these relationships must exclude all which separates, divides, or opposes the masculine and feminine genders, or which might cause any kind of conflict. The relationship should be peaceful, harmonious, and enriched by a complementarity which is not just outward and formal. Each of the genders should adopt the special qualities of the other, without confusion of genders or absorption of one by the other, maintaining their distinction and difference. Here we find a principle dear to Christianity. "Union without confusion" and "distinction without separation" apply at many different levels: the Persons of the Trinity; the two natures of Christ, divine and human; and the local Churches, whose faithful members are compared by St Paul to the different members of a body (cf. 1 Cor 12:12–27).

We have also seen that the harmonious relations which man and woman enjoyed in the beginning were broken by the sin of our first parents. They should have progressed toward perfection, but instead, they and their descendants plunged into the various passions which appeared and developed in their fallen nature. The first of these was egotistical self-love (*philautia*), and as St Maximus explains, this broke up the unity of human nature into many antagonistic parts.

St Maximus describes this nature, broken by discord and the clash of individual wills.[251] Then he presents Christ's work of reunification which each of us should appropriate by uniting with Him and practicing the virtues. These oppose the passions, and especially self-love, through the practice of true love for our neighbor.[252]

"Moreover, [Christ] reunites Himself to us, and each man to his neighbour, by renewing the power of love. This is the antidote to the poison of egotistical self-love (*philautia*) which is the father of the first fall, the first work of the Devil, and of all the passions which are born of it. He who drives it out through love shows himself worthy of God. At the same time, he drives away the whole pack of passions which henceforth has no root or reason to exist. For he becomes a stranger to pride, that sure sign of a presumption opposed to God, so perverse and complex. He no longer cares for passing fame which causes the fall of those it first swells then withers, precisely and firstly those whom it affects. He willingly welcomes his neighbor with goodwill. He cuts off at the root all anger, ideas of murder, mockery, resentment, irritability, avarice, and all which breaks up man's unity.[253] By uprooting egotistical self-love (*philautia*), the father, as I have said, of all evil, he also uproots all which usually flows from it. Without it, no form or trace of vice can survive. Instead, every kind of virtue comes in, enclosed in the power of love. It gathers up the fragments of mankind and restores his unity of thought and behavior, smoothing and removing all disparity and divergence of the disposition of the will (*gnômè*). Instead, it encourages another praiseworthy inequality where everyone deliberately draws his neighbor to himself and puts him in the higher place, just as formerly he pushed him away to take his place. By willingly separating himself from himself,[254] and breaking with the particular thoughts and reasons[255] he once nourished in his inmost self, each person comes to simplicity and oneness of mind [with the others]. Thenceforth none are separated from the community—all for one and one for all, or rather, all with God and with each other. They become one, bursting open the unity of their individual *logos* of being as regards nature and the disposition of the will."[256]

Although the grace to accomplish this work is given to humankind by Christ, St Maximus identifies Abraham as an Old Testament prophet who proclaimed and fulfilled it by anticipation:

"This was precisely what the great Abraham achieved by turning himself back to the *logos* of being and nature[257] ... he was worthy to see God in human form and to receive Him as a guest.[258] For, through his love of men, he restored himself to the *logos* of his nature. To rise to this level, he left behind the characteristics of what is separated and divided. He no longer considered any man other than he considered himself, seeking out the most unique *logos* and not the disposition of the will in which is trouble and division so long as it is out of tune with nature. He sought that nature in which is found the likeness in which we know that God shows Himself perfectly. He deigns to reveal Himself as good, embracing His own creatures. For the creature cannot, of itself, know Him as He is. Indeed, it is not right that he who is simple and identical should assimilate what is neither simple nor identical, still divided into many fragments through the disposition of the will regarding nature. For the disposition of the will of nature must first draw nigh through the love of men and show forth a unique *logos*, peaceful and free from dissension, which will never allow itself to stray deliberately to anything which is not from God.[259] Through it, nature remains undivided, and not broken in pieces, in those who receive this grace, that is, not divided into many conflicting opinions. For they no longer divide nature into this and that as if they were themselves divided. They remain the same without, each from his own point of view, looking at what divides and separates. Instead, each considers what they have in common and what is undivided in their common nature, gathering together the fragments which were separated. None of these fragments can, by himself, unite with the others. Thus it is that God manifests Himself to those in this state, conforming Himself to the special virtue of each through His love for mamkind. . . . This is the most perfect work of love, stretched to its limit: to bring about, through mutual relations, the sharing of the properties of those united by Him between all of them and what they are called."[260]

The restoration described by St Maximus applies generally to the whole vast range of human relationships, but especially to the relations between man and woman. The passages cited above reveal his idea that the *logos* defines them fundamentally and identically as human beings. This should prevail over their differences in the spiritual view they have of each other, an idea which here is strongly argued, and which brings us back to the same principle: the fundamental unity of humanity in the plan and the eye of the Creator, the unique cause, and the unique end of all creatures.

The process St Maximus describes of passing from the passions which divide to the virtues which unite, from egotistical self-love to the love of neighbor is not so easy as it might seem. It is the fruit of a long and painful ascesis,[261] for every man takes pleasure in the passions which attach him to his own ego and to the things of this world. Giving them up is most painful, accompanied by suffering, or, at the least, unpleasantness. The virtues are a source of spiritual joy, but more distant and less material, which makes them less immediately attractive than the pleasures of the senses linked to the passions.

The egotistical love of oneself is what seems natural and spontaneous to fallen humanity and not the love of one's neighbor.[262] So the Gospel gives us this unselfish love as a commandment (cf. Matt 22:36–40; Mark 12:28–31; John 13:34).

Christian love is more than a simple sentiment. It is a spiritual state which involves all the leanings and dispositions of man.[263] The passions are simply the various forms taken by man's attachment to himself and to the things of this world. His attachment to the things of this world comes from his egotistical self-love, since this attachment brings him the pleasures he desires; but the virtues are the different forms taken by man's spiritual attachment to God and his neighbor. The passions and virtues are at odds and cannot coexist. For as the Greek Fathers explain, the passions are none other than perversions of the virtues. What was originally and rightly directed toward God and neighbor is turned toward the ego and the world. Both are related to the same human faculties but turned to work in different directions.[264]

Spiritual life is a struggle where man's effort is helped by the grace of God to weaken the passions and make the virtues blossom in their place. It is a matter of conversion. This is why the word *metanoia* is so important in Christian spirituality. It is usually translated by "repentance," but literally it means a change of direction (*meta*) of the spirit (*nou*).

Everyday life is the place where spiritual life is applied to the relations between men and women. This is especially so for married life, destined to continue and last for longer with relations of greater intensity.

In the relations between men and women are to be found all the passions which affect human relationships in general. It is commonly held that the passions are made up of various kinds of abuse of the principal faculties of the human soul: the desiring power (*epithumetikon*); the aggressive or ardent power (*thumikon*); and the rational power (*logistikon*). The passions are surmounted through repentance, *metanoia* in Greek, which means conversion. Clement of Alexandria remarks that it is then that the genders are transcended as sources of division and opposition.

Anger and desire, strengthened by habit and raised in vice, cover the light of the intelligence with thick darkness. Through repentance these heavy fogs are dissipated, and the soul begins to meditate and concentrate on the single point of obedience to the Word; and then it is that, in the words of St Paul: In us "there is neither male nor female." The soul breaks free from its covering of flesh through which the sexes are distinguished and comes to unity; and "there is no more male or female."[265]

However, there are two special passions that specifically affect the relationships between men and women. The first is the passion related to sexuality to which the Greek Fathers gave the name *porneia*.[266] The second is the spirit of domination.

Continence, Chastity and the Love of Neighbor (*Agape*): Three Paths to the Ordering of Relations between Persons of Different Genders

A. The Virtues of Continence and Chastity

As we have seen, for Christian ethics sexual relations are only lawful within marriage.[267] The unmarried should therefore abstain from every sexual act.

They should permanently practice the virtue of continence (*egkrateia*). This name comes from the verb "to contain." It means to master carnal sexual passions; but it also means to master the desires which give rise to them and the thoughts which inspire them—thoughts, memories, and imaginations—from which they well up.

Conjugal relations are also concerned by this virtue. Christian ethics condemn all kinds of perverse sexual practices as the writings of St Paul suggest: "Marriage is honorable among all, and the bed undefiled" (Heb 13:4). In addition, the consent of both spouses is needed as another passage from the Apostle makes plain: "Do not deprive one another except with consent for a time, that you may give yourselves to fasting and prayer; and come together again so that Satan does not tempt you because of your lack of self-control" (1 Cor 7:5). For spiritual life can only intensify with pauses from conjugal relations which may be quite long.[268] St Paul advises us to do as much as our human weakness can stand: "But I say this as a concession, not as a commandment" (1 Cor 7:6). St Gregory of Nyssa goes further, writing: "He who practices [abstinence] to excess has a 'sick conscience' as says the Apostle, (Cf. 1 Tim 4:1–3) for he 'despises marriage.'"[269]

The virtue of chastity (*sophrosyne*) brings a state of inner purity as regards sexuality and applies equally to marriage and celibacy. To spouses, it first teaches them not to make sensual desire the aim and object of their union.[270] They should guard themselves from being dominated by pleasure.[271] They should neither become dependent on it nor seek it out so that in the end, it holds no more attraction for them. "As long as the slightest attraction to sensuality remains, one is not chaste," writes St John Cassian.[272] This does not mean that the pleasure naturally linked to sexual union is to be eliminated, but that the spouses should be detached from it. They should not be obsessed by it or exalt it. Pleasure should not be seen as the aim of their union but as its effect, like something extra.

Sexual union should not be sought for itself and the pleasure it gives. It has its role in the mutual love of the two spouses as a means of uniting their bodies. It is part of their total union, of spirit, soul, and body, which makes them, as Scripture says, "one flesh" as well as "one soul" and "one spirit." Chastity in marriage implies that this union of bodies is neither absolute nor self-sufficient but should be perfectly integrated into the superior spiritual union and psychological union of the spouses. St Basil of Ankyra writes of this: "When reason reigns in the soul and takes first place in the souls under its rule, it binds these souls together in what is clearly essential. It is then natural that this union should be joined to the lawful union of the bodies in which they dwell. But when the souls put something else in first place, the bodies in which they dwell seek pleasure for themselves and cause the souls to serve the passion which excites them. The souls are dragged along in the wake of these carnal passions which makes such sexual unions unlawful."[273]

A chaste marriage means that both man and wife are free from the rule of sexual desires and passions so that their union is not dominated by such things.[274] It is love that should preside over their union, not an impersonal instinct arising from their biological nature, nor yet desire, which is often the result of instinct or passion. So conjugal chastity requires a certain continence, a self-mastery which reins in the instincts, moderates desire, and drives off all thoughts or imaginations which could excite them. Thus, St Gregory of Nyssa (a married man) taught us "to use marriage with moderation and measure,"[275] "care and restraint,"[276] whilst St Gregory the Theologian recommends sobriety, giving little weight to the flesh.[277] This is the basis of a union where the person and freedom of the spouse are respected and not a simple vehicle to satisfy desire. This also ensures that husband and wife do not become "entirely flesh and blood"[278] and continually set the spiritual first in life and in their married life together.[279] For "the danger is not trivial," writes St Gregory of Nyssa, that man "beguiled by the experience of lust, comes to despise all good things which are not tasted passionately in the flesh. He will then become entirely carnal, his spirit utterly dead to the desire of spiritual blessings and will pursue, by all means, the pleasures offered by the flesh."[280] St Gregory of Nyssa emphasizes the awesome strength of the force of habit to bind men to lust. He gives examples of many people who, "once they had experienced such things turned all their powers of desire towards them. . . . They turned all the vigor of their thoughts of divine reality to ... these things and opened wide their inner self to the passions."[281]

In Christian marriage, lust implies a love of the other apart from God, purely carnal and opaque to the divine energies. Chastity implies love of the other in God and love of God in the other. Chastity transfigures love and raises it to the spiritual plane where it is entirely transparent to God. It gains a mystical meaning (cf. Eph 5:32). It becomes an analogy of the love of Christ for the Church as St Paul teaches in chapter 5 of his Epistle to the Ephesians, read during the office of marriage. Chastity cannot be seen as stable until it becomes a permanent habit.[282] All struggle ceases and is replaced by unchanging tranquility. St John Cassian writes: "such is the fulfillment of true chastity: it has no longer to struggle with the motions of carnal desire but detests them with utter horror and remains in steady and inviolate purity."[283]

One of its signs is that beings that arouse the passions leave the gaze and the heart unmoved.[284] St John Climacus maintains that he who is chaste "possesses at all times a gaze unaffected by the sight of perceptible bodily creatures, whatever their sex or their beauty."[285] He continues: "Perfect and most pure chastity has as its rule and characteristic to keep to the same disposition before living or inanimate bodies and before reasonable creatures and those without reason."[286] Moreover: "Truly happy is he who has reached perfect impassibility before any kind of body, flesh or beauty."[287] We may recall once more that in Christ "there is neither male nor female" (Gal 3:28). The difference in sex and gender is abolished as a principle of division, opposition, and domination; but it also vanishes as a source of sensual desire and passion. The other is perceived in his or her fundamental reality as a person whose nature bears the image of God. The other becomes an icon of God, transparent to Him and glorifying Him. St John Climacus testifies to the highest degree of this virtue: "I have been told of something which denotes a most extraordinary sovereign purity. Someone, I was told, who saw a body of the most exquisite beauty took this as an opportunity to adore and glorify with praise the Sovereign Beauty of which that body was the handiwork. He felt himself transported by the fire of divine love and melted into a river of tears. It was a true marvel to see that what might have caused another to fall over a precipice brought crowns to this person."[288]

B. The Virtue of Spiritual Love of One's Neighbor (*Agape*)

The virtue of charity, the spiritual love of our neighbor (*agape*), is Christ's second commandment, after the first: to love God. This is at the root of good relationships between all human beings for in this way tensions and conflicts are calmed down and avoided. It applies especially within the couple where relations are frequent and close which can make them more difficult.

The love of neighbor has a single nature, but, as St Paul says, it takes many and varied forms:[289] "Love suffers long and is kind; love does not envy; love does not parade itself, is not puffed up; does not behave rudely, does not seek its own, is not provoked, thinks no evil; does not rejoice in iniquity, but rejoices in the truth" (1 Cor 13:4–6). Love shows itself especially through benevolence, kindness, meekness, longsuffering, compassion, and well-doing. But, as the Apostle says, we must be humble, patient, indulgent, confident, and truthful.

Christ's commandment is that one should love our neighbor as oneself[290] (cf. Matt 22:38; Mark 12:31; Luke 10:27). So, its manifestations can be summed up in two precepts: do not to others that which you would not wish them to do to you; do to them what you would wish them to do to you.[291]

The first of these precepts, with its negative form, is given in the Old Testament by the righteous Tobit: "What you yourself hate, do not do to anyone" (Tob 4:15). St Paul puts it this way: "Love does no harm to a neighbor; therefore love is the fulfillment of the law" (Rom 13:10). He has left many recommendations in this vein, which have been taken up by the Fathers. We should not just avoid any act which could harm our neighbor or even make him sad.[292] We should also avoid any evil thought or intention toward him and any inward or outward attitude to him which could indicate that our spiritual relationship is perverse. So, love rules out any jealousy of our neighbor.[293] Loving him, we cannot despise him,[294] judge him badly,[295] rejoice in his problems and falls,[296] or, especially, wish him evil.[297] Nor can we be saddened by the good things which come to him.[298]

The second precept is positive. It is given in the New Testament by Christ Himself: "Therefore, whatever you want men to do to you, do also to them" (Matt 7:12; Luke 6:31). This means showing solidarity with all people and helping them as the Apostle recommends: "Bear one another's burdens, and so fulfill the law of Christ" (Gal 6:2); also, that one should be their servant (cf. Gal 5:13–14). The help given should fulfill all the needs of one's neighbor: his material needs and his spiritual needs, which are satisfied by word,[299] by service,[300] and especially prayer.[301] Love implies compassion: rejoicing with one's neighbor in all his blessings and weeping with him in all his afflictions[302] thus giving him consolation and comfort.[303]

To love one's brother as oneself as Christ commands means to be attached to him as much as one is attached to oneself. We may say, with Evagrios, that he who loves "is he who considers himself one with all, through the habit of seeing himself in everyone."[304]

Agape is the love of all men equally. One reason for this is that all men are essentially equal. They all have the same nature, and in Christian anthropology, as we have seen, this applies equally to men and to women. "We are all of one and the same essence, members of each other. So, we love each other deeply," writes St Anthony the Great.[305] St Maximus writes in the same vein that "perfect love admits no distinction based on difference of character between anyone, for we all share the same nature. Love beholds that unique nature and loves all men equally."[306] Elsewhere he remarks that love means honoring all men "insofar as the idea of nature requires it. For it grants to all equal honor and excludes from nature any inequality which the spirit might raise between this or that person, including them all in itself on the sole ground of identity."[307] "He who ... possesses perfect love," he continues: "makes no difference between himself and another, between slave and freeman, between man and woman. ... He simply sees in men their unique nature: he sees them all as equal and feels for them all in his heart."[308] St John Chrysostom echoes this idea saying: "as if the human race were but one single person."[309]

As I have shown elsewhere[310], love of neighbor is not rooted in psychology, even if it does draw on psychological faculties. It is spiritual. It is not a sentiment or an affection, though it has an affective side to it. It is a virtue: a spiritual state.

It comes through effort, an ascetic struggle joined to the gift of grace which goes beyond the confines of nature. This ascetic struggle is a fight against the passions which are all of them ways in which man worships his ego. The struggle seeks to weaken the passions until they become inactive. This is what led the Fathers constantly to maintain that impassibility—where the passions are overcome—is the essential condition for love. The love of man grows in proportion to the weakening and mortification of the passions.[311]

All the passions are born from man's rejection of God so as to cherish his ego and serve to express it. So, it is clear that love can only be possible when man purifies himself from the passions and lets go of his ego.[312] Only when he is pure of every passion can man love his neighbor with spiritual love. If he is not free from passion, he will love with a carnal love related to this or that passion. He may be conscious of this or not, for such love can arise for many reasons; and most of them are "stained by passion" being far from true charity.[313] Whilst man is affected by passion he cannot see his neighbor in his true reality, for "the passions hidden in [his] soul cloud [his] judgement."[314] It is only when he becomes impassible that he can relate spiritually to his neighbor, free from desire, free from all carnal intention or fancy (in the widest sense) which would pervert the relationship.

What has been said of love for one's neighbor in general clearly also applies to all relations between men and women and especially to the relations between spouses, who are the closest of neighbors. Love is the first rule of the life of the couple, with all the ascetic struggle it implies. Each spouse must strive to renounce all egotism, to esteem the other and give the other the better place. The sacrifice of each is to the advantage of the other. Far from being a loss, it is a gain for both: for by giving oneself to the other, one receives the other in return and is enriched.

Love does not just resolve conflicts but helps us to avoid them. It brings the wishes and desires of the spouses into harmony: compatible yet preserving their differences. It is like a musical score which unites harmoniously two different instruments, making them compatible. Sometimes they are in close harmony and sometimes quite distinct. Sometimes they part company, but around the same melodic line, each playing more quietly in turn to allow the other to sound forth. For the nature of love is to unite beings deeply, whilst preserving their personalities and differences.

Chapter 11

The Transfiguration of Gender in Married Life

How can words be found to describe
all the excellence and happiness of a Christian marriage?
Both are brethren, both servants of the same Master;
both conjoined in just one flesh and one spirit.
(Tertullian, *To his wife* II, 9)

The Foundations of Christian Marriage

A. The Divine Plan

It is usually thought that the first foundation of Christian marriage is found in the Divine plan expressed by these words in the book of Genesis: "And the LORD God said, 'It is not good for man to be alone. I will make him a helper comparable to him'" (Gen 2:18), and in the words of Adam after the creation of his wife: "This is now bone of my bones and flesh of my flesh" (Gen 2:23), and what he said next: "For this reason a man shall leave his father and mother and be joined to his wife, and the two shall become one flesh" (Gen 2:24). Their sexual union, which followed their sin, is described thus: "Now Adam knew Eve his wife, and she conceived and bore ..." (Gen 4:1).

The words: "Therefore a man shall leave his father and mother and be joined to his wife, and they shall become one flesh," (Matt 19:5–6) are mentioned four times in the New Testament (cf. Mark 10:8; 1 Cor 6:16; Eph 5:31). Christ Himself refers to it in Matthew chapter 19 after referring to Genesis 1:27. A parallel text is found in Mark 10:2–9:

> The Pharisees came and asked Him, "Is it lawful for a man to divorce his wife?" testing Him. And He answered and said to them, "What did Moses command you?"
>
> They said, "Moses permitted a man to write a certificate of divorce, and to dismiss her."

> And Jesus answered and said to them, "Because of the hardness of your heart he wrote you this precept. But from the beginning of the creation, God 'made them male and female.' 'For this reason a man shall leave his father and mother and be joined to his wife, and the two shall become one flesh'; so then they are no longer two, but one flesh. Therefore what God has joined together, let not man separate."

Note that Christ attributes these words to God, not just to Adam as some commentators do, following the literal sense of the text. He takes them on Himself which confers on them Divine authority.

Several characteristics of Christian marriage are defined in this passage: sexual otherness; monogamy; faithfulness of each spouse to the other; that the union is established, or sealed, by God.

B. Sexual Otherness

Christian marriage is only conceivable between a man and a woman. It is based on the complementarity of man and woman, physiological, psychological, mental, and spiritual, as willed by God from mankind's creation. (Gen 1:27–28; 2:22–23). Moreover, it is based on the couple's calling to bring forth children and to raise them within a normal family. This is God's Will, inscribed in humanity's nature. There should be one true father and one true mother, the first of the male sex and gender; and the second of the female sex and gender. This is the only way for children to be raised harmoniously, both psychologically and spiritually, in accord with Christian anthropology and ethics which are based on man's nature, created by God.

C. Monogamy

Christian marriage presupposes monogamy: each Christian man has but one wife, and each Christian woman but one husband. Many or several marriages are excluded as are extra-marital relations: the sin of adultery. However, on this point there is a rupture between the Old and New Testaments.

God created one single wife for Adam: "And the Lord God said, 'It is not good for man to be alone. I will make him a helper comparable to him'" (Gen 2:18) and He blessed their union: "For this reason a man shall leave his father and mother and be joined to his wife, and the two shall become one flesh"

(Gen 2:24). This might be interpreted as God establishing monogamy from the beginning as corresponding to His intention and His Will. It is true that throughout the Old Testament there are many famous examples of monogamy: Noah, the second patriarch and Moses for instance. Closer to the coming of Christ we find Joachim and Anna, the father and mother of the Mother of God, and Zacharias and Elizabeth, the father and mother of the Forerunner, St John the Baptist. Moreover, adultery is forbidden by the Ten Commandments and severely punished (Lev 20:10).[315]

However, we find polygamy amongst the descendants of Cain. The Bible also tells of the patriarchs and other famous men who practiced polygamy without their unions being rebuked by God. The first example of this is Lamech, "Then Lamech took two wives for himself" (Gen 4:19), and his brothers. Abraham also took a second wife, Hagar, since his first wife, Sarah, was sterile, and this with God's blessing (cf. Gen 16:1–16). Jacob had two wives and two concubines (cf. Gen 30:1–26). It was Solomon who had the most: "And he had seven hundred wives, princesses, and three hundred concubines (1 Kgs 11:3 NKJV [3 Kgs 11:3 LXX]). David also had many wives. This was blessed by God Who, through the mouth of the prophet Nathan reminded him how he had placed in his embrace the wives of his master and would have given him more if they were not enough (cf. 2 Sam 12:8). Deuteronomy also tolerates bigamy (cf. Deut 21:15). It even allows for polygamy since it asks the King not to multiply the number of his wives (cf. Deut 17:17). Taking prisoners of war (cf. Deut 21:10–14) and slaves (cf. Ex 21:1–11) as concubines is presented as normal. Moreover, in the Old Testament there is no mention of monogamy as an obligation.

Everything changes with the coming of Christ. He clearly teaches monogamy by his words in Matthew chapter 19:5–6: "For this reason a man shall leave his father and mother and be joined to *his wife, and the two shall become one flesh*? So then, they are no longer two but one flesh. Therefore what God has joined together, let not man separate." Though He does not condemn the woman taken in adultery (cf. John 8:3–11) He does not thereby justify adultery or polygamy but rejects any judgment of the person by another whatever her sins may have been. Elsewhere, Christ confirms the Old Testament's condemnation of adultery and makes it still stricter by treating even a lustful look at another's wife as a sin. After the story of the woman who had seven husbands (cf. Mark 12:19–25), Christ is asked: "Therefore, in the resurrection, when they rise, whose wife will she be?" (Mark 12:23). This sets monogamy as the norm, even though Christ's reply indicates that in the Kingdom of Heaven there will be no need for marriage.

St Paul clearly states that monogamy is the rule. In his first Epistle to the Corinthians he makes plain that every man should have his own wife and every woman her own husband (1 Cor 7:2 "let each man have his own wife, and let each woman have her own husband"). Writing to Timothy (1 Tim 3:12) and Titus (Titus 1:6) he teaches that the deacons and presbyters should each be "the husband of one wife." He does not teach that monogamy is just for the clergy but confirms through those who should be models for the Church that monogamy is instituted by God and henceforth applies to all.

Monogamy shows greater respect to the woman and makes the relationship between the man and his wife completely personal. Polygamy is justified by arguments which are foreign to Christian ethics: it is a way for a man to affirm his power and wealth, proportional to the number of his wives and concubines. It is also a means to produce more offspring, for in the Old Testament, a sterile woman is an inferior woman. In polygamy, a woman is in many ways a means to an end outside of herself. She is depersonalized and objectivized and becomes interchangeable. A man with several wives cannot give any of them an absolute worth nor yet perfect love in a true personal relationship, for by definition, this is unique: the person is characterized by being unique and irreplaceable.

D. Indissolubility

Another characteristic of Christian marriage is its indissolubility, which is closely linked to monogamy. This was also a revolution for the Old Testament regime, where divorce was possible. It was the same for Roman society, where divorce was common and accepted.

Indissolubility does not arise for sociological reasons: to preserve an institution which is a foundation of society. It arises for spiritual reasons. Marriage is seen as common life which extends throughout earthly life and beyond its confines, where it takes on a new character.

It is solidly based on the words of Christ. During the age of the Old Testament divorce was tolerated to allow for the weakness of men; but this did not correspond to the original intention and Will of God which should henceforth be respected: "The Pharisees came and asked Him, 'Is it lawful for a man to divorce his wife?' testing Him. And He answered and said to them, 'What did Moses command you?' They said, 'Moses permitted a man to write a certificate of divorce, and to dismiss her.' And Jesus answered and said to them, 'Because of the hardness of your heart he wrote you this precept. But from the beginning of the creation, God "made them male and female."' 'For this reason a man shall leave his father and mother and be joined to his wife, and the two shall become one flesh; so then they are no longer two, but one flesh. Therefore what God has joined together, let not man separate.' In the house His disciples also asked Him again about the same matter. So He said to them, 'Whoever divorces his wife and marries another commits adultery against her. And if a woman divorces her husband and marries another, she commits adultery'" (Mark 10:2–12).

"'Furthermore it has been said, "Whoever divorces his wife, let him give her a certificate of divorce." But I say to you that whoever divorces his wife for any reason except sexual immorality causes her to commit adultery; and whoever marries a woman who is divorced commits adultery'" (Matt 5:31–32; cf. Matt 19:9).

"Whoever divorces his wife and marries another commits adultery; and whoever marries her who is divorced from her husband commits adultery"[316] (Luke 16:18).

This permanent commitment and fidelity became the model for Christian marriage. It implies repentance and mutual forgiveness when one spouse harms the other. It requires ascetic, spiritual effort to keep life together harmonious and to make it bear fruit within the couple and the whole family.[317] It should be an image of the union of Christ with His Church as St Paul and the Fathers teach.

The Status of Husband and Wife in Marriage

The Gospels say nothing about what the relations between husband and wife should be within marriage. This is doubtless because conjugal love has a spiritual side and is a special example of love for one's neighbor. For the husband is the closest neighbor of his wife and she of her husband. In the New Testament it is this text from St Paul that sets the standard:

> Submit "to one another in the fear of God. Wives, submit to your own husbands, as to the Lord. For the husband is head of the wife, as also Christ is head of the church; and He is the Savior of the body.[318] Therefore, just as the church is subject to Christ, so let the wives be to their own husbands in everything. Husbands, love your wives, just as Christ also loved the church and gave Himself for her, that He might sanctify and cleanse her with the washing of water by the word, that He might present her to Himself a glorious church, not having spot or wrinkle or any such thing, but that she should be holy and without blemish. So husbands ought to love their own wives as their own bodies; he who loves his wife loves himself. For no one ever hated his own flesh, but nourishes and cherishes it, just as the Lord does the church. For we are members of His body, of His flesh and of His bones. 'For this reason a man shall leave his father and mother and be joined to his wife, and the two shall become one flesh.' This is a great mystery, but I speak concerning Christ and the church. Nevertheless let each one of you in particular so love his own wife as himself, and let the wife see that she respects her husband"
>
> (Eph 5:21–33).

A feminist reading of this text dwells one the phrase "the husband is the head of the wife," and on the comparison of the husband and wife to Christ and the Church which appears to institute a hierarchy with the man at the top. However, other readings of this complex text are possible. This has led other commentators, who refer also to other passages from his epistles, to consider that St Paul is ambiguous on this question.

An alternative reading starts from the first sentence of the passage quoted: "Submitting to one another in the fear of God." This indicates that submission should be mutual. It is not the will of the husband, nor yet of his wife, which should prevail, but *the fear of Christ*: the respect of his precepts.

The main body of the text does not refer to power or authority, but to the love that the husband should have for his wife and a strong emphasis on his duties. The injunction "Husbands, love your wives, just as Christ also loved the Church and gave Himself for her" emphasizes that this love should be all-embracing. The husband must be ready to sacrifice himself completely, just as Christ sacrificed Himself in His passion and death. Comparing the love of husband and wife with that of Christ for His Church is not justified by anthropology. Instead, it strongly emphasizes the love that a husband should have for his wife and the sacrifices he must make for her. There is no hierarchy here.

This interpretation is supported by the comparison St Paul makes a little further on: "So husbands ought to love their own wives as their own bodies; he who loves his wife loves himself. For no one ever hated his own flesh, but nourishes and cherishes it." Here is a fourfold reference: first to the "Second Commandment": "You shall love your neighbor as yourself" (Matt 22:39); secondly to the Church, which is the body of Christ which He loves as his own body; thirdly to the verse from the book of Genesis (2:24) quoted by the Apostle: "For this reason a man shall leave his father and mother and be joined to his wife, and the two shall become one flesh"; fourthly to the story of the creation which tells how the woman was formed from the rib of the man (cf. Gen 2:22). For the Fathers, this does not mean that woman depends upon man but that they share one and the same nature: essential solidarity.

This interpretation is confirmed by St John Chrysostom's commentary on this passage in his twentieth homily on the epistle to the Ephesians. It is seen as one of the greatest patristic texts on marriage.

> "A wise man who listed various blessings numbered among them the lot of "a wife and husband well-adjusted together" (WSir 25:1 LXX). Elsewhere, he ranks the perfect concord between husband and wife as a great felicity. From the beginning, God showed particular care for marriage. He treated man and woman as being one in these words: "male and female He created them"; and elsewhere: "There is neither male nor female" (Gal 3:28). In truth, there is less of a link between one man and another than between a man and a woman, joined in legitimate union. This is why a blessed person,[319] wishing to express his great affliction and sadness at the death of one of his closest friends[320] did not use the words "father" or "mother," "child," "brother" or "friend" said instead: "Your love to me was to be admired, surpassing the love of women" (2 Kgs 2:26 LXX [2 Sam 1:26]). For there is not; no, there is not any feeling more powerful than that. There are other lively affections, but this one unites liveliness and length. In the depth of our being a love is hidden which through a secret instinct brings about the union of the sexes. It is because of this that in

the beginning woman came forth from man, and from thenceforth man and woman come forth from man and woman. Do you see this perfect bond, this close embrace by which God provided that no foreign essence should penetrate ours? And see what care He took. He allowed man to marry his own sister, his daughter, or rather his own flesh. For the consummation of their perfect union, he started from the beginning as when one builds. He did not make the woman from another substance so that man should not see her as foreign to him."[321]

In the same homily, St John Chrysostom teaches that a husband should never inspire feelings of fear in his wife. At no time should he have a relationship with her based on forcing and dominating her. It is true that in Genesis God said to Eve: "Your recourse [desire] shall be to your husband, and he shall rule over you" (Gen 3:16), but here it is a question of the passion of desire, and the passion[322] of domination. God presents them as a consequence of the fall and the effect of sin.

The conflicts within a couple should be resolved by the struggle against the passions and the practice of Christian virtues. The greatest of these is spiritual love (*agape*). This love drives out fear (1 John 4:18), which leads St John Chrysostom to emphasize the duties of the husband:

"Even when your wife treats you with disdain, despite and insolence it is up to you to bring her round through the force of your goodness, love, and tenderness. For there is no stronger attachment than this, especially between man and woman. Through fear one may bind the hands of a servant, yet he will hasten to escape; but it is not through fear and threats that you will attach to yourself the companion of your life, the mother of your children and the source of all your happiness. You must use love and affection. What kind of a couple is it where the wife trembles before her husband? What joy is there for a husband who lives with his wife as with a slave and not as with a free woman? Even when you suffer something for her do not rebuke her, following in this the example of Christ...."[323]

St Paul teaches perfect equivalence between man and woman in their attitudes to each other in sexual relations.

"Let the husband render to his wife the affection [or debt] due her, and likewise also the wife to her husband. The wife does not have authority over her own body, but the husband does. And likewise the husband does not have authority over his own body, but the wife does. Do not deprive one another except with consent for a time, that you may give yourselves to fasting and prayer; and come together again so that Satan does not tempt you because of your lack of self-control" (1 Cor 7:3–5).

St John Chrysostom remarks that St Paul "calls that a debt to show that neither of the two is master of him(her)self but *each is the servant of the other*."[324]

Transfiguring Gender through Common Ascesis

St Paul prefers celibacy to marriage for the same reasons as those used later to recommend monasticism: to consecrate himself more fully to God unburdened by the cares and troubles of conjugal and family life. Yet, for all that, he did not reject marriage but justified it as the means of escape from sexual desires too strong to be tamed.

> Now concerning the things of which you wrote to me: it is good for a man not to touch a woman. Nevertheless, because of sexual immorality, let each man have his own wife, and let each woman have her own husband. Let the husband render to his wife the affection due her, and likewise also the wife to her husband. The wife does not have authority over her own body, but the husband does. And likewise the husband does not have authority over his own body, but the wife does. Do not deprive one another except with consent for a time, that you may give yourselves to fasting and prayer; and come together again so that Satan does not tempt you because of your lack of self-control. But I say this as a concession, not as a commandment. For I wish that all men were even as I myself. But each one has his own gift from God, one in this manner and another in that. But I say to the unmarried and to the widows: It is good for them if they remain even as I am; but if they cannot exercise self-control, let them marry. For it is better to marry than to burn with passion.
>
> (1 Cor 7:1–9)

For this reason, St John Chrysostom considered that marriage is good to support the weak, but "unnecessary for the strong and robust."[325]

Another justification of marriage is procreation. The Old Testament is deeply preoccupied by the need to multiply one's descendance, but this idea is not present in the New Testament, either in the Gospels or in the Epistles. Nonetheless, many Fathers use this argument to justify sexual relations within the couple.[326] For if God gave sexuality to mankind, it was, as we have seen, to allow humanity to reproduce, develop, and last through time. There is also a spiritual element to this argument since conception itself is not enough. It must be followed by the birth and raising of children in a family community where parents and children should be united: an important element in the blossoming and happiness of the couple.

St Paul is often accused of providing feeble arguments for marriage. This reproach is not entirely well founded since chapter 5 of the epistle to the Ephesians, quoted above, praises conjugal love. It calls the relation between husband and wife a "great mystery," setting the highest value upon it by comparing it to the love between Christ and his Church.

The two main aims of marriage given by St Paul, the taming of sexual lust and the bearing of children, do not concern everyone. For many men, and even more women, love grows through an affection stronger than sex. Moreover, some couples are sterile, yet their union still has great meaning, for with human beings, fertility is not just biological.[327] The greatest aim of marital life is the spiritual development of the spouses in their common life, overcoming its difficulties and enjoying its blessings.

From the second to the fifth century, the Fathers of the Church greatly praised consecrated virginity.[328] Then, from the fourth century onwards, they praised monasticism which had largely replaced it. They did not simply put forward the qualities of these two ways of life, marked by celibacy. They also showed how they had the advantage over marriage as they were free of the cares arising from married life and children.[329] They were, of course, almost all celibate which must have inclined them to value this condition, consecrated to God, and to emphasize the problems of marriage which they observed from outside.[330]

However, they never rejected marriage and struggled with great vigor against the sects which condemned it.[331] The struggle with these sects led them to teach that it is legitimate and of great value.[332] Thus, they came to teach that monastic life and married life were two roads that led to the same ends. The means used were partly the same and partly different.[333] They often considered virginity and monasticism as superior[334] since they were radical and maximal[335] in restoring man and woman to their life in paradise and making them like angels and giving them a foretaste of life in the Kingdom of Heaven. Yet marriage also can sanctify the Christian, providing him with a specially fruitful framework for spiritual life. Indeed, St John Chrysostom describes the Christian family as a "tiny Church."[336] Furthermore, we should recall that Christ Himself sanctified marriage by His presence at the wedding of Cana and His first miracle which He performed there. He never expressed any reservation about it and some of His disciples, Peter, the foremost, and Philip,[337] were married.

Amongst those who praise marriage Tertullian stands out. In his magnificent letter to his wife, he shows the advantages of the community of life which allows the spouses to help each other and work together. Their common efforts bring growth to their spiritual life:

"Where can one find the words to express all the excellence and happiness of a Christian marriage? The Church draws up the contract which is confirmed by the divine offering and sealed by the priestly blessing. It is witnessed and registered by the angels, and the Heavenly Father ratifies it. How sweet and holy is this alliance of two believers who carry the same yoke and are united in the same hope with the same vow, the same obedience and the same dependance! Both are brothers, both servants of the same Master. Mingled in the same flesh they become one flesh, one spirit. They pray together, bow together, fast together, Each teaches the other, encourages the other and puts up with the other. You will meet them together in the Church, at the divine banquet. They share poverty and riches, the fury of persecutions and the consolation of peace. Between them are no secrets to reveal, no surprises to discover. They live in complete confidence, eager to help the other, never bored, never sickened. They need not hide from each other their visits to the sick, their help to the destitute. They have no need to hide from each other their charity, their unfeigned sacrifices, or their daily practice of holy things without constraint. For them, there is no need to hide the sign of the cross, to be timid in their salutations or dumb in their thanksgiving. Their mouths, free as their hearts, sing pious hymns and holy canticles. Their only rivalry is to see who will better sing praise to the Lord. Such are the unions which rejoice the eyes and ears of Jesus Christ upon whom He sends His peace."[338]

We may also quote the text of Clement of Alexandria who shows how a spiritual life led in common brings unity, harmony, and fruitfulness. Everything is in common in a relationship where man and woman are equal in every respect yet maintain their difference of gender.

"Let us give ourselves up entirely to the Lord. Let us bind ourselves with ropes to the vessel of faith and let us be convinced that the virtues which we are bidden to pursue are equally the preserve of men and women, If they have indeed one and the same God, they have also one and the same Teacher, one and the same Church. Moderation, temperance, and chastity are virtues common to both sexes. They feed on the same foods and unite in marriage. They have all in common, their breath, their sight, their hearing, their intelligence, their hope, their inclination to hear the commandments of God and their charity. If man and woman have the same way of life, they also partake of the same graces and the same salvation. They are beloved of God with the same love and instructed with the same care. 'The sons of this age,' the Lord tells us 'Marry and are given in marriage.' This is the sole difference between them."[339]

There are difficulties in every form of community life since different personalities are thrown together with their different desires and wills. Life in a Christian community, be it monastic or a marriage, requires an ascetic struggle with its inevitable effort and self-denial. Each must fight his or her own selfishness, called by the Greek Fathers *philautia*. This egotistical self-love is, in their eyes, the principal passion and mother of every other. Each person must accept and respect the other's different personality. One's self-will and personal desires must not be set up as an absolute but should be harmonized with the desires and will of the other through sometimes costly compromise. In monasticism this comes about through the common reference point of a rule and through obedience to the abbot and a spiritual father. In a married couple, concord comes from a common reference to the Divine Will, expressed in the Gospel commandments. The couple may come to have "one heart and one soul" (Acts 4:32; cf. Phil 2:2), and to "be of one mind" (1 Pet 3:8) through their common faith and common will by which they reach an ideal that surpasses them and to which both agree. Neither seeks his or her own but the good of the other, and so the common good. This is the general rule. However, in the details of daily life there must be an ascetic struggle with the passions which bar the way to perfect concord, especially those linked to aggression, pride, and lust for power.[340] The virtues must also be practiced assiduously, especially patience, meekness, and humility. Obedience, the pillar of monasticism, is also found in the couple, not just obedience to the Divine Will, but also obedience to each other. For, as St Paul writes, submit "to one another in the fear of God" (Eph 5:21).

This kind of ascesis does not simply lead to concord. It also leads to common spiritual growth over the years. Love becomes ever stronger for it is free of all those attractions which are outward and foreign to the Love of God, the love of neighbor, and the love of wife and children.

The rite of crowning, so characteristic of the Orthodox wedding ceremony, is rich in symbolism. Traditionally, crowns are for kings, for the athletes of old who won the victory and, spiritually, for martyrs. They signify honor, royal dignity, power, and reward for a great feat. All these are present in the rite of crowning.

The spouses receive a royal dignity. As the priest says in the prayers, the couple are crowned with glory and honor. This is not in a worldly sense but signifies the new spiritual dignity to which they acceded through marriage.

The spouses become king and queen for each other. Each will respect and honor the dignity of the other. Each, like a king serving his people, will care for the well-being and safety of the other, ready, if needed, to sacrifice himself or herself in this task.

They are called to become king and queen of the passions which may arise in this new way of life as well as those which they have inherited from their former state.

In their marriage, the two spouses should pursue their personal ascetic efforts to which they should add the ascetic effort of life together. They need self-mastery and self-sacrifice. The Greek word, *askesis*, is a synonym of *athlesis* which means an athletic exploit or feat. In Russian the equivalent word is *podvig*, meaning achievement. The crowns of the two spouses symbolize the reward that they will receive for victory over their passions, obtained through their ascetic struggle [*podvig*] in their common life, a reward which will reach its full flowering in eternal life. As St Paul writes, "And everyone who competes for the prize is temperate in all things. Now they do it to obtain a perishable crown, but we for an imperishable crown" (1 Cor 9:25). So, the crown represents not only "the crown of justice" which rewards those who "have fought the good fight," have finished the race," and "have kept the faith" (2 Tim 4: 7–8), but also "the crown of glory that does not fade away" (1 Pet 5:4).

Married life and the family are founded upon love, a true Christian and spiritual love, which requires ascetic struggle. This means mortifying the passions and sacrificing oneself in a form of martyrdom, which is one of the themes of the wedding service.

A marriage lived spiritually as the way of spiritual fulfillment through perfect unity transfigures gender. The genders are not denied, but the oppositions of one to the other, provoked by the passions, are surpassed. The difference between the genders is no more a source of rivalry or conflict but of mutual enrichment in complementary harmony.

Chapter 12

The Status of Woman in Christianity

Woman is of the same nature as man.
They both have the same capacities.
(Didymus the Blind, *On Genesis*)

The Asymmetry of Man and Woman in the Epistles of St Paul and of St Peter, and in the Writings of the Church Fathers

In the epistles of Sts Peter and Paul, and in the writings of the Fathers, the status of man and woman is seen as asymmetric. Woman appears as inferior to man, to whom she must submit, and is excluded from all public office. In life in the Church, this gives rise to certain obligations and restrictions and in married life, to certain duties, all of which apply mostly to the woman. This asymmetry has been emphasized in the feminist movement and in gender studies but is also discussed in biblical and patristic studies. As regards the Fathers, we will summarize the main lines of their thought, referring to all the texts where it appears. However, we will look in more depth into the texts of Sts Peter and Paul because of their special authority on which the thought of the Fathers is founded.

A. The Texts of St Paul

In the epistles of St Paul, chapter 5 of the epistle to the Ephesians is most important for the status of women, especially verses 21 to 24: Submit "to one another in the fear of God. Wives, submit to your own husbands, as to the Lord. For the husband is head of the wife, as also Christ is head of the church; and He is the Savior of the body. Therefore, just as the church is subject to Christ, so let the wives be to their own husbands in everything" (Eph 5:21–24).

There is a clear asymmetry in this passage: man takes the place of Christ, and his wife that of the Church. Christ is more than the Church. Christ is the head, and the Church, the body, and, of course, in the human being, the head directs the body.

Chapter 11 of the first epistle to the Corinthians (verses 3–16) emphasizes the hierarchy by making the man an essential intermediary between the woman and God, whilst man relates directly to God. It is also in this passage that women are enjoined to cover their heads, whilst man should not, since he is "the image and glory of God," which seems to imply that woman is not. The head covering is also said to be "a symbol of authority" over her. The woman is enjoined to keep her hair long "for her hair was given to her for a covering." St Paul also justifies his affirmation of woman's inferiority by saying: "Man is not from woman, but woman from man," and: "Nor was man created for the woman, but woman for the man." These two references to the text of Genesis are both interpreted to give the sense of a hierarchy:

> But I want you to know that the head of every man is Christ, the head of woman is man, and the head of Christ is God. Every man praying or prophesying, having his head covered, dishonors his head. But every woman who prays or prophesies with her head uncovered dishonors her head, for that is one and the same as if her head were shaved. For if a woman is not covered, let her also be shorn. But if it is shameful for a woman to be shorn or shaved, let her be covered. For a man indeed ought not to cover his head, since he is the image and glory of God; but woman is the glory of man. For man is not from woman, but woman from man. Nor was man created for the woman, but woman for the man. For this reason the woman ought to have a symbol of authority on her head, because of the angels. Nevertheless, neither is man independent of woman, nor woman independent of man, in the Lord. For as woman came from man, even so man also comes through woman; but all things are from God. Judge among yourselves. Is it proper for a woman to pray to God with her head uncovered? Does not even nature itself teach you that if a man has long hair, it is a dishonor to him? But if a woman has long hair, it is a glory to her; for her hair is given to her for a covering. But if anyone seems to be contentious, we have no such custom, nor do the churches of God.
>
> (1 Cor 11:3–16)

Later, in the same epistle, St Paul orders women to be silent during the assembly: "…as in all the churches of the saints. Let your women keep silent in the churches, for they are not permitted to speak; but they are to be submissive, as the law also says. And if they want to learn something, let them ask their own husbands at home; for it is shameful for women to speak in church" (1 Cor 14:33–35).

Some interpreters have weakened this text by suggesting that it refers simply to gossip,[341] but it is clear that it also refers to simple questions, asked for the sake of instruction. It is also clear that this passage renews the call to submission.

The first epistle to Timothy completes this teaching: women are obliged to remain silent since they are not "to have authority over a man." From the beginning, the passage reminds women of their duty to submit to their husbands since they are seen as inferior. Woman was created from Adam, and it was she who was first deceived: "Let a woman learn in silence with all submission. And I do not permit a woman to teach or to have authority over a man, but to be in silence. For Adam was formed first, then Eve. And Adam was not deceived, but the woman being deceived, fell into transgression" (1 Tim 2:11–14).

B. The Texts of Saint Peter

The first epistle of St Peter also teaches, in two places, the submission of woman. He also criticizes outward adornment. This theme is taken up frequently by some of the Fathers, notably Tertullian and Clement of Alexandria. Woman is presented as a more fragile creature than man. Her fragility is seen as more psychological than physical since St Peter advises husbands to be to be understanding with their wives in their life together (cf. 1 Pet 3:1–7).

C. The Church Fathers

The Church Fathers adopt the same asymmetry in their conception of man and woman as we find in St Paul and St Peter. They develop and complete it, using various different arguments.

There are anthropological arguments, based on the account of the creation of man and woman in the book of Genesis: woman was created after man;[342]

she was created for man;[343] man is the image and reflection of God, but this is not so for woman.[344]

There are also moral arguments from the text of Genesis: (1) it was woman who was first beguiled by the Serpent;[345] (2) it was she who led man to sin in his turn;[346] (3) she therefore bears the primary responsibility for original sin and its consequences, and transmits, through inheritance, its guilt right down to our day;[347] (4) as a consequence of her sin, a woman is ruled by her husband according to the judgment of God: "Your recourse will be to your husband, and he shall rule over you" (Gen 3:16).[348] From this, one may deduce that it was God Himself Who made woman dependent on man.[349] It is the episode of the Eve's seduction by the serpent and her subsequent seduction of Adam which deprive her of authority. So, she is forbidden to teach, for "she once assumed authority and caused evil" and: "she once took upon herself to teach and taught badly."[350]

There are also psychological arguments: a woman is preoccupied by her appearance,[351] light-minded, frivolous,[352] and superficial; she is greedy for vainglory,[353] anxious to seduce, and so is to blame for arousing in men desires which lead to their perdition.[354]

Next come intellectual arguments. A woman is not a deep thinker. In the couple of man and woman, it is man who represents the spirit of reason, whilst the woman represents the *psyche* or *anima*, the animal soul and sensitivity.[355] From these flow impulses, emotions, and feelings which are unstable and undermine psychological equilibrium.[356] Compared to man, woman has a weaker intellect,[357] incapable of thinking with rigor and wisdom.[358] Her words carry less weight than those of men.[359] Her teachings are often false and even ridiculous.[360]

There follow physiological arguments. Woman has a weaker bodily constitution than man,[361] and this implies and justifies man's role as dominator[362] and protector.[363]

There are also physico-psychological arguments. Woman is passive, physically in relation to her sexuality and to conception, and psychologically, whereas man is active. So, it is normal for man to direct and dominate. Woman is thus intellectually, psychologically, and physically "the weaker sex."[364]

Then there are social arguments. (1) Woman submitting to man, as to a chief, allows good order and peace to be preserved within the couple and the family.[365] (2) It is right to respect the order established by custom and law: woman is inferior to man[366] so that in society, man is concerned with public affairs whilst woman takes care of the household.[367] Woman's abstention from public matters helps to preserve social order.

There are theological arguments too. The superiority of man is based on the order established by God, and this Divine order is reflected in nature and society.[368] Moreover, the social roles of man and woman correspond to the will of God. Man is occupied with public matters, whilst woman looks after domestic matters.[369]

The Relativization of This Asymmetric Concept

There are several factors which lead us to relativize this asymmetric teaching.

A. It Is Only Taught by Certain Fathers in Scattered References

The arguments given above are presented all together, and it is only for this that they seem impressive. They are not distributed evenly amongst the Fathers. Some are common to all, and the name of St John Chrysostom appears often. Whilst they do all witness to feminine inferiority, they are far from forming a system.

These ideas do not represent the teaching of the Fathers as a whole, though some make the mistake of believing that they do. Amongst the multitude of the Fathers, only a few have written on this subject, the most prolific being Tertullian and St John Chrysostom. The others—Clement of Alexandria, Origen, Cyprian of Carthage, Diodoros of Tarsus, Epiphanios of Salamis, Ambrose, Jerome, Augustine and Cyril of Alexandria—have simply left a few short remarks in the vast body of their works.

It must also be remarked that some modern critics have exaggerated the positions of some of the Fathers to tar them all with the brush of a misogyny that was absent from their thought.[370] Even if some Fathers, such as Tertullian or Augustine, clearly have some accounts to settle with the female race, there is no trace of hatred or disdain of women in their work. Moreover, some of their writings, which are rarely quoted, witness to the contrary.

B. Their Position Is Softened and Even Sometimes Contradicted in Other Parts of Their Work

Commentators on the epistles of St Paul and on the Fathers of the Church have observed that they all hold an ambiguous, or even contradictory position on these matters.[371] Beside the texts that teach an asymmetry in the relations of man and woman there are others that teach a perfect symmetry in these relations. As we shall see, they teach fundamental equality, based on nature and destiny. For they both share a common spiritual activity toward the same end, led by the same Master, Christ, to Whom both submit equally.

C. Explaining the Contradiction

The ambiguity and contradictions in the teaching of the Apostles and the Fathers can be explained by the fact that they address two different levels: a social level and a spiritual level.[372] The asymmetric teaching found in certain passages from the epistles of St Paul and St Peter show that they were referring to concepts generally accepted in their times. They were found in all the societies of antiquity—Jewish, Greek, and Roman—and included the ideas of Greek philosophy, especially those of Aristotle,[373] as well as the physiology of their time. Their teaching should also be set in the social order of that time[374] which had lasted thousands of years, and which, for many reasons, could not then be disturbed.[375] These ideas about the status of women would be imprinted on the societies of the Middle East and the West[376] for many more centuries and thus would influence a part of Christian thought.[377]

The Apostles and the Fathers had a different perspective on these matters which came from the New Testament. Nonetheless, they were obliged to conform to some extent to the ideas of their time so as not to be completely cut off from social life, which would have stopped their preaching being acceptable to the people of their day.[378] In general, Christianity treats this world as ephemeral, passing, and inconsistent.[379] It preaches another world, eternal and of infinite worth: the spiritual world of the Kingdom of Heaven. It is yet to come in its fullness but may be partly experienced in this world through inner life and life in the Church.

In all ages, Christianity has formally accepted the social structures of its time, or has, at least, tolerated them. It has never fought them directly, but rendered to Caesar the things that are Caesar's, (cf. Mark 12:17; Matt 22:21; Luke 20:25) if they did not compromise the essence of the Faith. But it transcended them through its *ethos*: its own special life. In particular, it taught a new way of life to the established structures of the couple and the family which changed their meaning positively, transfiguring them with transcendent value.[380]

Though Christianity, in its early centuries, did not at once change the social status of man and woman, it gave new meaning to their lives. They could accept their condition in a positive spirit, drawing spiritual riches from it, something far greater than any other consideration.

The Christian Revolution

Christianity may not have been able to change the reality of woman's inferior social status. Yet it taught a new conception and a new *ethos* which in many respects are revolutionary.

A. The Soteriological Revolution: Christ's Restoration of Fallen Humanity

The central message of Christianity is the gospel, or good news, *evangelia* in Greek. It is the salvation of fallen humanity, its healing and restoration. This was made possible by the Word of God assuming the whole human reality with no distinction of sex or gender so that He might transform it in His Person through the power of His divinity. In Christ and in the new humanity He inaugurated; the effects of ancestral sin are abolished.

Through his baptism, man is freed from any bondage to sin or to the power of the devil, "the prince of this world." Through this new birth he comes into a new life, a spiritual life, which transcends all biological and sociological determinism. All who receive grace and bring it to bloom through their spiritual life (asceticism in the widest sense) will put off the "old man" and put on the "new man" (cf. Col 3:9–10; Eph 4: 22–24).

I have written elsewhere[381] about the doctrine of original sin developed by St Augustine and amplified by the Latin tradition. It teaches that each man inherits at birth the sin of Adam and each woman the sin of Eve and both bear the blame for these sins. This gave rise to the idea of "sin nature" which is quite foreign to the teaching of the Greek Fathers. They taught that it is the effects of ancestral sin which are inherited. The sin itself of Adam and Eve is personal and is not transmitted. The blame remains their own personal responsibility and is not inherited. Note that these Fathers prefer to speak of "ancestral" not "original" sin.

Some writings teach that every woman inherits the sin of Eve and is to blame for it. This is not the thought of the Greek Fathers. Even if one supposes that the sin of Adam and Eve is inherited, humanity would have been cleansed of it by Christ. He is described by St Paul as "the last Adam" (1 Cor 15:45) and by the Fathers as "the second Adam" or "the new Adam."[382] Adam represents the prototype of all humanity, both men and women. The Virgin Mary, Mother of God,[383] is described as "the new Eve." She is not set in parallel with the new Adam but is the prototype of all women restored by Christ to the state they once had in Paradise, saved and deified.[384] Proclus of Constantinople wrote: "By Mary, all women are blessed. Woman is no longer damned for she has gained a glory surpassing even that of the angels. Eve is now healed."[385]

Seen from this angle, none of the faults of sinful Eve can be ascribed to Christian women renewed in Christ by baptism. Nor can any of the faults of sinful Adam be ascribed to any of his baptized male descendants. Men and women, united to Christ in baptism, are placed by Him in Paradise. They become representatives of the equality which humanity once had when first created by God. Seen from this point of view, the idea that woman's submission to man, which God presents as the consequence of the sins of Eve (Gen 3:16), should remain in effect is illogical. For the effects of ancestral sin have been abolished by Christ in the new humanity He has raised up.

B. The Anthropological Revolution: The Proclamation of the Fundamental Equality of Men and Women

1. Back to the Origins

The salvation brought by Christ allows, in principle, the restoration of the state of mankind in Paradise. There, the norm is the fundamental equality of man and woman which they had when created.

Genesis relates that woman was created after man from his rib; but as we have already seen, this in no way implies that woman is inferior to man. It is true that there are passages from St Paul and some patristic commentaries that suggest it. However, other patristic commentaries see woman's creation from man as a sign of their ontological unity, common essence, and natural equality.

St John Chrysostom reminds us that inequality came in through sin, but that it was not so in the beginning. There is no principle of inequality.

"Today, it is useful to tell you ... what kinds of slavery sin has brought into the world. Like a tyrant decreeing slavery in many forms, with what a range of shackles has sin bound our nature. The first of these is the subjection which places women under the power of men. This subjection took place after the sin, for before her disobedience woman was the equal of man. When God created her, he pronounced the same words as He did when creating man. Just as He said: 'Let us make man in our image and likeness,' rather than: 'Let man be made', so for woman. He did not say: 'May woman be made,' but: 'let us make him a helper.' Moreover, he did not simply say 'a helper', but also 'comparable to him,' (Gen. 2:18) to show once more equality in honor. . . . Such were His words before the sin."[386]

In what follows this passage, St John Chrysostom shows that ancestral sin changed the situation. However, in another text he refers to the incarnation of the Word as another justification of the equality of men and women. He says that Christ is of the same flesh as both men and women: "He participates in the same material as we do, the flesh of Eve and the flesh of Adam."[387] When the creed proclaims that the Word was made man, by man it means the human being (*anthropos*), which includes equally both man and woman. Just as Christ participated in both man and woman, so do man and woman participate equally in Him: "So, just as the Son of God participates in our nature, we also participate in His substance. Just as He bears us within Himself, so we bear Him within ourselves."[388] The formula of St Paul, "in Christ there is neither male nor female" is here confirmed by the theology of the Incarnation.

This is stated still more clearly in a text of St Gregory the Theologian. He counters the patristic writings cited above by reminding us that in the beginning, the woman did not sin more than the man. Then Christ accomplished the economy of mankind's salvation equally for men and women. Indeed, this work favors woman above man since He was born of a woman and is called son of David since from David she descended:

"If you look on the bad side of things, the woman sinned, but so did Adam. The serpent tricked them both. Neither was stronger than the other. But will you look on the good side? Christ saves them both through His sufferings. Was Christ made flesh to save man? It was the same for woman. Did He die for man? Woman is also saved by His death. He is given a name from His descendance from David: do you think that this is an honor for man? He was born of a woman, and this is in woman's favor."[389]

2. *Perfect Equality on Every Level*

Amongst the Fathers, Theodoret of Cyrus teaches that the basic equality of man and woman concerns their fundamental nature just as much as their intellectual, moral, and spiritual capacities. Their only difference is their sex which is secondary and physical:

"[God] did not make woman from some other material but took all that was needed to create her from man so that woman herself could not take a different path to man on the grounds that her nature was different. This is why God gave the same commandments to both men and women since the difference between them is purely a question of the body and not of the soul. Just as man is endowed with reason, so is woman, able to understand and to be aware of her duty. Like him, she knows what should be avoided and what should be sought out. At times, she judges better than men what is useful and gives good advice. It is not just men, but women too who should enter the divine temples. The law which enjoins men to partake of the divine mysteries does not forbid them to women but enjoins their initiation into them and partaking of them, just as for men. Moreover, the law grants to women, just as to men, the rewards of virtue since they struggle together to reach it."[390]

St John Chrysostom uses the biblical story of creation to affirm the equality of essence (or substance, or nature) between man and woman. He teaches that they are like brother and sister or father and daughter:

"God allowed man to marry his own sister, or rather his daughter, his very own flesh. To make their union perfect He started from the foundations, as when one builds. He did not create the woman from some other substance so that man would not see her as foreign to him."[391]

St Asterios of Amasea takes up the same idea to justify the indissolubility of marriage:

"Marriage unites both bodies and souls. It mixes two spirits and joins two bodies of flesh. How can you break this without pain? How can you separate, without torment, from her to whom you have bound your life? She is not just a servant but a sister and a wife: a sister according to the original creation. You are both formed from the same earth, from the same clay."[392]

This text of Genesis 2:24: "For this reason a man shall leave his father and mother and be joined to his wife, and they shall become one flesh," leads St

John Chrysostom to emphasize the unity of the human nature of the man and the woman, and how the children which they will conceive will share it:

"Henceforth father, mother and child are all of one flesh through marital union: for the joining of the seeds produces the child so that all three of them are of just one flesh."[393]

The reference to conception also allows St John Chrysostom to emphasize that it is achieved through cooperation of the man and the woman. He uses this to correct Aristotle's theory and the physiological ideas of his day which attributed the dominant role in conception to the man. At the same time, he balances the words of St Paul which at first teach the supremacy of man over woman since she was created after him and for him. Then, referring to the Apostle, he shows that the question of who is first is a false question, since all comes from the Creator to Whom all is due:

"After giving great superiority to man and saying that the woman was taken from him for his sake and set under him, [the Apostle] fears lest man should be exalted beyond measure whilst woman is too greatly humiliated. See how he corrects his words: 'Nevertheless, neither is man independent of woman, nor woman independent of man, in the Lord.' Be careful not just to see the beginning, the first creation. If you look at what followed you will see that each gives rise the other; or better still, neither gives rise to the other. God alone is the cause of all beings, hence these words: 'For as woman came from man, even so man also comes through woman.' ... In truth, these magnificent works are not of man but of God. So, the Apostle adds: 'But all things are from God.'"[394]

St John Chrysostom counters the arguments of certain writers, some of them Fathers, by emphasizing that woman is in the image of God as much as man. The sexual difference is irrelevant:

"As both infallible reason and the witness of the Apostle declare, it is not after the shape of the body but after the reasonable soul that man was made in the image of God. For, to think that God is restricted and limited by a certain configuration of our members is a wretched opinion without foundation. Does not the same blessed Apostle say: 'Be renewed in the spirit of your mind .... that you put on the new man which was created according to God' (Eph 4:23–24). Elsewhere he says more openly: 'Put off the old man with his deeds, and put on the new man who is renewed in knowledge according to the image of Him who created him' (Col 3:9–10). If, therefore, we renew ourselves in the spirit of our soul, and if this spirit is the new man who renews himself according to the image of Him who created him, there is no doubt that man was made in the image of his Creator, not after the body, nor after some part of the soul, but after the reasonable soul itself, where alone the knowledge of God can dwell. According to this renewal, we also become children of God by the baptism of Christ. Putting on the new man, we also put on Christ through faith. Who can exclude women from participating in this, for they also coinherit grace? And the Apostle says elsewhere: 'For you are all sons of God through faith in Christ Jesus. For as many of you as were baptized into Christ have put on Christ. There is neither Jew nor Greek, there is neither slave nor free, there is neither male nor female; for you are all one in Christ Jesus' (Gal 3:26–28). Have women of faith lost their bodily sex? No! But just as they have been renewed in the image of God where there is no sex, man also has been made in the image of God where there is no sex, in the spirit of his soul. So why should a man not cover his head, being the image and glory of God, whilst the woman should cover hers since she is the glory of man, as if she had not renewed herself in the spirit of her soul which is renewed in the knowledge of God? It is because her sex sets her apart from man, and the veil which covers her body is a sign of that part of her reason which is occupied with ordering temporal matters. For the image of God resides only in that part where the human soul is fixed on the contemplation and consultation of things eternal, a part which is clearly woman's just as much as man's."[395]

Didymus the Blind starts from another text of Genesis, the creation story, to emphasize that man and woman have the same nature. They both are equally in the image of God and have the same aptitudes on the most fundamental spiritual level.

"'He made them.' According to the literal sense we may say that we have here the proof that woman is of the same nature as man. Both are of the same kind which leads to the words: 'let us make man.' The words 'male and female' though, indicate the distinction which God set up between them to allow a descendance. They also show that woman too is in the image of God and that they both have the same capacities to imitate God, to acquire the Holy Spirit and to gain virtue."[396]

Clement of Alexandria emphasized the perfect equality of man and woman at every level of spiritual life:

"Let us embrace ever more closely this saving obedience; let us give ourselves wholly to the Lord; let us bind ourselves tightly to the ropes of the vessel of faith, convinced that the virtues to which it calls us are equally the preserve of man and woman. If they both have one and the same God, they also have one and the same Teacher, one and the same Church. Moderation, temperance, and modesty are virtues common to both sexes. They are nourished by the same foods; they unite in marriage. Breath, sight, hearing, intelligence, hope, the hearing of God's commandments and charity, they have all these in common. If man and woman lead the same life, they participate in the same grace and in the same salvation. They are beloved of God with the same love, taught with the same care and partake of the same graces and salvation. 'The children of this world marry' says the Lord, 'and are given in marriage.' This is the only difference between them."[397]

St Basil of Caesarea emphasizes the identical nature of man and woman and their equality in virtue. He reminds us that God gave them equal dignity:

"Blessed is the man who walks not in the counsel of the ungodly. . . . Why does the psalm proclaim only the man to be blessed? Are women excluded from this blessedness? In no way! There is not one virtue for men and another for women, for the creation of the one and the other has the same dignity. So, both will receive the same wages. Listen to Genesis: 'God created man in His own image; in the image of God He created him; male and female He created them.' Those who have one and the same nature have identical deeds, and those whose deeds are identical receive the same wages. Why, then, is man mentioned and woman passed over in silence? Since the nature of both is one and the same. The psalmist considered that the whole could be indicated by the part which is mentioned first."[398]

He repeats these arguments in another passage where the central idea is the creation of both man and woman in the image of God: "So that no one, through ignorance, should take the word 'man' to mean simply the masculine sex, Scripture adds: 'Male and female created He them.' The woman, like her husband, also has the privilege of being created in the image of God. Their two natures are equal in honor, equal in virtue. Their rewards are equal and their condemnation the same. . . . Since the image of God certainly has equal honor, the virtues of both and the manifestation of their good works are equally honorable."[399]

The equality of man and woman is confirmed in practice by the personal experience of St Gregory The Theologian of the relationship of his parents:

"They were superior to all others, but they never crushed each other, so great was their equality."[400]

St Basil places in the mouth of the martyr Julitte, whose life he wrote, the following words addressed to the women around her:

"We are formed from the same dough as men. We were created like them in the image of God. The Creator made women as capable of virtue as men. And so, are we not in every way of the same race as men? To create woman, it was not just the flesh which was taken but also bone of his bone. So as regards firmness, strength, and patience we are the equals of men, and this we owe to our Creator."[401]

3. *The Argument from Salvation: Christ Saves All Human Beings in the Same Way*

Christ came to save all human beings in the same way with no distinction of sex or gender: a weighty argument. Christ indeed assumed in Himself the whole of humanity, men and women together indiscriminately, not setting one over the other. He was born, suffered, and died, raising from the dead all without distinction.[402] All have become in Him the adopted children of God the Father, all with the same value in His eyes. So, as St Peter writes husbands and wives are "heirs together of the grace of life" (1 Pet 3:7), so women have their share of honor, equal to the share of men. It is also on this level that St Paul's words apply: "In Christ there is neither male nor female" (Gal 3:28).

Woman and man receive the grace of salvation and deification equally. Of course, each person appropriates this grace in his or her own way as befits his or her dispositions. Gender and sex play no part in this. Each person is equal to another in the opportunities received and the objectives that can be reached.

St Gregory the Theologian emphasizes that man and woman are not only of equal nature in God but also in destiny:

"The same Creator for man and for woman, for both the same clay, the same image [of God], the same law, the same death and the same resurrection."[403]

St Peter Chrysologus admirably evokes the common life of man and woman as a union without separation or confusion. Each discovers him(her) self in the other in their common activity yet neither is confused with the other nor with the whole they form as a couple. Each brings to the other his or her own qualities: sex, gender, and personality: "Christ calls at once both man and woman whom God unites, whom nature brings together giving them in a wonderful correspondence the same gestures and the same tasks. God causes, through the bond of marriage that two beings become one and that one should be two. Man discovers there his own self in another without losing his uniqueness or being confused with the couple."[404]

4. *The Eschatological Argument*

In the Kingdom of Heaven those who are saved are equal, "though there are many rooms in My Father's house" (cf. John 14:2), says Christ, "in the resurrection" people will "neither marry nor are given in marriage; but are like the angels of God in heaven" (Matt 22:30). In other words, the distinction of sexes will endure but sexuality will be abolished with all that belongs to it.

The Kingdom of Heaven is a new world where all human beings are renewed, and the laws of this present world apply no more. For Christians, who are already called to be new creatures (cf. 2 Cor 5:17; Col 3:9–10), a foretaste of life in the Kingdom of Heaven can be lived here and now in the Church: a different society from civil society, superior to it and inhabited by human beings who, through baptism, are born into a new life. This is no longer a biological and sociological life, but a spiritual life with its own ethics.[405] As France Quéré writes: "Before God, the Christian loses all particularities [biological and sociological]: nationality, trade, rank, sex and age, and becomes a creature burning with zeal, earnestly desiring to meet God in eternity where all distinctions are abolished." "In this sense," she continues, "the woman escapes from the family, from the supervision of father and of husband: a radical emancipation."[406]

However, though the Kingdom of Heaven is already amongst the faithful (cf. Luke 17:21), they can only participate therein in part. Everyone living in this world is subject in the body to the laws of fallen nature, and to the laws of society. All must "render therefore to Caesar the things that are Caesar's, and to God the things that are God's" (Matt 22:21; Mark 12:17; Luke 20:25).

C. The Legal Revolution: Equality of Duties and of Rights

The Fathers taught new principles which gave woman the same dignity as man, and therefore the same social rights and duties. Though they respected the laws of the societies in which they lived, some of them raised their voices against the legal privileges given to man, notably in the case of adultery, and sought equal rights for women.

St Gregory the Theologian was one who protested against the unequal treatment of men and women in the case of adultery and the guardianship of their children. It is remarkable in that he criticizes the legislation head-on, and blames the social custom on which it rests, teaching that it is contrary to the principles of Christianity which recognize perfect equality between man and woman.

"[Concerning chastity], I see that most men have false ideas and that their law is unjust and inequitable. Why do they punish the woman and allow the man to go free? The wife who dishonors the bed of her husband is an adulteress and must bear the severe penalties of the law; but the husband who is untrue to his wife goes unpunished. I cannot accept such legislation; I do not approve this custom. It is men[407] who have passed such laws, which is why they are directed against women. They also leave the children in the care of the father and completely neglect the interests of the weaker sex.

God did not act thus but said: 'Honor your father and your mother' ... which is the first commandment with promise 'that it may go well with you'; then: "'Anyone who curses their father or mother is to be put to death.'" He both praised what is good and punished evil. He goes on: "'For the blessing of the father establishes the houses of the children; but the curse of the mother uproots their foundations' (WSir 3:9 LXX [Ecc 3:9]). Notice the equality of the commandment: a single Creator of man and of woman; the same dust from which they both arise; one single image, one single law, one single death, one single resurrection! We are born of both man and woman and the children are in the same debt to both of their progenitors.

So how can you require chastity if you do not observe it? How can you ask what you do not give? How can you legislate for a body of the same dignity in such an unequal way? 'And they,' said [God], 'become one flesh,' so let this single flesh be honored equally!"[408]

St Basil of Caesarea also condemns the different treatment given to man and woman in cases of adultery. He criticizes established custom:

"The decision of the Lord, taken literally, applies both to men and women: a marriage cannot be broken save for the cause of adultery. In our customs, it is not thus, for we find the strictest provisions applied to women ...—'whoever keeps an adulterous wife is senseless and impious'—whereas custom obliges wives to keep their husbands even if they are adulterous ... but if the man is abandoned, he is excused, and his new wife is in no way condemned."[409]

Finally, we will quote St Jerome who defended Fabiola who was accused of leaving her husband who had mistreated her:

"I will not praise the convert before justifying her who has been blamed. Her first husband, it is said, had vices such that even a courtesan or a vile slave could not have borne them. If I were to describe them, I would discredit the virtue of a woman. For she preferred to suffer all the wrongs of a divorce rather than defame the one who had become part of her body and reveal his filth. I will simply present what is enough for a modest woman and for a Christian. The commandment of the Lord is that the women should not be repudiated save for the case of fornication (Matt. 5: 9 and 19:9), and should she be repudiated she should thenceforth remain celibate. So, all that is commanded to men applies equally to women. If an adulterous wife may be repudiated, a wife cannot be obliged to keep a depraved husband. "He who is joined to a harlot is one body with her" (1 Cor 6:16). So, she who keeps company with the fornicator and the immodest becomes one body with him. There are the laws of Caesar and there are the laws of Christ. ... The pagans relax the reins of modesty in favor of men: only debauchery and adultery are condemned. However, at their pleasure they may satisfy their passions in the brothels and with young slaves as if social rank, rather than their lust, created the crime. With us, what is forbidden to women is also forbidden to men. The obedience is the same and so is the status."[410]

D. The Conjugal Revolution

1. Woman Is Recognized as a Free and Independent Person through the Requirement of Mutual Consent for Marriage

One of the essential foundations of marriage in the eyes of Christianity is the free consent of both the man and the woman to their union. Without this, it would be seen as invalid. The marriage service itself implies that this free consent should be clearly expressed by both spouses before God, the priest, and the congregation. This was a break with the forced marriages practiced in the society of Antiquity. It might be the man who forced the marriage, through physical force, psychological domination, or abduction. It might be the family which arranged a marriage without the consent of the bride.[411] Indeed, these practices persist in some societies to the present day. So, Christianity was a counterweight to the power of the male and the authority of parents.

2. *The Status of Women Enhanced by the Rule of the Indissolubility of Marriage*

The indissolubility of marriage, taught by Christianity, was a true revolution for the laws and practice of the Old Testament and for the Judaism of Antiquity. It was the same for the Greek and Roman societies of the time, where the husband could repudiate his wife with a simple formality whilst the opposite was impossible. A husband could change his wife whenever he wished.

Indissolubility was not just a formal rule. It helped to give woman a dignity which she lacked. She was no longer an object to be changed at will, but a unique and irreplaceable subject. This gave her rights which she had lacked, limiting the formerly absolute rights of her husband.

3. *Reciprocal Duties: Mutual Sacrifice, Service, and Love*

St Paul compares the relations between husband and wife with those between Christ and the Church. He places them in the context of reciprocal love, with an especially strong idea of sacrifice for the husband. For Christ suffered and died for His Church after humbling Himself in total self-abasement.[412] This is the theme of kenosis[413] which St Paul develops in his epistle to the Philippians with a vibrant call to brotherly love:

> Therefore if there is any consolation in Christ, if any comfort of love, if any fellowship of the Spirit, if any affection and mercy, fulfill my joy by being like-minded, having the same love, being of one accord, of one mind. Let nothing be done through selfish ambition or conceit, but in lowliness of mind let each esteem others better than himself. Let each of you look out not only for his own interests, but also for the interests of others. Let this mind be in you which was also in Christ Jesus,

> who, being in the form of God, did not consider it robbery to be equal with God, but made Himself of no reputation, taking the form of a bond-servant, and coming in the likeness of men. And being found in appearance as a man, He humbled Himself and became obedient to the point of death, even the death of the cross.
>
> (Phil 2:1–8)

Commenting on the injunction of St Paul—"Let the husband render to his wife the affection due her, and likewise also the wife to her husband" 1 Cor 7:3)—St John Chrysostom remarks that in marriage, the man and woman are servants of each other.[414] As regards the verse which follows: "The wife does not have authority over her own body, but the husband does. And likewise the husband does not have authority over his own body, but the wife does," he writes: "This saying shows the intention to create complete equality: just as the husband is the master of his wife's body so is the wife mistress of her husband's. Why therefore did He institute perfect equality? It is that ... once it is a question of continence and chastity, man has no more his prerogatives with regard to his wife and suffers the same punishment should he break the laws of marriage. This is perfectly reasonable. For if your wife has come to you, if she has left her father, her mother and all her family it is not so that you should offend her; ... it is not to suffer unceasing conflict. You took her to be your companion, your partner, so that she should be free and enjoy the same rights as you yourself."[415]

It is clear that the mutual gift of oneself into the hands of one's spouse is not simply of the body and its sexuality, but also of the whole person and all goods possessed in common. A husband explained this to his young wife who had not yet understood that marriage means sharing: "You say: 'It's mine'? What do you claim as your own? I don't know. I have nothing of my own! Why do you say: 'It's mine'? Everything belongs to you! And I also belong to you."[416]

4. *The Collaboration of the Spouses*

The passages just quoted suggest that the relationship between the spouses does not simply mean helping each other and submitting to each other but also involves collaboration. France Quéré writes: "The rigid theories which make man the master and the wife his servant must be abandoned. . . .

From the teachings of the Fathers and their observations and reflections on conjugal life a very simple model arises. Husband and wife work and converse together. Neither takes on anything without consulting the other. The symmetry implied by the intimacy of life together and a close common interest is spontaneously restored."[417]

We have seen how St Gregory the Theologian wrote that his parents "never crushed each other, so great was their equality."[418] We have also read how St John Chrysostom described the wife as a "partner" of her husband. In the same vein, St Augustine writes of the couple: "United side by side they walk forward together and together fix their gaze on the same horizon."[419]

E. The Sexual Revolution: Consent for Sexual Relations

In the ancient world, a woman was entirely dependent on the desire of her husband. Sexual relations were often forced and imposed by the man on the woman without her being able avoid them; but from the start, Christianity taught the principle of mutual consent for sexual relations in marriage. St Paul writes that the husband should fulfill his marital duty to his wife, and likewise the wife to her husband. "The wife does not have authority over her own body [but yields it to her husband]. And likewise the husband does not have authority over his own body [but yields it to his wife]. Do not deprive each other except perhaps [by mutual consent] for a time, that you may give yourselves to fasting and prayer; and come together again so that Satan will not tempt you because of your lack of self-control" (1 Cor 7:3–5).

The advice that that the husband should fulfill his marital duty to his wife, and likewise the wife to her husband, sets out that each should be ready to reply to the desire of the other; for, in the eyes of the Apostle, sexual relations served to regulate this desire and avoid extra-conjugal relationships: "It is good for a man not to touch a woman. Nevertheless, because of sexual immorality, let each man have his own wife, and let each woman have her own husband" (1 Cor 7:1–2).

The statement "The wife does not have authority over her own body but the husband does. And likewise the husband does not have authority over his own body but wife does" is not to be understood as treating the body as an object to be possessed. It signifies the sharing of a treasure which, through marriage, has become common to both man and woman: "one flesh" (cf. Gen 2:24; Eph 5:31).

The advice "Do not deprive each other except perhaps with [mutual] consent," signifies that consent is also required for abstinence, in view of a common spiritual goal.

F. The Maternal Revolution: Re-evaluating Motherhood

In every age motherhood has been valued, but often this is based on the quality (male or female) of the children born and their quantity, without giving much credit to the mother. Instead, she might be personally despised if she were sterile. Indeed, the Old Testament saw sterility as shameful and as a reason for divorce. Christianity changed the way these things were seen, setting great spiritual worth on motherhood, and giving less importance to the idea of fertility.

1. The Spiritual Appreciation of Motherhood

Christianity sees motherhood in relation to the mother herself. She is not just valued for her biological and social qualities but for her spirit as in St Paul's first epistle to Timothy (2:15): women "will be saved through childbearing if they continue in faith, love, and holiness with self-control." The conditions for salvation show that a woman will not gain it merely by giving birth. A virtuous life is also required, suggesting that this virtue should imbue the raising of the children. For motherhood goes far beyond the biological and physiological function of gestation and birthgiving to include spiritual birth. The father is also called to participate in this spiritual birth. He should be at the children's side to train them as they grow both psychologically and spiritually. He should raise them in the literal sense of the word.[420]

2. Fertility Relativized

The value placed on biological fertility in the Old Testament as a divine blessing may lead people to believe that this is the timeless teaching of Christianity. The idea is reinforced by the promotion of families with many children by Catholicism from the middle of the nineteenth century and the opposition of the Roman hierarchy to any kind of artificial birth control. However, a careful look at the teachings of the early Fathers shows that this is in no way true.

—Against an Apocalyptic Background to History—

From the earliest times, right up until at least the fifth century, the Fathers saw history against an apocalyptic background. The end of all things seemed close which made the idea of a numerous descendance absurd.

For most of the Fathers, of the fourth century especially, the duty to procreate does not seem to have been important or a fundamental duty. They generally interpreted the commandment: "Increase and multiply" (Gen. 9:7) allegorically: a call to spiritual growth and multiplication of the virtues. These Fathers considered that it is no longer necessary to procreate in the way it was at the start of humanity. To the one who opposed him with the word of Scripture: "Be fruitful and multiply," St Basil of Caesarea replied: "I laugh at him who does not mark in what age the commandments were given."[421] He interprets this commandment of Genesis 1:28 as meaning that man should grow from childhood to maturity, intellectual, moral, and spiritual. "It is the animals," he says, "who have been commanded to multiply physically. Man should grow in reason and multiply in good works."[422] Eusebius of Caesarea asks the natural question as to why Christians, unlike the Jews, neglect marriage and childbearing. He gives three answers: (1) the Jews are concerned with the beginning of the ages and the Christians by the end of all things; as St Paul writes: "The time is short" (1 Cor 7:29), so it is vain to worry about the future; (2) the holy Jews were few in number and were obliged to procreate so as to pass on the revelation to others; but in the present time, the doctors and preachers of the Word have no need of a physical descendance; crowds without number await the Gospel, and those who teach it give birth to a divine and bodiless descendance; (3) between their activities and the worship they render to God, Christians have no time to found a family.[423] Many Fathers feel that they are in a world which is full up[424] threatened with overpopulation[425] and whose end is nigh.[426] They no longer encourage procreation,[427] but virginity which anticipates the Kingdom whose coming, for them, would not tarry. This gave rise to many treatises on virginity[428] of which the best known are those of St Athanasius of Alexandria, St Gregory of Nyssa, St Basil of Ankyra, and St John Chrysostom. It also led to such a huge growth of monasticism that people had the impression that the cities were emptied to fill the deserts.[429] Clearly, Christianity had little interest in population growth at that time.[430]

The main concern of the Fathers was to bring about a growth in the quality of humanity rather than its quantity.

Consequently, procreation is not seen as the justification of marriage nor even its principal reason. Although many Fathers emphasized procreation as the exclusive aim of marriage, this was to counter the Gnostics and Manicheans who denied this aim. They also attacked pagan customs which gave much importance to perverse sex which was unconnected to marriage and aimed entirely at pleasure.

Freed from these considerations. Some Fathers took a clearly different position where sexual union is seen as having purposes other than procreation. Paradoxically, this position finds a firm foundation in St Paul's first epistle to the Corinthians:

> Now concerning the things of which you wrote to me: It is good for a man not to touch a woman. Nevertheless, because of sexual immorality [*porneia*], let each man have his own wife, and let each woman have her own husband. Let the husband render to his wife the affection due her, and likewise also the wife to her husband. The wife does not have authority over her own body, but the husband does. And likewise the husband does not have authority over his own body, but the wife does. Do not deprive one another except with consent for a time, that you may give yourselves to fasting and prayer; and come together again so that Satan does not tempt you because of your lack of self-control. But I say this as a concession, not as a commandment. For I wish that all men were even as I myself. But each one has his own gift from God, one in this manner and another in that. But I say to the unmarried and to the widows: It is good for them if they remain even as I am; but if they cannot exercise self-control, let them marry. For it is better to marry than to burn with passion.
>
> (1 Cor 7:1–9)

This teaches that consecrated celibacy, virginity and monasticism, is the ideal. Marriage is a way of life for those who cannot reach this ideal because of their weakness. They cannot master sufficiently their sexuality and find it too hard to remain entirely continent, or abstinent. So, marriage is seen as an inferior condition; but this does not devalue it. Just as celibacy, it is seen as a personal charisma (each of you has your own gift from God). All commentators have noticed that nowhere is procreation seen as the aim of marriage. The only explicit aim is, through marital sexual relations, to avoid sexual passions and what goes with them: adultery, whoring, homosexuality, and the like. "Because of sexual immorality, let each man have his own wife, and let each woman have her own husband."

The views of St John Chrysostom are particularly representative. They are expressed many times in his work and deserve to be examined in detail.

He recognizes that it is certain that the primary aim of marriage is procreation.[431] However, he sees this as the first aim of marriage long ago, at the beginning of humanity and under the law of the Old Testament.[432] It has become secondary with the coming of the New Testament. He raises several arguments to support his position. The main one is that marriage was instituted after the ancestral sin to allow the human race, now become mortal,[433] to be preserved. However, this is now no longer the main aim: (1) the earth, which was once empty is now full;[434] (2) the hope of resurrection has been given to men by the saving economy of Christ, so they no longer need to seek to live on in the image and traces of themselves which they leave in their descendants;[435] (3) it is henceforth possible to have children without recourse to marriage, through spiritual fatherhood and motherhood.[436] Another reason to consider that the sole aim of marriage is not procreation is the existence of sterile couples who profit nonetheless legitimately from marriage.[437] Finally, it seems to St John Chrysostom that procreation "is not so much the result of marriage, but of that word of God: "Be fruitful and multiply; fill the earth" (Gen 1:28)."[438] The polygamy practiced in the Old Testament was perfectly adapted to this commandment, whilst monogamy in marriage, in the strict sense, did not then exist and was brought in with the New Testament when the earth was largely inhabited.

We see that the patristic arguments we have presented are influenced by two factors: the first is the idea that the end of the World is imminent, an idea which is rare today outside various marginal groups; the second is the wish of the Fathers to justify the biological sterility of monastic life which they so strongly encourage. However, they never lose sight of procreation as the final aim of sexuality, and this allows them to reject sexual perversions which all imply sterile unions.

Procreation as an end in itself is seen as relative. To have as many children as nature allows is no longer a duty. The union of man and woman has other more important aims than procreation: love in all three dimensions of the human person, spiritual, psychological, and bodily. Here is the positive teaching of Christianity. Biological sterility is not a curse, and God's blessing on a couple is not in proportion to the number of their children.

Through Periodic or Permanent Abstinence

St Paul recommends that couples should abstain "for a time" to give themselves "to fasting and prayer." In the Church, this time of abstinence has been formalized and extended over time through the institution of periods of fasting and abstinence throughout the year. There are the four fasts: Advent, before Christmas; Great Lent which precedes Pascha/Easter; the fast of the Dormition which precedes August 15 and the fast of the Apostles which precedes June 29. There are also almost all Wednesdays and Fridays and the days before taking Communion. In all, this comes to about half the days of the year.

Although these rules appeared gradually, fasting and abstinence were practiced from the beginning of Christianity. For instance, Clement of Alexandria (ca. 150–ca. 215) sets out the right times for them.[439] St Gregory the Theologian advises one of his spiritual daughters: "Know how to refuse. Teach your husband that on holy days you should abide in chastity."[440]

Like fasting, these periods of sexual abstinence have a spiritual goal,[441] but naturally reduce the number of births.[442]

By Promoting Consecrated Celibacy

The Fathers encouraged widows not to remarry, and from the earliest times they were consecrated as a clear group in the Church. Virginity was also encouraged and later monasticism, all of which shows that procreation was not a priority for the Fathers. Instead, births were limited, particularly in the fourth century when the monasteries multiplied and the cities were emptied: the deserts filled up with monks and nuns, living as hermits or in communities. Whilst encouraging these three consecrated orders, the Fathers also emphasized the shortcomings and difficulties of marriage, but for all that, they did not exclude or devalue it.

Consecrated celibacy requires strict discipline and demanding sacrifice, but the Fathers presented it as a way to be free of the many constraints of marriage. St Ambrose mentions two in particular: the anguish and pain of birthgiving and submission to a husband:

"Marriage should not be shunned as if it were a sin but avoided as a burden. The law [of nature] compels the wife to give birth in anguish and pain, and to turn to her husband so that he may dominate her. The married woman's lot is to give birth in pain and sorrow, but not the widow's. The wife submits to the man's domination, but not the virgin."[443]

On this second point, St Ambrose places the following words in the mouth of his friend, Julienne: "Firstly, marriage is a chain which binds the wife to her husband and binds her in submission. For sure, love is a good chain, but a chain nonetheless. Should she wish to free herself, the wife is powerless. Nor can she dispose of herself freely. For the Apostle said truly: 'The wife does not have authority over her own body, but the husband does.' (1 Cor 7:4). And why be surprised at this, since the husband has no authority over his own body, but his wife? If the stronger cannot freely dispose of himself still less the weaker! So mutual dependance does not disengage the woman but binds her more strongly. ... My children, I have lived through the pains of marriage and the discomforts of the married state and with a good husband! Even with a good husband I was not free; I was subject to my husband, and I sought to please him."[444]

However, it seems that the husband was no freer. As Mariella Carpinello remarks: "Olympias in Constantinople, Emmilie in Cappadocia, Julienne and Paula in Italy all describe their husbands as their unhappy companions in slavery rather than as enemies who deserved reproach."[445] However, the constraints of married life extend yet further, enhancing further the freedom of the one who prefers monastic life.

The biological sterility of this life seems insignificant to the Fathers compared to its potential spiritual fertility, so much greater than in marriage. This could be seen as anticipating some of the claims and experiences of radical feminists and of the queer movement. But there is a difference: the framework of a Christian perspective, where abstention from marriage and the choice of celibacy do not arise from selfish or individualistic motives. There is no phobia, no disdain, no rejection or hatred of the opposite sex. The aim is higher: a more perfect union with God which can only come about through the sacrifice of the ego—which alone allows one's true self to appear—and the unconditional love of one's neighbor.

G. The Moral Revolution: Chastity as the Virtue Which Brings Mutual Respect

The virtue of chastity has been mentioned in two previous chapters of this book, on marriage and on monasticism. Here, it is important to emphasize its key role in the status of woman. This virtue, which should not be confused with abstinence, is based on the words of Christ in the book of Matthew: "You have heard that it was said to those of old, 'You shall not commit adultery.' But I say to you that whoever looks at a woman to lust for her has already committed adultery with her in his heart" (Matt 5:27–28) This teaches a man to avoid any sexual approach to a woman who is not his wife, and a woman to any man who is not her husband. Even lustful looks and desires are to be avoided. Another way of behaving and looking at the other is required, pure and free from any sexual connotation. Chastity implies absolute respect for the other's person. The other should not be seen as an object of desire or sexual pleasure but should be treated as a person in the wholeness of his(her) being with all the dignity which goes with it.

In the passage quoted, Christ speaks only of the man's approach to woman. The Fathers often do the same, even though virtue also involves woman's approach to man. For man's nature and sexuality make him the one responsible for this problem in the great majority of cases.

In the society of Antiquity debauchery was trivialized and often valued.[446] Men were often brutal toward women[447] whose social inferiority made them vulnerable to the sexual desire of the male. So, Christianity's promotion of the virtue of chastity was a revolution in the relations of men and women. They came to be seen in a new way and Christians enshrined them in a new way of life which set an example to the rest of society without imposing itself.

H. The Spiritual Revolution: The Transfiguration of the Relations of Men and Women through *Agape*

The spiritual love for neighbor (*agape*) is Christ's second commandment (or precept) after the love of God (Matt 22:39) and St Paul states that it contains all the fullness of the law (Gal 5:14). It is the foremost of all Christian virtues in the domain of human relations and profoundly changes their nature since all men and women become spiritual brothers and sisters. It is in this love that the word of St Paul finds its full expression: "There is neither Jew nor Greek, there is neither slave nor free, there is neither male nor female; for you are all one in Christ Jesus" (Gal 3:28). Through spiritual love of neighbor between men and women, all the oppositions and hierarchies linked to sex and gender disappear. Perfect equivalence appears with peaceful and harmonious relationships. Fleshly concerns are no more, and all which belongs to the body and mind are transfigured by a spiritual vision of the other.

I. The Family Revolution: Esteem for the Wife as Mother, Teacher, and Mistress of the Household

St Paul writes of woman: "She will be saved in childbearing" (1 Tim 2:15). The Fathers also esteem a woman for childbearing, and especially for raising her children, for they do not consider that motherhood can be reduced to a biological function."[448]

Modern feminism, even the most moderate, has worked hard to dissociate maternity from women and women from maternity. Contraception and abortion are encouraged, and abortion is ever more common as a form of contraception. As a result, in our days, children are conceived through in vitro biological techniques, and the task of gestation is devolved to surrogate mothers, poor women who are hired for this task. The mother herself is not involved. Instead, there is surrogacy, a new form of exploitation of women and a marketing of the human body in a totally impersonal world where everything can be bought and sold. This inhumanity and depersonalization reach icy depths in the main justification given by feminists for abortions of convenience:[449] the woman is said to be mistress of her own body, as if the child existed only as an outgrowth of her body, a kind of parasite without his(her) own life or personality, with no rights. So, with chilling logic, the child can be seen as something insignificant, whose elimination is of no importance.

Of course, in former times women were frequently pregnant. This was partly due to the physiological needs of men who might force sexual relations. It was also to compensate for a high infant mortality. Yet this could be extremely inconvenient for women, and as we have seen, the Fathers of the early Church saw no problem in limiting births by the natural means of periodic or permanent abstinence.[450]

However, modern feminism in its most radical form goes so far as to refuse motherhood entirely. This is closely linked to the individualist concept of freedom promoted by the modern world. Limitless individual pleasure is the goal, a totally egotistical conception of life.[451] Maternity and raising children are seen as obstacles to individual freedom and pleasure. The role of the mother and housewife is completely downgraded, especially as a woman's role in society is seen as salaried work, her main way to freedom.

France Quéré writes: "Today, everyone proclaims loudly that the independence and dignity of women come from taking part in professional life. Such ideas would have seemed laughable in the time of the Fathers: it would have meant abolishing the rights of free and noble women to reduce them to slavery. For them, freedom was reached by quite different methods which we, today, no more understand than they would understand ours. We see them as extra burdens imposed on women, but they called them happiness and freedom."[452]

The condition of a woman in her home was obvious to the ancient world, so no woman complained of it.[453] It is only in the eyes of modern feminists that it is a form of slavery, just as they systematically see marriage and maternity as forms of slavery. In the Christian perspective taught by the Fathers, whose writings tell us of the incarnation, the life of the woman in her home is of great value. The home is seen as a place of freedom where woman blossoms. But man's social activities in the outside world are seen as a burden because of the constraints they impose, the energy they require, and the cares they bring. In both these cases, the Fathers see freedom as an inner attitude and not the result of special social status.

St John Chrysostom give an excellent description of this twofold life, where the home is seen as a place of peace, favorable to those intellectual and spiritual activities which make everyone blossom:

> Under the Old Testament, God withdrew His people from the society of the wicked. He separated the Jews from the Egyptians and led them into the desert to teach them, to instruct them in His laws and precepts. He exhorts us to do likewise, to flee the public square, the tumult of the crowd and to enclose ourselves in our secret chamber [Matt 6:6] there to offer peacefully our prayers. A vessel which is not shaken by the tempest makes a prosperous voyage, and the soul, free from every care, lives in peace and tranquility as if she had already reached her harbor. This is why women, who usually keep to their homes, should be more immersed than men in philosophy and in the contemplation of heavenly

> things. This is why Jacob, who dwelt in his home, far from tumult, was a simpler man than Esau: for it is not without reason that Scripture says of him that "he dwelt in the tent of his father." [Gen 25:27]
>
> ... Man is almost always in the public sphere and the courts. He is troubled by many things foreign to him, like a vessel on the high seas, tossed by the waves and beaten with the wind. But woman, seated at home as in a school of philosophy, can collect her thoughts. She can apply herself to prayer and to reading and to all the other exercises of philosophy. And just as those who dwell in the desert are troubled by no one. So woman, always enclosed in her home, can enjoy continual rest. Though she may sometimes be obliged to go into the town, she is not, for all that, exposed to the troubles of the mind. She goes to Church, and she goes to the bath. It is often necessary for her to go out, but usually she remains at home to keep it. There she can practice the study of wisdom.[454]

Formally, it was man who had power, through his outward activity and the rights, superior to woman's, given him by society. Yet woman remained the mistress of her household and there was superior to man. Historians have verified that this was so in the societies of the past, and sociologists have seen that it persists today in those societies that have preserved a traditional structure. St John Chrysostom, as we will see below, sees that the mistress of the home does more than care physically for her husband. She supports him psychologically and educates him morally, not just by teaching, quite legitimate in this context, but also by advice, and especially by her example.

It hardly needs saying that the power of the woman is seen and applied fully in the raising of her children. Though she was barred from public education in the ancient world, the woman gave vital education to her whole household,[455] transmitting the values she and her husband kept. This played a basic role in the development of early Christianity.

Monique Alexandre writes: "From the beginnings of Christianity to its triumph, the power of women was that of their outgoing faith. More easily freed from political and social constraints, and from the religious and cultural traditions of the cities of Antiquity, they often seem well ahead of the men in their families. Their influence in the home helped convert their loved ones, and they played a vital role in the spread of the Faith."[456]

It was women, through their grip on the family, who helped Christianity to take permanent root. During the persecutions of old and of recent times it was the mothers and grandmothers who kept the Faith in the face of the coercion put in place in society by the States which sought to eradicate it.[457]

However, though the Fathers praise the advantages of home life they do not see it as the only path for women, just as they do not see maternity as their only goal. This is shown by their ideas on the limitation of births and consecrated celibacy described above. In the previous text they also praise the intellectual and contemplative activities of women, showing that they do not think woman's material tasks in the home to be the better part, for they follow Christ's teaching when he visited Martha and Mary (cf. Luke 10:38–42). So, the home is not valued for itself, nor for the material tasks it brings to women. Indeed, in well-to-do families these tasks may be delegated to domestic staff. The home's value lies in its being a special place for spiritual blossoming. This leads St John Chrysostom to write: "The women who are almost always confined to their homes should be better Christians than men."[458] France Quéré writes that in Christianity: "An incessant dialectic would develop between self-recollection and the inner world which, paradoxically would show that enclosure is the great opening into the liberty of God."[459] What goes for the enclosure of the home goes even more for the monastic enclosure. In his *Life of Saint Macrina,* St Gregory of Nyssa shows how changing their family home into a monastery was its perfect fulfillment.[460] In a similar way, St John Chrysostom describes the home as "a miniature church."[461] Moreover, in the earliest days of the Church there were no church buildings. The church was a private building owned by a Christian and placed at the disposal of the community.

J. A Certain Superiority of Woman

The Fathers sometimes affirm that woman is superior to man. For instance, St John Chrysostom sees women as often surpassing men in spiritual warfare: "It is accepted that woman should stay at home whilst man is occupied with the business of the city.... But in divine combat and bearing the burden of work for the Church it is not the same. Woman often surpasses man in valor when it comes to giving such battles and bearing such burdens."[462]

This can be seen especially in monastic life.

> You will see that Egypt . . . places all its glory in the Cross of Jesus Christ. These are the miracles which Egypt shows forth, not only in the cities but more so in the deserts.[463] Everywhere can be seen the soldiers of Jesus Christ, an august and royal company of solitaries and an image of the life of angels. This glory is not just for men: women share it with them. They have no less strength than men, not for riding horses or for the skill of bearing arms as ordained by the weightiest of the Greek law-makers and philosophers, but for a far fiercer war which they share with men. For they, like men, must fight the Devil himself and the powers of darkness without being prevented by the weakness of their sex. For such battles require, not bodily strength, but the good disposition of the soul and the heart. This why, in this kind of war, women often show more courage and great heartedness than men and win more glorious victories.[464]

Though St Paul writes that women should not teach and advises that "if they want to learn something, let them ask their own husbands at home" (1 Cor 14:35), St John Chrysostom "encourages women to set to work and give their husbands useful advice." He says: "Instruct your husbands, not just with your words but also by your deeds."[465]

St John also emphasizes more fully the authority and power of a wife over her husband on the spiritual level (which completely determines his behavior).

> The wife usually remains at home, keeping the household. She may engage in the study of wisdom and calm the troubled spirit of her husband when he returns home. She can calm him down and drive off the useless and troubling thoughts which torment him. Then she can let him go back to his work, freed from the cares and burdens which were weighing him down, taking with him all the goodness he has learnt from his wife. There is nothing, truly nothing, which has more strength and virtue

> to guide and lead a man than the goodness of his wife when she is wise and prudent. She may indeed turn his spirit where she will at her pleasure. He will place less confidence in his friends, his doctors, or even in princes than in the opinions and advice of his wife. For the great tenderness which a husband feels for his wife makes him receive her counsels with pleasure. I could here give many examples of coarse and undisciplined men who were polished and civilized by their wives. The wife is the companion of the man, at table, in the bed and in the procreation of children. In her he confides his secrets and his deeds. What more can I say? Bound to her husband in everything she is as closely joined to him as the body is to the head. She will be of more service to her husband than anyone if she is honest and sensible.
>
> This is why I urge wives to take in what I have just said and to give good and salutary examples to their husbands. For … a wife is well able to provoke her husband to virtue.... It was Nabal's wife who saved him from death. Another woman [Esther] saved a whole nation. Deborah, Judith and yet others have been perfect as generals of the army. Saint Paul says: "For how do you know, O wife, whether you will save your husband?" (1 Cor 7:16). And Scripture teaches us that in the blessed century of the Apostles, the women like Persis, Mary and Priscilla [cf. Rom 16] bravely exposed themselves to Apostolic combats.
>
> Imitate these holy women. Edify and instruct your husbands, not only with your words but even more by your good example.[466]

St Gregory the Theologian provides us with a concrete example of how a wife taught her husband and how powerfully this improved him. He describes how his mother was a true spiritual and intellectual teacher for his father: "The wife who God gave to [my father] Gregory was not simply a helper for him. That would be a small thing and not worth recording. For him, she was a guide and teacher of his thoughts. The example she gave in her life and her good words raised him to the highest virtues. Though she obeyed her husband in everything, as the laws of marriage command, yet she did not blush to be the mistress who brought him to the faith and piety. If it is for this that we admire him, then we should admire at least as much the docility of his companion."[467]

K. The Social Revolution: Women Take Their Place in Community Life

Though the Fathers praised the home as the place where the woman could blossom in her role of raising her children and in her spiritual and intellectual activities, they did not intend to restrict her to its boundaries.

France Quéré remarks: "The Fathers put the ancient absolute of the home into perspective. The traditional work of women, which was to perpetuate human life, lost its meaning if life was to cease. Those men who proclaimed the second coming of Christ had little reason to maintain women in this condition or to be sensitive to the differences between sexes. Even were this life to last longer, the material care for people was not "the better part": it was better to seek God. So, the fathers sought to surpass domestic life even while moralizing about it in their preaching! They clearly sought something other than this existence sheltered by walls and roofs. Faith deserved broader spaces. So, when, in our times, people say that a woman's place is not only in the home, they make hardly any advance on the thought of the Fathers. There is just this difference. The virtues of emancipation which are now said to come from entering professional life were then seen to arise simply from faith in Jesus Christ,"[468] and, we may add, from the zeal employed to support it, to defend it and to spread it.

Though Christianity conformed to the social structures of its time, we can easily see that it greatly contributed to freeing women from the ideas and structures of Judaism and the societies of Antiquity.[469] There were still inequalities between men and women in Western societies, said to be "Judaeo-Christian," in second half of the twentieth century. Yet historical studies have shown that these arose from influences foreign to Christianity. They first arose at the end of the Middle Ages and then in the sixteenth century.[470] More recently, there were influences from the nineteenth century. (In France, specifically from the Napoleonic Code.)

Sophie Malick Prunier writes: "The renounciation of marriage and procreation allowed some women access to written culture,[471] but sometimes they could even go further and take on veritable 'paraclerical' roles, to adopt and expression of P. Brown:[472] roles of advice, of instruction, and of protection.[473] ... This affirmation of the leading role of some women, and of new expressions of feminine life beyond the narrow circle of the family, but within the first Christian communities, can well be considered ... as one of the fundamental contributions of Christianity to women's emancipation."[474] However sometimes there were also married women who played this role. From the first centuries and throughout the history of Christianity there are "great women," seen in the Church and in society, alongside "great men." They do not just shine with brilliance equal to men's in spiritual and ascetic life but have, as well, a high social standing, a brilliant and acclaimed culture, and wield economic and political power equal or superior to that of men.[475]

1. *Women in the Gospel*

The revolutionary aspect of Christianity can be seen in the Gospels. Christ left no teaching that might prefigure or justify the unequal positions we find in St Paul or in certain Fathers, but instead gives women an unprecedented place.[476] He overturned all the conventions and hierarchies that applied to socially despised women who were condemned and cast out, and rejected religious, moral, and social exclusions. He talked spontaneously to a stranger, a schismatic woman whose community was rejected[477] by the Jews: His meeting with the Samaritan woman (cf. John 4:5–29). He did not join in blaming the woman taken in adultery and rejected the Mosaic Law which sentenced her to stoning. He taught her judges not to judge her, just as He did not judge her (John 8:3–11). He healed the daughter of a Canaanite woman who was not of "the household of Israel" (Matt 15:22–28). He told the pious folk who were listening to Him that the prostitutes would go into the Kingdom of Heaven before them (Matt 21:31).

Though He chose His twelve Apostles amongst men, which is explained by their liturgical function[478] and their future missionary role,[479] certain women were very close to Him in everyday life. They spoke with Him and received His teaching just like the Apostles. One of the most remarkable of these women is St Mary Magdalene, venerated by the Orthodox Tradition as "equal to the Apostles." Other remarkable women emerge, such as the friends of Jesus, Martha and Mary of Bethany, Mary mother of James, Mary Salome, the wife of Zebedee and Joanna who came to the tomb before the Apostles and were the first to discover and bear witness to the Resurrection of Christ. His meetings with other women, like the Samaritan at the well of Jacob with whom he spoke, the woman with an issue of blood whom he healed miraculously, or the woman taken in adultery whom he did not judge, were all occasions when Christ underlined their qualities and which he used to teach deep truths.

Some recent works have emphasized the leading place of these great female figures in the Gospels and their significance for the deepest Christian ideas of the role of women.[480]

Mary, the mother of Christ, has a modest place in the Gospels, but as time went by, she was given greater and greater honor. The Fathers stress that it was by her fiat ["Let it be done unto me according to your word." (Luke 1:38)] to the Archangel Gabriel that she allowed the Word to be incarnate amongst men. She is Christ's first and principal coworker in His saving economy. She was officially proclaimed "Mother of God" (mother of the Word in the flesh) by the Council of Ephesus in 431. In the iconography of the Church, in its feasts, its piety, and in its liturgical texts she takes the next place after Christ. She is the first amongst all human beings, being seen as the first creature to be saved and deified, with a power of intercession greater than all the saints.

2. *The Coworkers of the Apostles*

In the epistles of St Paul, the Acts of the Apostles, and certain other writings such as the Acts of Paul, women are seen as precious coworkers in the Apostolic mission of evangelization. St Paul himself shows that he was no misogynist, despite his reputation, when he gives women such a high place in his apostolic mission,[481] going far beyond the roles they were given in the societies of that time. He calls them "coworkers,"[482] "apostles,"[483] and "deaconesses."[484] He gives them the same titles as men calling them "sister" (Philemon 2; Rom 16:1), "countrymen" (Rom 16:7), and "helper" (Rom 16:2). They teach in private,[485] they gather the communities and enliven them.[486] They look after the needs of itinerant preachers, lodging them and opening their houses to those who follow their teaching.

3. *The Martyrs*

Women are seen amongst the first martyrs in great numbers. They often surpass men in the strength of their confession of faith, their endurance under torture, and their bravery in the face of death. Amongst the best known are St Thekla,[487] St Blandina of Lyon,[488] Sts Perpetua and Felicity,[489] St Agnes of Rome,[490] and St Julitta of Caesarea.[491] Their courage aroused the admiration of the pagans like the orator, Libanus, who exclaimed: "Oh, what women we find amongst the Christians."[492]

4. *The Ascetics*

There were many women, widows, virgins, and then nuns, who shone as ascetics equaling or even surpassing the monks. Some, such as Theodora, Sarra, or Syncletica, are mentioned in the *Apothegms*.[493] The lives of others are recorded in Palladius's *Lausaic History*,[494] and still others individually, for example, the life of St Macrina,[495] the life of St Syncletica,[496] and many others. Some of them were collected and translated into French in the seventeenth century by Arnaud d'Andilly. It should be noted that the first of his three volumes has the title: *The life of holy men and women*, whilst the whole work is entitled *The lives of the holy Fathers of the desert and various holy writings by the Fathers of the Church and other ancient Greek and Latin ecclesiastical authors.*[497] In the first part of this volume, he gives us the lives of nine great male ascetic saints, and in the second part the lives of eleven ascetic holy women, more women than men. They are, Sts Fabiola, Marcella, Lea, Azella, Marina, Thais, Mary, Pelagia, Mary of Egypt, and a more recent Western saint, Raingard.

5. *The Deaconesses*

This ordained ministry for women existed in the very first years of the Church as shown by the epistles of St Paul (cf. Rom 16:1; 1 Tim 3:11) Its initial role seems to have been to assist the Apostles, but its exact nature is not revealed in the sources and remains unclear. In any case, Several Fathers consider that Phoebe, referred to by St Paul (Rom 16:1) was truly a deaconess and not just a servant or assistant.[498] It was only in the third century that the word "deaconess" appears—particularly in the *Didascalia*—with well-defined attributes. Their ministry was to adult women: they anointed the women before the priest baptized them for he could not do this "for reasons of decency";[499] they welcomed and instructed the newly baptized women[500] and also visited and assisted the sick[501] to whom they would bring Holy Communion.[502] They looked after poor women whom the deacons were unable to succor themselves "because of the opinion of the ill-willed."[503] In the church they watched over the doors on the women's side[504] and gave the kiss of peace to the women during the liturgy.[505] However, the *Apostolic Constitutions* decree that, like the deacons, "they do not bless, and accomplish none of the tasks of the presbyters and deacons,"[506] that is, their liturgical functions. They were indispensable for women wishing to address a deacon (the bishop's assistant) or the bishop himself.[507] The diaconate of women flourished especially in the fourth and fifth centuries when the wife of St Gregory of Nyssa, St Theosebia, was a deaconess. So was Olympias, a well-known spiritual daughter of St Gregory the Theologian then of St John Chrysostom. There are several other deaconesses amongst the saints: Melania (commemorated December 31), Xenia (January 24), Apollonia (February 9), and Gorgonia (February 13). The council of Nicaea[508] and the *Novels* of Justinian listed deaconesses as members of the clergy. Novel 3, dated March 16, 535 lets us see their number: of the 425 clergy serving in Hagia Sophia forty were deaconesses. They seem to have been ordained (χειροτονία[509]) and not just instituted (χειροθεσία[510])—by the Bishop with a prayer similar to the one used for the ordination of deacons.[511] The ceremony was also similar. They were ordained in the sanctuary, before the altar, during the Liturgy and after the epiclesis. They wore the *orarion* and communed in the altar,[512] all of which seems to place them on the same level as the deacons.[513] Deaconesses could not be ordained before the age of forty (canon 15 of Chalcedon). They were to be chosen by the Bishop amongst the "faithful and holy women."[514]

The female diaconate seems to have withered away during the seventh century when the baptism of adult women became rare, so the essential function of the deaconess in this rite was no longer needed.[515] Moreover, some of their other functions were gradually subsumed into other orders whose roles were extended.[516] However, during the subsequent centuries and right down to our days, women continued to help the Christian community in the same way as the deaconesses had done, but without bearing the title.

6. Educators and Spiritual Mothers

Although they were forbidden to teach in public by the epistles of St Paul (which can be explained by the social attitudes of Antiquity), women were always foremost in the moral and spiritual education of their children. Moreover, as we have seen, some of the Fathers of the Church encouraged them to advise and train their husbands in Christian ethics when they had drifted away. Thus, many women have had a fundamental role in the training and spiritual direction of men who came to have a leading role in the Church.[517]

Of special note is St Macrina, who helped to educate her whole family, especially her brothers, Basil of Caesarea and Gregory of Nyssa.[518] Noteworthy also is St Monica who educated her son, St Augustine.[519] The well-known adage "Behind every great man is a great woman" proves true in many cases. Alongside many saints, the Synaxarion[520] also commemorates their mothers,

The *Apothegms* describe the main events in the lives of the ascetics of the Egyptian and Palestinian deserts and their edifying words. Alongside the fathers, we find also spiritual mothers[521] such as Amma [Mother] Theodora,[522] Amma Sarra,[523] and Amma Syncletica.[524] This last Amma is very famous. By the fifth century her life and teaching had been written down and published widely.[525] Palladius mentions Olympias, a daughter and wife of prefects, who "abandoned all her goods and gave them to the poor." She became a nun, "catechized many women and spoke with reverence to the priests," and is counted as a confessor of the Faith.[526] It was she who was the spiritual daughter of St John Chrysostom, and who supported him spiritually during his many trials: persecutions, exile, and sickness. Marcella, in the same way, gave St Jerome precious spiritual support.

One of the greatest ascetics is St Mary of Egypt. She is such a great example of spiritual life for every Christian that the Orthodox Church devotes the fifth Sunday of Great Lent to her memory. Her life, composed in the VI century by St Sophronius, patriarch of Jerusalem, is now read solemnly in every Orthodox Church on the Thursday of the fifth week of Great Lent.[527]

As hermits and abbesses, "spiritual mothers" fulfilled the same needs as "spiritual fathers." They gave spiritual advice and direction to nuns and lay women and also to men living in the world, to monks and even sometimes to bishops. This can be seen throughout history right down to our days.[528] There were also double monasteries[529] in the Byzantine Empire and in the West. These could be led by an abbess just as easily as by an abbot.[530] In the West, during the Middle Ages, a male monastery could be ruled by an Abbess.[531]

7. *Women as Patrons*

There were women who were patrons of the Apostles and Fathers, financing their activities. They created a whole social structure which allowed

Christianity to carry out its work of teaching and social assistance. They opened schools, libraries, hospitals, and orphanages. They provided material help to the dispossessed and psychological and spiritual help to those in distress. They also founded monasteries and convents.

Some examples of the foundresses of monasteries are the following, some of whom became their abbesses. There is Macrina, the sister of St Basil of Caesarea and of St Gregory of Nyssa. She transformed their family household, including her parents and their servants, into a monastic community.[532] Melania the elder came from Rome to found a community in Jerusalem.[533] Marcella, as a widow, transformed her house on the Aventine into a convent.[534] Paula founded a male monastery and a convent in Bethlehem to which she added a hostelry to lodge pilgrims. St Macrina, abbess of her monastery, undertook works of charity, caring for the aged poor and sheltering stray children.[535]

Once Fabiola had left her first husband who treated her so badly and had then been widowed from her second husband shortly after their wedding, she spent her huge fortune on helping the poor. She founded the first hospital in the West at Ostia, and in the Roman Port the first hostelry for destitute pilgrims.[536]

St Melania the elder gave financial support to the monks of Egypt. In Jerusalem she gave assistance to exiles and founded a monastery. For twenty-seven years she lodged pilgrims and gave gifts and food to the clergy. Palladius writes of her:

"It is not for me, but for those who live in Persia, to say how much of her wealth she spent in her fiery zeal for God. Indeed no one escaped her good deeds, neither in the East nor in the West, nor in the North nor in the South. For thirty-seven years, though she lived abroad, she spent her substance on helping churches, monasteries, foreigners, and prisoners. Her family, her own son and her servants provided the money."[537]

Melania the younger was married to Pinien. After seven years together they both agreed to become monastics and likewise gave away their immense fortune. It was so great that the politicians of the day opposed their generosity, fearing that it might harm the economy of the State:

"She gave her silver and gold to be managed by a priest, Paul of Dalmatia. She had him send money by sea: to the Orient, to Egypt and to the Thebaid ten thousand coins; ten thousand coins to Antioch and its dependencies; fifteen thousand to Palestine; ten thousand to the isles and places of exile; and she herself provided equally for the Churches of the West....Then, after selling her estates in Spain, in Aquitaine, in Tarasconnais, and in Gaul, she kept for herself just her lands in Sicily, Campania, and Africa and used them to support the monasteries."[538]

Apart from this, the couple freed six thousand slaves and gave each of them three gold pieces. Melania founded a monastery and a convent on the Mount of Olives. Her biographer, the priest Gerontios, praises not only her limitless generosity but also her ascetic heroism and her spiritual power.[539]

Olympias was a rich heiress of Constantinople who gave part of her wealth to the poor and placed the rest in the hands of St John Chrysostom for him to use more strictly in support of various charitable institutions.

"[Imitating] those disciples who, at the start of the preaching of the Gospel, brought to the feet of the apostles all they possessed, she gave him ten thousand pounds of gold, a hundred thousand pounds of silver and all her lands and properties in the provinces of Thrace, Galatia, Cappadocia Prima, and Bithynia. Moreover, she also gave him the buildings she owned in the capital. Close to the Great Church [Hagia Sophia] was 'the House of Olympias' with the buildings of the courts of justice, the well-furnished baths and all the buildings around them as well as the Silignarion. Then, next to the public baths of Constance there was the house which she owned and where she dwelt; and another of her houses known as 'the house of Evandre', and all her property in the suburbs.... Inspired by God, His true servant Olympias also gave to the Great Church through the hands of the most holy Patriarch John all her other properties scattered throughout the province and all the rights she possessed to public subventions."[540] She also owned a group of houses beside Hagia Sophia where she founded a monastery which soon was home to two hundred and fifty nuns.[541]

8. *Intellectuals and Theologians*

There were women who, being especially cultivated, created discussion groups with leading intellectuals. Some of them set up libraries which they placed at the disposal of all who wished to learn.

Palladius mentions the case of Julienne. She was a virgin of Caesarea who sheltered Origen for two years and comforted him after he had fled the uprising of the pagans. He found books in her house which he found instructive even though he was immensely cultivated.[542] St Catherine of Alexandria (287–305) was trained in all the liberal arts. She held her own in debates with the emperor and his court orators on philosophy and theology. Olympias (ca. 368–after 408) was the spiritual daughter first of St Gregory the Theologian then of St John Chrysostom. She was also a co-worker with St Gregory of Nyssa. He dedicated his *Homilies on the Song of Songs* to her as a homage to her contribution to this work which he undertook at her suggestion.[543]

Marcella (325–410) supported St Jerome in his various labors.[544] She stimulated him in his works of translation and interpretation of the Bible by her questions and comments. She helped him in the same way to handle his theological controversies, so much so that she may be considered his collaborator in a part of his work. She raised problems which caused Jerome to go deeper into his subject, and he wrote to her: "You have harassed us with important problems: my mind, deadened by leisure, was instructed by your questions."[545] "She debated, then prayed and read the Bible so as to compose an address. Her reflections were expressed in the dialogue and her religious practices imbued her projected work."[546] Jerome summarizes Marcella's culture thus: "What virtues, what a talent, what holiness, what purity have I found in her. No one would believe it. I will content myself with this: all that we have gathered within us of science through long study she has drunk in. She has learnt it and made it her own so well, that after I leave this life, if there were any controversy about any texts of the Scriptures it would be submitted to her judgement."[547] Marcella turned her palace on the Aventine into a true center of biblical studies for many women. She was both an interpreter of Scripture and a theologian, so she actively supported Jerome in the controversy over the *Treatise on principles* of Origen in which he opposed Rufinus of Aquila,[548] and in his criticism of the positions of Jovinian.[549]

When Jerome left for Palestine, it was Paula and her daughter, Eustochium, who became his collaborators. When Jerome set about translating the Bible into Latin, learning Hebrew to compare the Greek and Hebrew texts, Paula learnt Hebrew so well that "she could speak it without any trace of Latinisms." She debated with him the best interpretation of the biblical text. She also supported him in his controversy with Origenism.[550] Their monastery in

Bethlehem became a true center of biblical and theological studies for these two women and their companions.

Melania the elder (350–410) was also engaged in theological controversy, but in support of Rufinus. She supported the bishops and priests in Palestine who were persecuted for their faith by the anti-Nicene Emperor Valens. She also helped Rufinus to end the Paulinian schism in Jerusalem.[551]

Her granddaughter, Melania the younger (383–439), was trained in grammar, rhetoric, Greek, philosophy, mathematics, poetry, music, and the study of the sacred texts. As mentioned above, she gave her immense fortune to the Church and became a nun. She took part in debates on the developments which led to Nestorianism. She received in her home "many wives of senators and other persons of the highest culture to discuss with her the Orthodox Faith. She, in whom dwelt the Holy Spirit, ceased not, from morning to night, to speak of theology, bringing back to Orthodoxy many of those who had strayed and supporting others who doubted, helping, in a word, through her teaching inspired by God all those who sought her out."[552]

Other Christian women were also involved in politico-religious disputes. There were Proba, Juliana, and Demetrias, of the prominent Roman family of Anicia, who afterward played an important role in the monasticism they adopted.[553]

Later, the wives of Byzantine emperors, or their regents, took part in the theological disputes of their time. Sometimes they supported heretics, like Theodora, the wife of Justinian, who supported the Monophysites. Sometimes they defended Orthodoxy, like Pulcheria who played a major part in the victory over Monophysitism at the Council of Chalcedon in 451.[554] Another Theodora (ca. 815–ca. 867) summoned a Council which condemned iconoclasm. In the thirteenth century, the unionist policies of the Byzantine Emperor Michael VIII were strongly opposed by his sister, Eulogia, and his two nieces. Later, Irene Choumnaina and the wife of John Kantakouzenos took sides against Palamism.[555] It is clear that there were many women with a very high level of education in every kind of culture in the Byzantine Empire between the twelfth and fourteenth centuries.[556]

It is true that all the women we have mentioned belonged to the aristocracy which gave them easy access to a good education; but women of more modest origins could also study. Women's monasteries often ran schools within their precincts which were open to all. They educated the nuns, and with them, children who lived nearby. During the Middle Ages, the education of children, both boys and girls, was encouraged as many episcopal instructions attest.[557]

It is true that few women were authors, apart from their correspondence with certain Church Fathers. However, in the West, Herrade of Landsberg, Abbess of the Convent of St Odile in Alsace in the twelfth century, wrote an illustrated Christian Encyclopedia, *Hortus delicarum* (*Garden of delight*). At the same time, Hildegarde of Bingen wrote treatises on spirituality, botany, medicine, and linguistics. She also composed religious chants. This all bears witness to her encyclopedic knowledge and her undoubted genius, so that the Roman Catholic Church proclaimed her a Doctor of the Church.

9. *Powerful Women*

From the first centuries and throughout history some women wielded considerable power. They were mothers and wives of emperors or kings both in the East and in the West. They inspired their sons or their husbands and collaborated with them. Some even held power in their own right. As mothers they acted as regents for their sons, or as widows they assumed the power of their late husbands.

In the Byzantine Empire the general rule was that wives of aristocrats took part in politics alongside their husbands.[558]

The fate of cities or countries might sometimes depend on a woman: St Genevieve for Paris, and Joan of Arc for France. In some countries, it was women who first brought the people Christianity, St Nino in Georgia and St Olga in Kiev. There were also the abbesses of great convents. They not only had spiritual authority but could also wield considerable economic and political power.[559] In the Middle Ages there were even abbesses who ruled over the monasteries of men.[560]

10. *Women in the Professions*

Women being able to work outside the home in a profession is not, as some believe, a feminist victory of the twentieth century. It is true that this was not common in the first centuries, and, for the reasons given above, the Fathers placed great value on the life of women in the home. Nonetheless, the teachings of Christianity had nothing against it. For instance, in the Acts of the Apostles Priscilla is described as a tentmaker, like Aquila, her husband.[561]

We know little of the professions of Christian women in the first centuries, but we know more of the strongly Christian societies of the Middle Ages. They allowed women freedom to take on all manner of employment, even what is nowadays considered to be only for men.[562] Women had an important place in the economy. They often ran a business, sometimes a big one, by themselves; and they also farmed independently.[563] In the West, women worked in a great range of professions. They were hairdressers, barbers, bakers, millers, cheese mongers, milkmaids, chicken farmers, brewers, secondhand dealers, fishmongers, inn keepers, embroiderers. furriers, glove makers, hatters, grocers, tapstresses, greengrocers, candle makers, washerwomen, laundresses, chambermaids, seamstresses, cutlers, locksmiths. armorers, boilermakers, blacksmiths, jewelers, bookbinders, and messengers. Women sometimes worked in partnership with their husbands, and sometimes alone and independently if they were widows or single and even if they were married. Women were not restricted to being craft workers. They were also librarians, teachers, and doctors, often preferred to men by their patients.[564] Some women exercised legal functions. There were the *prude femmes* [respectable women], the ancestors of the French court of *Prud'hommes.* They were chosen by each trade guild to regulate its methods of working and the quality of the goods it provided.[565]

L. Developments Unfavorable to Women Arising from Unchristian Ideas

Feminist studies have become so ingrained with certain prejudices that they are commonly accepted as facts. They have rightly fought against the inequalities between men and women for over a century, yet these are not the result of Christian law, as they suppose, but of the more regressive legal systems which gradually replaced it. Historians have established that the social position of women and their status as wives and mothers began to deteriorate in the thirteenth century when Europe began to re-adopt Roman Law which was very unfavorable to women.[566] Between the fifteenth and seventeenth centuries, women were progressively driven from the labor market whilst the universities closed their doors to them, thus excluding them from the liberal professions. This movement to denigrate the work of women and to exalt of the status of men ran its course until the nineteenth century when the values of the bourgeoisie were enshrined, keeping a woman in the home in complete submission to her husband. In France, the Napoleonic Code pushed restrictions on women to the limit. So, what Feminism rightly criticizes is in no way the result of twenty centuries of Christianity. It arises from the modern era which, especially since the Renaissance, has steadily abandoned and opposed Christian values, returning to the values of Greek and Roman Antiquity.

Nonetheless, we have seen that there is a certain ambiguity toward a woman's place in the epistles of St Paul. This is not found in the Gospels but is echoed in the writings of some of the Fathers. The principles of complete equality are affirmed, but these principles are rather timidly applied. Complete liberation from the social structures and established traditions of the time was impossible. For that would have prevented the spreading of these principles and could have imperiled their existence. Social structures have evolved, and in our age, there is a strong egalitarian mentality. Apart from some of the deviations, excesses, and confusions linked to this mentality,[567] it is nonetheless more in tune with the basic principles of Christianity than the mentality surrounding and affecting the Christians of the first centuries. It is only Christianity which can give this egalitarian mentality a positive sense by infusing it with love (*agape*). Without this basic grace, nourished by ascetic works, differences change into opposition or are denied on the grounds of a false identity.

M. The Freedom of Christianity

We have seen how some of the teachings of St Paul and some of the Fathers align with the society of their era. The social status of men and women is not challenged but the spiritual means of surpassing its limits are proposed.

The Christian is in the ambiguous position of being both a citizen of this world and a citizen of the Kingdom of Heaven (Phil 3:20) which is not just to come but already amongst us. Christians must render unto Caesar the things that are Caesar's (cf. Luke 17:21) and to God, the things which are God's (cf. Luke 20:25). They inherit the effects of ancestral sin and remain imperfect. They still bear within them "the old man" (cf. Rom 6:6; Eph 4:22; Col 3:9) but through baptism have put on "the new man" (cf. Eph 4:24; Col 3:10), and work through ascetic endeavor, in the widest spiritual sense, to purify and perfect themselves. They are always people of their times and their society who, through their spiritual life beyond time, touch on eternity where historical factors are left behind. Through their spiritual life, Christians can meet the needs of every situation, transcending its limits and transfiguring it.

Today, the structure of the couple and of the family is generally considered to be patriarchal. Yet, when love reigned in their couple and family, almost all Christian women accepted it and lived with it happily for twenty centuries. In a way, it is feminist thought which, in retrospect, has decried this structure as unhappy. It sees the relationship between man and woman in terms of domination, opposition, and conflict, and maternity as an alienation. Most women have, for centuries, been content to accept the status of man as "head of the family" since this status is more formal than real. Historians and sociologists are unanimous as regards leadership in the couple and the family: in the past, the wife was the true mistress of her household, and still is in traditional societies. Even in the West this is so for couples who have chosen to live in a traditional way. Most women also see themselves as mothers, whose finest act of creation is to give life to new persons and to raise them as good people. It is for this that most women of years gone by thought their position as wives and mothers more noble, interesting, and fruitful than work in a factory or an office.[568] They also found they were in a more peaceful situation than their husbands, weighed down by the cares of public life.

Nonetheless, the Fathers who lived at the time of the development of monasticism strongly emphasized the difficulties of marriage both for man and woman. In its early days, Christianity offered another way to those who were not attracted to this way of life. They were offered a celibate way of life consecrated to God, as virgin, monk, or nun. They could surpass the limits of conjugal and family life. Though childbearing was seen as the main (but not exclusive) aim of marriage, it was never an obligation. Indeed, some Fathers discouraged large families leading to contraception by abstinence in accord with Christian ethics.

During the twentieth century in the West, the relationships within the couple changed greatly from those of former times. These deep changes are partly due to the influence of the feminist movement on mindsets, but also to the massive movement of women into professional life. This has often been seen, correctly, as liberating and empowering; but is also strongly linked to the development of capitalism, something which is rarely mentioned.[569]

At all events, rights for women equal to those of men, sharing in domestic tasks, and raising the children together do not contradict Christian values. They agree better with their sense of the equality of man and woman in nature and dignity and also in rights and duties. But for this agreement to be perfect, equality and identity must not be confused. For this would lead to an identity that would abolish every difference, depriving the relationship of all the riches of the complementarity of sexes and genders.

The life of the couple should not be defined entirely by the will of one of its members: by authority. It should develop with reference to Christian values, where Christ is the head. In this way Christianity can accommodate many kinds of relationship in its bosom. It infuses them with spirituality, which gives them all the form of happy and harmonious collaboration.

The feminist movement denigrates marriage, motherhood, and the life of the woman in her household and considers professional activity almost obligatory. Christianity, through the Spirit, gives a woman the ability to live with many kinds of social situation. She may be married or single, submitted to her husband, equal to him, or dominating him; she may live at home or go out to work; but in all these things she remains free. Her spiritual life enables her to move in her inner, higher world, linked to heaven. It allows her to be detached from her outer circumstances and the world here below and to transcend them. Like the Christian man, the Christian woman is first and foremost a citizen of the Kingdom of Heaven. She is a new person who is no longer constrained, like her old self, by the laws of this fallen world. Through ascetic life, she is freed from the passions which bind the individual to the ego and to this world. Christianity sees the first things in light of the first chapters of Genesis and the last things in the affirmation that: "In Christ there is neither male nor female." Both agree that man and woman are human beings, basically equal in their natures and their destinies. They are called to collaborate harmoniously in their spiritual life which should unite them and lead them both toward the same goal.

Chapter 13

The Transfiguration of Gender in Monasticism

Though lower than the angels in its nature, the human race does violence to its own faculties and strives with all its might to rise to their level.
(John Chrysostom, *Virginity*, XI, 1)

Consecrated virginity throws an interesting light on the question of gender. It was praised by many of the Church Fathers from the second to the fourth century after which it developed into monasticism, not just for women but also for men. Some feminists, filled with the libertarian mindset of the 1960s have struggled for sexual freedom of every kind without limit.[570] More recently, others have rejected any kind of relationship with men which might have a sexual connotation even if there is no physical contact, be it flirtation or even gallantry.[571] Critics of gender theory and radical feminism have often remarked, and criticized, their resemblance to the attitudes of religious sects. They see in them attitudes and teachings which are like the Christian sects of the first centuries rejecting all sexuality. They also resemble certain Protestant communities with their strict and intolerant moralizing and their proselytizing.

So, Bérénice Levet has given a subtitle to her book *La théorie du genre*: "ou Le monde rêvé des anges" [or the dream-world of angels]. In a section entitled "Gender: the new Puritanism," she writes of this, showing the messianic character of its militants who dream of building a new world and a new mankind:

> Nowadays it is not Christians or those who are supposed to be narrow minded and uptight who tie ever tighter the moral corset. It is the most progressive ideologies which, despite the 20th century, continue to believe in the end of history, in a world at peace with itself, delivered from all the darkness, the shadows and the roughness of the human condition. Confident in their beliefs in this law of history, they try to remold

> humanity to conform to it. We no longer have need of religion to preach abstinence, continence, and the strictest asceticism. Gender theorists do the job fine.... Their ideal would be to have no sexual organ. For what is it but a wretched appendage which condemns us to a sexual identity? At best, it is useless; at its worst it is complicit in the heterosexual order as an instrument of reproduction. Indeed, an article in *Le Monde* which conveyed the opinions of queer artists stated that it is "an organ which one could well live without, or which one could leave unused for years."[572] Unable to be sexless, there is the possibility of ignoring sex and of denying it as part of the human condition, The apostles of Gender explain that we no longer pass from one sex to another but from one person to another.... In other words, there are no longer special natures of feminine bodies and of masculine bodies, nor should there be. Their bodies should be seen as objects of little significance, divorced from any sexual appearance. The ambivalence of erotic desire, ... inherent in our incarnate nature, would thus be overcome since we are both soul and body.[573]

Refusing relationships with sexual connotations is quite understandable in certain types of persons. There are prudish and timid people. There are those whose sexual appetite is small, both men and women who once used to be the majority of the unmarried in society. There are also feminists who refuse a culture where women are seen as an object of sexual pleasure for men. More positively, this attitude may also reveal an aspiration toward relations between men and women where they are not simply reduced to sexual objects but where they are all seen in the wholeness of their being, as true persons. Total rejection of sexuality itself can be criticized when it extends to the legitimate bonds of marriage. But we can approve those who reject the banal sexuality found in a hedonistic society which systematically perverts relations between men and women, turning both into psychological and/or physical objects of sexual pleasure.

Michel Onfray published a review of the work of Bérénice Levet quoted above. He wrote: "In a work which goes against the flow, the philosopher Bérénice Levet shows that gender, paradoxically, achieves the Christian aim: a body with no organs, aspiring to sexless neutrality like the angels."[574]

Of course, this remark does not truly reflect the Christian position. To begin with, Christianity has never aimed at a body without organs. God created the body with its organs, including sexual organs, so we respect it in its wholeness. Moreover, Christianity has never aimed at "sexless neutrality." The sexual attributes of mankind are a property given to the creature by the Creator. It would be better to say, "not sexualized" than "sexless."

Virgins, monks, and nuns retain their sexual attributes, but their calling enjoins them to abstain from all sexual activity, bodily or psychological. Monks and nuns make vows of chastity when they are professed by which they promise to abstain from all sexual acts and thoughts. This, with their vows of obedience and poverty, sets them apart from other Christians.

The total sexual abstinence in monasticism is formally justified by the monk not being married, but alone (*monos*); and for Christian ethics, sexuality is only blessed in marriage. The aim of monasticism is complete consecration to God. The monk does not marry so as to have no care but God to Whom he directs all his desire and love, all his intelligence and strength. As St Paul writes, "He who is unmarried cares for the things of the Lord—how he may please the Lord" (1 Cor 7:32) and "The unmarried woman cares about the things of the Lord, that she may be holy both in body and in spirit" (1 Cor 7:34). Both are "without care" for the things of this world (cf. 1 Cor 7:32). As for the married, "He who is married cares about the things of the world—how he may please his wife.... But she who is married cares about the things of the world—how she may please her husband" (1 Cor 7:33–34). If the Apostle thinks it good that man and woman should remain single (cf. 1 Cor 7:26) it is so that they "may serve the Lord without distraction" (1 Cor 7:35).

If every Christian is called "to put off … the old man" and to "put on the new man" (Eph 4:22–24), the monk does this in the most radical way. Through bodily asceticism, he lightens the weight of his flesh inherited through ancestral sin, what the Bible symbolically calls "garments of skin" (Gen 3:21). He fasts strictly to weaken his desire for food. He keeps night watches to free himself, as far as possible, from the pressure, the numbness, and the unconsciousness which come from sleep. He remains continent and chaste, steadily to free his body and soul from every sexual thought or impulse. The icon expresses the new state of body and soul of those who have successfully followed this path, the saints: their bodies slim, their faces thin, and their eyes open wide.

Monasticism seeks to return again to Paradise where man and woman were sexually distinct but had not yet expressed this in sexual acts. We have already seen that the Fathers with one accord consider that sexual desire is not part of the original nature of mankind. It does not belong to mankind's essence but came in as a result of the fall when Adam and Eve began to turn their desire away from God. So, as St John of Damascus writes, "Virginity was original and engraved in the nature of mankind. When, through sin, death came into the world, it was only then that Adam knew his wife and she gave birth."[575] St John Chrysostom says the same: "It was only after their disobedience and their exile that Adam and Eve came together. Before, they had lived as the angels. . . . Thus, in the sequence of time, virginity has priority."[576] This is why the Fathers saw in virginity a way for man to recover the nature he had in Paradise,[577] which, as the Fathers all agree, makes him like the angels.[578] It is significant that the "Great Schema" which monks and nuns put on at their solemn profession of vows is called "the Great Angelic Schema."

The angelic nature of monastic life develops from the rigorous ascetic struggle which frees human nature from the weight of the flesh. Thus St Gregory the Theologian writes of the virgin: "Is she not close to the angels, for though bound to the flesh, she does not live according to it but surpasses it?"[579] Monasticism, in a way, also prefigures and anticipates the life of heaven[580] according to the word of Christ: "For in the resurrection they neither marry nor are given in marriage, but are like angels of God in heaven" (Matt 22:30).

It is important to realize that monastic chastity and celibacy have no value unless they are consecrated to God with a view to perfect union with Him. Thus, St John Chrysostom emphasizes that virginity alone has no value. It is the intention alone which gives it value. "Amongst pagans it is sterile and fruitless since they do not practice it for God."[581] He also harshly criticizes those for whom it is simply an escape from marriage rather than a way to heavenly union.[582] He even says that in such cases, "virginity is more shameful than licentiousness."[583] Virginity has no value in itself. It is valuable when it helps man and woman to give themselves more fully to God. St John Chrysostom remarks, "The Apostle, speaking of virginity, attributes its excellence less to the chastity of the body than to the means it gives us to consecrate ourselves to God and to devote ourselves to piety." He adds: "Those who make the vow of chastity propose not just to preserve their purity, but especially to be occupied with nothing but the things of God and His service."[584] St Augustine advises the virgins: "To allow [Christ] to take all the space in your soul which you were unwilling to devote to marriage."[585]

Though sexuality is inactive in monasticism, sexual differences do not disappear. Nuns keep their feminine characteristics just as monks remain masculine. Though as we will see, spiritual life can bring about a certain gender fluidity which allows each gender to take on some of the characteristics of the other.

There is a strong nuptial dimension in feminine virginity which is often mentioned by the Fathers. Spiritually, the virgin becomes the fiancée of Christ, Who is often designated as "The Bridegroom." The monks maintain a close spiritual relationship with the Virgin, Mother of God. This is especially obvious on Mount Athos, the summit of masculine Orthodox Monasticism.

Certain radical feminists and members of the LGBTQI+ movement reject heterosexual relationships and denounce relationships between men and women as systematically stained with sexual connotations. Usually, their rejection of the other sex, which broadly means anyone with a different sex to theirs, comes from fear of the other. An associated problem is the form of this rejection, which is often spiteful and violent. Radical feminists sometimes describe their attitude as a "sex strike," and often take part in what they call "the war of the sexes." Here, there is a distortion of a legitimate claim to mutual respect in a peaceful relationship which takes the form of a rejection of sexuation. This offends the nature of both sexes and fails to rise above the fleshly condition. It has no superior goal. There is no transfiguration.

Monasticism fights the passions which may lead to opposition of sexes and genders and mortifies them. Both monks and nuns seek the same goal using the same means. The capacities of each applied to this end are at the same level. Their spiritual progress and the levels of sanctification they progressively reach are identical.

The "desert" is the place of monastic life, apart from the world with its oppositions and hierarchies. The Fathers of the Church who lived in the world were not completely free of the male-dominant categories of their time, but the Fathers and Mothers of the desert were free of them. As John Chryssavgis remarks, "the desert signified a radical break with the social restrictions and discriminatory constraints of the day."[586] The *Apothegms,* which recount their remarkable words and deeds, accord all of them the same admiration and veneration and show that they all esteemed each other equally.

Chapter 14

A Kind of Gender Fluidity as the Fruit of Christian Spirituality

> "O more noble than males in steadfastness, and more courageous than men in endurance!"
> (4 Macc 15:30 NRSVA)

In practice, the psychological characteristics linked to the two sexes and corresponding genders, masculine and feminine, are partly fluid. These characteristics are not uniformly shared by all. They vary with natural factors and with influences from the family and society and can be altered by a choice of personal development. All men and all women have both masculine and feminine traits. Generally, men have predominantly masculine characteristics and women feminine characteristics; but the proportions vary from one person to another, and they can evolve throughout life, influenced by the factors mentioned above. Spiritual factors also influence this evolution. Several spiritual texts and lives of saints witness to the manliness acquired by women who are martyrs or ascetics. Indeed, manliness is set up as an ideal for them to achieve. In men, however, the acquisition of other Christian virtues goes with the acquisition of certain feminine characteristics. This shows that there is some degree of gender fluidity, but its nature and forms need further description.

Manliness as an Ideal for Woman

Several writers have noticed that some of the Fathers, and also the Mothers, see manliness as an ideal for Christian women to attain.[587] However, it is an ideal which can be understood in different ways.

A. Manliness as Rising above Certain Feminine Weaknesses

As we saw above, the Fathers reprove some of the weaknesses of women, not the noble side of their nature, but the preoccupation with their physical appearance, which is so common amongst them, their clothes, jewels, make-up, and perfumes. They also reprove their desire to seduce and their sensuality, their desire for comfort and luxury, and their attraction to what we now call consumerism.[588] Such femininity is today exploited by advertising. Just as in times past, it gives woman a hypersexualized image, filled with the desire which she arouses, and inspiring desire for the objects she promotes. Just as modern feminists struggle against this ignoble image of woman, so too the Fathers fought against it. This led them to see manliness as its opposite and an ideal to be achieved. St John Chrysostom writes of this:

> I maintain that [woman is a helper of man in spiritual things] when, while remaining physically a woman, she rises above her nature to raise up also the virtue of blessed men. She will not win her husband by her grooming and attire in a life of pleasure where she asks him for ever more money to spend with prodigality. She will win him when she rises above all these matters and engraves in herself the style of life of the apostles. She needs great moderation, great modesty, a deep scorn for money and great forbearance. She should say: 'With food and clothing we will be content' and put into practice this philosophy. Laughing at bodily death, she will see our earthly existence as nothing and will believe with the prophet that all the glory of this world is as the flower of grass.[589]

Often, however, the Fathers also had in mind certain faults which the mindset of their times attributed to the feminine gender: a kind of psychological weakness, linked to physical weakness and a timorous character; a tendency to give way to emotions; weakness in the face of great suffering and fear in the face of death. So, St Basil asked himself: "if it were still right to call a woman someone who had overcome the weakness of feminine nature through the greatness of her soul."[590] So the martyrdom and ascetic exploits of Christian women show that these faults are not intrinsic to the feminine gender and can be surpassed.

B. Manliness Before or During Martyrdom

Many lives of martyrs show us how women acquired, or desired to acquire, virile characters in the face of martyrdom. In his *Homily on the Holy Martyrs Bernice, Prosdoce and Domnina* St John Chrysostom is amazed at these "women, or rather these men, who conquered death." This is also the case with St Perpetua to whom we will refer later.

The mother of the Maccabees is another well-known case. In the Bible it is said of her: "She encouraged each of them in the language of their fathers. Filled with a noble spirit, she stirred her womanly reasoning with manly courage" (2 Macc 7:21). Also, this is said of her: "O more noble than males in steadfastness, and more courageous than men in endurance!" (4 Macc 15:30 NRSVA). The text also sees a virile character in her love, which surpassed the love of a mother: "But devout reason, giving her heart a man's courage in the very midst of her emotions, strengthend her to disregard, for a time, her parental love" (4 Macc 15:23). The way this mother faced the martyrdom of her children, with spiritual impassibility, not emotional but compassionate, is also seen as manly by St Gregory the Theologian and St John Chrysostom. The former says of her: "A manly soul in a woman's body!"[591]

C. Manliness in Asceticism

Some spiritual texts and lives of saints present manliness as a quality and a characteristic of ascetic women. Palladius in his *Lausaic History* gives us lives and portraits of the saints of his time and says of the women: "But it is necessary in this book to mention the manly women … ."[592] And the author of the life of St Melania writes of her: "It is true to say of her that she surpassed the measure of her sex and acquired a manly mind."[593]

The ascetic women themselves also claimed to have acquired the quality of manliness. Amma Sara said: "By nature I am a woman, but not in my spirit,"[594] which shows also that she saw manliness as a spiritual quality. She was also well aware that not every man has systematically this quality. It is above nature and must be acquired, so she said to the brothers who had withdrawn, like her, into the desert: "I am the man, and you are women."[595]

Theodoret of Cyrus begins the chapter on women ascetics in his history of the monks and nuns of Syria by remarking that they were not just at the same level as their male contemporaries but often surpassed them: "After recounting the deeds of these heroic men I believe that I should make mention of those women who were no weaker in their struggles and often stronger."[596]

D. The Meaning of Manliness

Some commentators to conclude from these texts that, in their own perspective, the woman is fulfilled when she has acquired the characteristics of manliness, so that man—the male—is the model of perfect humanity. However, this is a hasty and simplistic generalization. The texts should be seen in their social and cultural context and with regard to the limits which the Fathers and Mothers set to the idea of manliness and the notion of man (the male).

The idea of virility or manliness has been based historically on three qualities: (1) physical strength, courage, and heroism in war; (2) Dominating masculinity; (3) sexual potency.[597] The manliness referred to in the texts above refers to the first quality. It was clearly dominant in Greek and Roman Antiquity and in the world where Christianity developed. It contrasts with what is seen as virility today. It implies especially force of character, rather than weakness. It is not oversensitive but masters the emotions and rises above sufferings.[598] This corresponds to what ascetic writings refer to as impassibility[599] (*apatheia*). It especially refers to strength, endurance, and courage: the ability to confront fierce trials, dangers, and death. These last three qualities can be seen as defining the idea of manliness in almost all the texts where it is set up as an ideal.

It should be remembered that the Greek word *andreia* and the Latin word *virtus* which signify courage come from the words *aner* (genitive *andros*) and *vir* which both refer to the male. Virility, or manliness, is a virtue of the fighter and warrior, which was the role of many men in the society of Antiquity, and which also served as a measure of heroism.

The women martyrs and ascetics are also seen as fighters and warriors. Both wage a spiritual war, of different intensity and length, which implies suffering and death. The martyr faces, unflinching, death and the tortures that precede it. The ascetic mortifies the passions, facing, unflinching, the death of the old man and the pain this involves. In general, both martyr and ascetic are soldiers of Christ.[600]

Before her martyrdom St Perpetua had a vision of herself in the arena: "They undressed me, and I became a male. My seconds [trusted representatives] then rubbed my body with oil as one does before the fight."[601] This in no way implies that woman is naturally inferior, nor yet Aristotle's idea that woman is an imperfect man and finds perfection in becoming male.

Women have, potentially or actually, the same capacities, the same qualities, and the same virtues as men in their manliness. This is because they are equal to men by nature since both were created in the image of God. This is what St Basil exposes in his eulogy of the holy martyr Julitta:

"She exhorted all the women with her to suffer all kinds of tortures with a great heart for love of Christ without falling back on the weakness of their nature, 'For,' she said: 'we are of the same dough as men. We were created, like them, in the image of God. The Creator has made women capable of virtue as much as men. Indeed, are we not, in everything, of the same nature as men? To create woman, He did not just take flesh, but bone from bone. So, as regards firmness, strength, and patience we are the equals of men, and this, we owe to our Master.'"[602]

It is also true that some males do not possess these qualities. It is warriors who are the reference point: those who fight without flinching and face death bravely.

Presenting virility, or manliness, as the ideal for woman might be thought to support the idea that she is weaker than man; but highlighting her manly virtues refutes this idea, showing that it is based on prejudice. So, some interpreters see the ideal of becoming manly not as becoming male (ἄρσεν, ἀνήρ, *vir*), but more as becoming a fulfilled human being (ἄνθρωπος, *homo*), what St Paul calls "a perfect man," come to "the measure of the stature of the fullness of Christ" [603] (Eph 4:13). It was with this in view that St Jerome wrote: "If woman desires to serve Christ more than the world, she will cease to be a woman (*mulier cessabit*) and one will call her manly (*vir*), for we all seek to draw close to the perfect man (*perfectus vir*)."[604]

It could be said that manliness is presented as an ideal to be acquired partially with the virile virtues mentioned above. It is not to be totally absorbed, eclipsing all feminine characteristics and showing all the characteristics of virility in the widest sense.

As many writings testify, the manly strength of woman surpasses that of many men. For instance, St John Chrysostom writes:

"So that you may see that women are not simply as brave as men, but that they come, as one may say, as far as possible to the impassibility of angels, let us take the example of one who was woman by nature but through her energy and philosophy reached heaven: the mother of the Maccabees.... Shall we simply call this woman a man, and not say that she is infinitely greater than men themselves?"[605]

This leads Rachael Moriarty to consider, correctly, that the ideal of manliness which the Fathers teach is not hierarchical. Man is not superior to woman, for this ideal lies beyond gender, and is an ideal for both.[606] Clement of Alexandria affirms that this is so:

"When woman is freed from the cravings of the flesh, she can reach perfection in this life. Souls are of neither one sex nor the other, neither masculine nor feminine when they no longer marry or are given in marriage. So, woman can then, so to say, change to man (*eis ton andra*), and losing her femininity, become manly (*andrike*) and perfect."[607]

There is also the advice of St Syncletica: "Put away the mentality of a woman and clothe yourself with valiance and manliness. For in the Kingdom of Heaven 'there is neither male nor female' but all women who please God take the rank of man."[608]

John Chryssavgis correctly remarks that the desert Mothers "threw off any associations of social 'weakness' expected of women and were completely identified with men on a level beyond separation and segregation."[609]

Praising his sister Macrina, St Gregory of Nyssa says that in truth she surpassed nature: "It is a woman who is the subject of our tale, if she may truly be called a woman. For I do not know if it is right to describe her in terms of nature when she has transcended nature."[610] This transcendence of her nature concerns not just her feminine character but also the manly character he attributes to her.

The supernatural quality of manliness is also indicated in the story of St Melania's visit to the Cells, a locality in the mountain of Nitria where dwelt many monks: "The most holy Fathers in that place received the saint like a man. It is true that she had surpassed the measure of her sex and gained a mind which was manly, or rather heavenly."[611]

Theodoret of Cyrus evokes the ascetic life of two hundred and fifty nuns in the desert, just as hard as the life of men. He goes on to emphasize the unity in Christ of the spiritual nature and the destiny of men and women:

"Since the day when Christ our Master honored virginity by being born of a Virgin, nature has brought forth virginal meadows and offers the Creator the perfume of incorruptible flowers with no distinction between the virtue of men and of women. Neither is philosophy[612] divided into two kinds, for the difference lies in the body and not the soul. For, as the divine Apostle says: 'In Christ Jesus there is neither male nor female.' One unique Faith was given to men and women. 'One Lord, one faith, one baptism; one God and Father of all, who is above all, and through all, and in you all' (Eph 4:5–6). It is one unique Kingdom of Heaven that the agonothete[613] offers to the victors, the common reward fixed for their struggles."[614]

The manliness attributed to women is also seen as a virtue which surpasses the natural world since it is rooted in the supernatural, in a grace given by God. When the keeper of the jail where St Felicity was imprisoned before her martyrdom saw her suffering the pains of childbirth he said: "If you groan now, what will you do when you are thrown to the wild beasts?" She replied: "Now, it is I who suffer what I suffer; but there another will be within me who will suffer for me since it is for him that I will suffer."[615] And in the story of the passion of St Blandina it is said that "she who was small, weak and insignificant put on the great and invincible athlete, Christ."[616]

It was by bearing this grace of Christ that the holy women martyrs rose to a spiritual manliness which surpassed the natural. It lies far above the hierarchy of sexes and genders, higher even than their distinction. St Augustine refers to this in his sermon on the holy martyrs Perpetua and Felicity:

"Can anything be more glorious than these women whom men find easier to admire than to imitate? But this glory belongs above all to Him in Whom they placed their trust, in Whose Name they fought with great-hearted and faithful emulation. Beside Him there is, for the inner man, no distinction of sex. Thus, it appears that in these holy women their sex disappears beneath the vigor of their spirit, and we no longer see in their bodies what does not show in their deeds."[617]

The Feminization of the Christian Male

In the times when these Christian texts praising manliness were written, it is rare to find femininity presented as an ideal for men. It would not have sent the right signal in a society which had inherited the mentality of Antiquity, where femininity was held to imply weakness, emotional behavior, or inconstancy. However, a few texts, whilst teaching that women should acquire manly virtues also teach that men should acquire the virtues of women.[618]

Verna Harrison has shown us that many of the virtues that became monastic virtues were seen as feminine in Graeco-Roman culture; for instance: chastity, silence, humility, receptivity, inwardness, obedience, and withdrawal.[619]

It may be surprising that one of the faults attributed by the Fathers to women—weakness[620]—is praised by St Paul: "Therefore I take pleasure in infirmities, in reproaches, in needs, in persecutions, in distresses, for Christ's sake. For when I am weak, then I am strong" (2 Cor 12:10). Weakness here means humility: it is by being humble that the Christian, man, or woman, becomes strong through Divine Grace which then comes to dwell within.

To reach the likeness of Christ, both man and woman must acquire Christian virtues through ascetic struggle, some of which are more in line with feminine nature. One is humility, which we have just mentioned, but there is also meekness and most of the means which express the love for neighbor, which Christ described as the greatest virtue after love for God.

The Christian man is called to replace the hardness of his heart of stone with the tenderness of a heart of flesh (cf. Ezek 36:26), to replace aggression with meekness and pride with humility. He should be humble and put away his vanity, which leads to a spirit of conquest and domination. He should replace his indifference and coldness with compassion, and his selfishness with altruism.

Tears, which were despised in Antiquity as feminine weakness, are exalted in Christian spirituality. According to their nature, they may show the virtue of compunction (*penthos*) at its highest degree[621] or deep compassion linked to a spiritual love of one's neighbor or of the creatures of the world: animals and plants.[622]

Even the Father, in trinitarian theology, is seen as being maternal. Clement of Alexandria writes of God: "Compassion makes Him a mother," and: "The Father, by loving us, has become feminine."[623]

St Macarius compares the bond between the faithful Christina and God to the bond between a child and his mother. For God relates to him like a mother:

"Even if a tiny child can do nothing by himself and cannot even go to his mother on his own legs, at least he rolls around and cries as he seeks her. And the mother takes pity on him, rejoicing to see that the little one seeks her with all his strength of body and voice. So, since the child cannot go to her, she herself, in her love for him, takes him up in her arms seeing how much he desires her. She caresses him and feeds him with great tenderness. And this is also what God, the lover of mankind, does for the soul which comes to Him with ardent desire."[624]

The Transfiguration of Gender in the Practice of Shared Virtues

What has just been said shows that the transfiguration of gender is accomplished in the practice of virtues common to both men and women. They are rooted in Christ in whom "there is neither male nor female." As we have seen, the practice of virtue leads to a kind of gender fluidity where the feminine gains virility and the virile the feminine. Yet genders are also surpassed, so that women can be superior to men as much as men can be superior to women. The virtues bring about spiritual states which surpass the physical and psychological characteristics, which distinguish genders, and which lead to opposition and hierarchy. Their limits are left behind and all opposition vanishes. In modern speech one might say that virtues are inclusive.

The virtues require each gender to rise above itself. It must not only leave behind its social habits but also its nature, tainted by the fallen state of humanity. Gender is not totally abolished. Indeed, there is a masculine way and a feminine way of practicing the same virtue, but gender is now what it was in Paradise when both man and woman were in the state in which God created them. This is also the new state of mankind which is anticipated by Christian life lived here and now when it reaches holiness. It will be perfected in the Kingdom of Heaven.

The virtues exalt and transfigure the psychology of both man and woman. They embrace it but remain above it. Though the seeds of virtues can be found in human nature, as it was before the fall, their model is in Christ, and they reach fulfillment and perfection through grace, which gives them a supernatural character. They are where man and woman meet, a center of concord and unity when practiced by both. On them rests the unity of the faithful in the Church: "the Body of Christ," and the perfect unity of the couple and the family. The virtues also bring man and woman to relate socially as equal human beings, with respect and love. Sex and gender do not distort their interactions. Instead, the differences linked to their sexes enrich both in a complementary and harmonious relationship.

Notes

Introduction

1 These are the different roles and characteristics which society attributes to men and women: what is considered proper to a particular sex as regards personality, attitudes, behavior, values, relationships, power, and social influence.

Chapter 1

2 This is the status of scientific theories themselves, which are considered as hypotheses which have not yet been falsified.

3 One of the two main works of the leading gender theoretician, Judith Butler, is entitled *Undoing Gender.*

4 See A Fausto-Stirling, "The five sexes: Why male and female are not enough," *The Sciences,* April–May 1993, pp. 20–24; "The five sexes revisited," *Sciences,* vol. 40, no. 4, 2000, pp. 18–23. The other three sexes proposed by the author, who took the idea of a spectrum from J. Money, are various kinds of hermaphrodism. The author has no qualms about putting them in the same category as the two sexes, male and female, even though the proportion of such people in the population at large is estimated to be about 0.018%. (See J. Sax: "How common is intersex? A reply to Anne Fausto-Stirling." *Journal of Sex Research,* vol. 39, no. 3, August 2002, pp. 174–178.)

5 For instance, Christine Delphy.

6 Preface to his translation of J. Butler, *Troubles dans le genre.*

7 A favorite saying of another great gender theorist, Monique Wittig.

8 Money set forth his theory in a work of popularization: *Man & woman, boy & girl: Gender identity from conception to maturity,* Northvale 1996. His main articles, including those which he wrote with the Hamptons, are in the work *Venuses penuses, sexology, sexosophy and exigence theory.* Amherst, 1986.

9 His theory is set out in *Sex and gender I: On the development of masculinity and femininity,* New York City, 1968; *Sex and gender II: The transsexual experiment,* London, 1968.

10 *L'existentialisme est un humanisme,* Paris, 1946.

11 *Le deuxième sexe,* t. 2, ch. 1, Paris, 1949.

12 It was called "The French Theory." The various philosophies involved are disparate and have little to do with gender theory or woke culture. Several American intellectuals combined and interpreted them on the basis that they all are centered on deconstructivism and the denial of norms in every field. See François Cusset, *French Theory, Foucault, Derrida, Deleuze & Cie et les mutations de la vie intellectuelle aux États-Unis,* La Découverte, Paris, 2005. On the influence of "French Theory," see Helen Pluckrose, "How French 'intellectuals' ruined the West: Postmodernism and its impact, explained," *Areo,* 27 mars 2017; Helen Pluckrose, James Lindsay, *Cynical theories: How activist scholarship made everything about race, gender, and identity – and why this harms everybody,* Pitchstone Publishing, Durham (NC), 2020.

13 See M.-C. Cadeau, "La pensée de Jacques Derrida aux fondements du gender et du queer," dans *Dossiers de l'École Pratique des Hautes Études en Psychopathologies,* sur le site de l'EPHEP.

14 See R. M. Rodriguez Magda, *Michel Foucault et la généalogie des sexes,* Paris, 2013.

15 See L. Mozère, "Devenir femme chez Deleuze et Guattari," *Cahiers du genre,* 8 2005, pp. 43–62. J. Watson, "Guattari and Gender," *Women: A Cultural Review,* vol. 16, no. 3, 2005, pp. 267–270.

16 See *La Domination Masculine,* Paris 1998.

17 There are two main schools of thought in moderate feminism: liberal feminism and essentialist or differentialist feminism. There are many schools of thought in radical feminism which often vary from one country to another (e.g., *Radical feminism* and *Cultural feminism* in the United States, and in France materialist feminism, socialist or Marxist feminism, intersectional feminism and queer feminism).

18 Professor at the University of California, Berkeley. Her best-known works are *Gender trouble: Feminism and the subversion of identity,* London, 1990, and *Undoing gender,* New York, 2004.

19 Professor of Biology at Brown University (USA). Her main works are: *Myths of gender: Biological theories about women and men.* 2nd edition New York, Basic Books, 1992 and *Sexing the body: Gender politics and the construction of sexuality,* New York, Basic Books, 2000. Her best-known article is "The five sexes: Why male and female are not enough," *The Sciences,* April–May 1993, pp. 20–24.

20 A French woman, she wrote most of her work in the United States. Her best-known work is a collection of articles: *The straight mind,* Beacon Press, Boston 1992.

21 An American attorney. See: *Towards a feminist theory of the state.* Harvard University Press, Cambridge, 1998.

22 A researcher at the CNRS. Her numerous publications include: *L'ennemi principal,* tome 1: Économie politique du patriarcat, Paris, 1998; *L'ennemi principal,* tome 2: *Penser le genre,* Paris 2001.

23 In France, there are about 200 such people.

24 We use the definitions given in the article by S. Bourcier, "Le Dictionnaire des 52 nuances de Facebook" on the site slate.fr.

25 They are enumerated in the introduction to a speech of Deputy Steffen Königer, AfD, to the Parliament of Brandenburg. He addresses those deputies who are potentially representatives of these identities, and who propose to legislate in favor of them. See the video at https://www.youtube.com/watch?v=H3pntGBylho.

26 A pretense, since all white males are grouped together and considered blameworthy.

27 See especially: Helen Pluckrose and James Lindsay, *Cynical theories: How activist scholarship made everything about race, gender, and identity – and why this harms everybody,* Pitchstone Publishing, Durham (NC), 2020; Jean-François Braunstein, *La philosophie devenue folle: Le genre, l'animal, la mort,* Paris, Grasset, 2018. Pierre Valentin, *L'idéologie woke,* vol. 1 et 2, Fondapol, Paris, 2021. Michel Vlahos, "Church of woke: The next American religion?," *Humanitas,* vol. 34, nos 1–2, 2021, pp. 113–122. Jean-François Braunstein, *La religion woke,* Grasset, Paris, 2022. Nathalie HEINICH, *Le wokisme serait-il un totalitarisme?* Albin Michel, Paris, 2023. Sylvie Perez, *En finir avec le wokisme,* Cerf, Paris, 2023.

Chapter 2

28 See the article in Wikipedia "Demographic statistics on sexual orientation," which breaks the figures down by country. Homosexuals make up between 1 and 4 percent of the population and less than 1 percent are bisexual. Less than 1 percent of adults identify with a gender that does not correspond to their biological sex.

29 There are many studies of mainstream thought (in French, la pensée unique) which are obviously critical of it. Those who hold to mainstream thought are not often ready to recognize what they are doing and fail to test it by self-criticism.

One work amongst many is the collective work which brings together the writings of authors who follow different schools of thought: Jean-Marc Chardon et Denis Lensel (ed.), *La pensée unique. Le vrai procès*, Economica, Paris, 1998.

30 This can be seen in all Western countries and applies also to woke thought. In the universities it is the same as in the media. The situation in the United States has been described by Anne Appelbaum, "The new Puritans," *The Atlantic*, August 31, 2021 (online version) and October 2021 (printed text).

31 A lobby, interest group, pressure group, or influence group is a group of people created to promote and defend special interests, private or otherwise. They exert pressure and try to influence people or institutions in positions of power.

32 Gender theory was officially adopted by the UN at the Peking Summit in 1995.

33 Nongovernmental Organizations.

34 See M. A. Peeters, *Le gender, une norme mondiale?* Mame, Paris, 2013, pp. 41–55. E. Montfort, *Le genre démasqué*, Peuple libre, Valence, 2011, pp. 33–41. M. A. Peeters is a specialist of international organizations and E. Montfort a former European Deputy.

35 Which starts in the eighteenth century.

36 *La société assiégée*, Éditions du Rouergue, Rodez, 2005.

37 See M. A. Peeters, *Le gender, une norme mondiale?* Paris, 2013, pp. 41–55.

38 *The revolt of the elites and the betrayal of democracy*, W. W. Norton & Company, New York, 1996. This tendency was imported to Europe from the United States.

39 A good analysis of this phenomenon can be found in the works of Jean-Claude MICHÉA, especially: *L'Empire du moindre mal: essai sur la civilisation libérale*, Climats, Paris, 2007; *Le Complexe d'Orphée: la gauche, les gens ordinaires et la religion du progrès*, Flammarion, Paris, 2011; *Notre ennemi, le capital*, Flammarion, Paris, 2016; *Le loup dans la bergerie*, Flammarion, Paris, 2018. In particular, Michea shows how part of the left helps, paradoxically, to promote neoliberalism.

40 The word *ethos* in Greek is equivalent to the Latin word *mores*. They refer to modes of life.

41 *La Vie en miettes. Expérience postmoderne et moralité*, Fayard, Paris, 2003; *La Vie liquide*, Éditions du Rouergue, Rodez, 2006; *Le présent liquide*, Seuil, Paris, 2007.

42 See, amongst others: Zygmunt Bauman, *Le coût humain de la mondialisation*, Fayard, Paris, 2011; Cynthia Gorrha-Gobin (with sixty collaborators), *Dictionnaire critique de la mondialisation*, CNRS Éditions, Paris, 2012.

43 A clear explanation is given in Jean-Paul Sarte's book *L'existentialisme est un humanisme,* Nagel, Paris, 1946. *Existentialism is a humanism,* Yale University Press, 2007.

44 See especially his *Essai sur les fondements de l'inégalité parmi les hommes.*

45 These anthropological and ethnological studies were conducted in the United States especially by Margaret Mead (*Moeurs et sexualité en Océanie,* Plon, Paris, 1963; *L'un et l'autre sexe. Les rôles d'homme et de femme dans la société,* Denoël-Gonthier, Paris, 1966), and in France by Claude Levi-Strauss (see *Les structures élémentaires de la parenté,* Paris, 1949; *Race et histoire,* Paris, 1952).

46 See the historical study by Guillaume Cuchet, *Comment notre monde a cessé d'être chrétien. Anatomie d'un effondrement,* Seuil, Paris, 2018.

47 "Du féminisme émancipateur au fascisme sexuel," *La pensée libre,* janvier 2012, p. 2. For a more detailed analysis, see Jean-François Braunstein, *La religion woke,* Grasset, Paris, 2022 which demonstrates the religious character of other parts of woke thought. He writes: "This is not simply a new ideology, but a new religion" (p. 28). He also remarks that its intolerance, its proselytism, its rejection of reason and science, and its lack of transcendence make it precisely "a political and social sect" (p. 29). Michael Vlachos believes that in the United States what he calls "The Church of Woke" is becoming the dominant religion. "Church of Woke: The next American religion?," *Humanitas,* vol. 34, nos 1–2, 2021, pp. 113–122.

48 *Le genre démasqué,* Peuple libre, Valence, 2011, p. 82.

49 "Le mépris du corps sexué," dans P.-O. Arduin et C. Geffroy, *L'imposture du gender,* La Nef, Paris, 2011, p. 39.

50 See Rod Dreher, *Live not by lies: A manual for Christian dissidents,* Sentinel, New York, 2020, which proposes a resistance to "the soft totalitarianism" of woke thought using the methods of the dissidents in Communist societies. On woke totalitarianism in which is included gender theory and its applications see Nathalie Heinich, *Le wokisme serait-il un totalitarisme?* Albin Michel, Paris, 2023.

51 A French Minister who introduced the teaching of gender theory into the educational system said this clearly in his "*Letter to the Rectors of the Academy*" dated January 4, 2013: "The Government is resolved to lean on the young to change minds."

52 In France, the teacher's union, Sud Education, strongly supports the teaching of gender theory in schools and helping children who wish to change gender. It recommends the following to its members: "Above all, do not mention

trans-identity to any member of the family without an explicit request." In the same document, we find under the heading "How to sensitize pupils and staff" a recommendation to call on LGBT associations. (Sud Éducation, "Fiches et analyses—Transition d'élève: accompagner, soutenir, protéger," September 21, 2021.) This is one of the principles of totalitarian societies to remove family influence from education.

53 As linguists have shown, we think through concepts, which require a verbal support. By changing words, we may change concepts and thus change thought.

54 AMAB (Assigned Male at Birth) and AFAB (Assigned Female at Birth).

55 Pressure from radical feminist associations has succeeded in 2012in banishing the term "Mademoiselle" from French law as being discriminatory. See the critique by Eugénie Bastié, *Adieu Mademoiselle,* Cerf, Paris, 2016.

56 The LGBT associations continue their struggle for total eradication. On January 11, 2021, the association "Stop Homophobie" opened a case before the CNII against the SNCF which persists in asking customers to tick "man" or "woman" for purchases online. They say that this shows it "conforms to old fashioned gender stereotypes." It "excludes individuals who identify as non-binary" especially trans and intersex individuals, "genderfucks," and queers. It also excludes those who do not wish to restrict their identity to masculine or feminine, who may wish to alternate between the two. (See Annick Berger, "Plainte contre la SNCF qui impose de cocher la case "M." ou "Mme"," *Capital* du 13 janvier 2021.)

57 The instructions were sent to the Bishops by Mgr. de Metz-Noblat, president of the Council for canonical questions of the Conference of the Bishops of France in a letter dated December 13, 2018. He writes that henceforth "the family situation of the baptized person will simply be noted without their being any moral judgement." This is strange, since those who have issued baptismal certificates have never made moral judgements on the situations of the father and mother of the one baptized. When the father was unknown, he was simply not declared. If the parents were in an irregular situation, this was not mentioned. In a circular letter dated February 28, 2020, the author made it plain that the aim of this reform was that "baptismal certificates should not be subject to attack as discriminatory by those concerned." This shows the terror inspired in the depths of the Catholic Church by the repressive judicial system set up by the State under pressure from LGBTQ+ lobbies. On this subject, see the article by Stéphane Kovacs, "Des actes de baptême sans mention de 'père' et de "mère"," *Le Figaro* du janvier 14, 2020.

58 The linguistic rules for medical personnel in the UK are given in *A guide to effective communication: Inclusive language in the workplace.* 2016, British Medical Association. Those imposed in American medical faculties and the sanctions for not conforming are given by Katie Herzog: "Med Schools are now Denying Biological Sex" *Common Sense*, July 27, 2021. Harriet Alexander writes of the linguistic recommendations of the American Cancer Society: "American Cancer Society is slammed for saying 'individuals with a cervix' instead of 'women' in their latest pap test guidance," *Mail Online*, 31 January 2020.

59 A neologism meaning the capacity of someone to act on the world, on things and on beings to change or influence them. It comes from the works of Judith Butler and is frequently used by gender theorists.

60 This term seeks to suggest a correlation between various kinds of oppression and discrimination (of race, of class, of sex, or of gender).

61 The past tense of the verb 'to wake.' It is intended to suggest that one is aware of the injustices suffered by minorities, ethnic, sexual, or religious. See A. Maad, "Qu'est-ce que la pensée 'woke'? Quatre questions pour comprendre le terme et les débats qui l'entourent," *Le Monde*, 24 septembre 2021. A critical analysis is given by Jean-François Braunstein, *La religion woke*, Grasset, Paris, 2022.

62 Exaggeration is a tactic recommended by Christine Delphy, a pioneer of radical feminism: "When a feminist is accused of exaggeration, she is on the right track."

63 See the criticism of these attitudes by Elisabeth Badinter in her book *Fausse route*, Odile Jacob, Paris, 2003.

Chapter 3

64 The writings of Judith Butler, the main foundress of gender theory, are particularly abstruse.

65 The force of culture was emphasized by Pascal: "Custom is our nature" (*Pensées*, 89); "A different custom will cause different natural principles. This is seen in experience; and if there are some natural principles ineradicable by custom, there are also some customs opposed to nature, ineradicable by nature, or by a second custom. This depends on disposition" (*Pensées*, 92); "Custom is a second nature which destroys the former. But what is nature? For is custom not natural? I am much afraid that nature is itself only a first custom, as custom is a second nature" (*Pensées*, 93).

66 To be is to perceive or to be perceived.

67 Jean-François Braunstein remarks: "With gender we are confronted for the first time with the development of a kind of radical solipsism which not only believes that consciousness is all that exists but also that this consciousness creates the world. This solipsism has become a mass delusion, encouraged by the development of a virtual world. The idea is simple. I say that I have this or that gender so everyone must treat me as if I truly had this gender. So, the legal system must be completely changed, starting with civil status. Everyday language must be completely remolded since the usual definitions will no longer apply." *La religion woke,* Grasset, Paris, 2022, pp. 150–151.

68 We may recall Socrates's objection to Protagoras who had said: "The individual is the measure of all things." This means that Protagoras's opinion has no more value than anyone else's and cannot pretend to be universal. Plato *Theaetetus* 151e–183c.

69 Commenting on Butler's work, Jean-François Braunstein remarks: "Gender identities, once they are disconnected from any reference to biological sex can always be questioned. It is this radical view of 'gender fluidity' which is now becoming popular with transgender movements." *La religion woke,* Grasset, Paris, 2022, p. 114.

70 Judith Butler developed the concept of performativity from linguistics: it is enough for one to think and affirm that one is of a given gender for it to be true.

71 This is emphasized by the essay of Kathleen Stock, the philosopher well-known for her work on fiction and imagination, *Material girls. Why reality matters for feminism.* Little, Brown and Co. Boston 2021. See also Jean-François Braunstein, *op. cit.,* sections entitled "Le monde imaginaire du genre," pp. 121–141, et "La guerre à la réalité," pp. 150–158.

72 Biology and science in general are denounced as creations which serve the patriarchy.

73 See Jean-François Braunstein, *op. cit.,* chapitre II, "Une religion contre la réalité," pp. 105–158.

74 In the show, "Arrêt sur images" of June 29, 2018, there is a dialog between the host, Danie Schneidermann, and an individual who appears entirely masculine but who claims to be nonbinary. He is most offended to be introduced as a man. It is typical … (https://www.youtube.com/watch?v=yvaHqraKsOw).

75 Training has a very limited effect on them.

76 Alain De BENOIST writes: "Our biological identity does not arise only from our inherited constitution. It is also influenced by our interaction with the setting in which we live, which takes place within the limits of our inherited

capacities." (*L'idéologie du genre,* dans *Les démons du bien,* Paris, 2013, p. 110.) Sylviane Agakinski agrees: "The constructivism (of gender theory) believes that culture can absorb nature completely. It is as if cultures came down from above with nothing to do with our conditions of life: nothing to do with our needs, our birth and death and of course on our sexual condition" ("Métamorphoses de la difference sexuelle," A paper given to the meeting of Semaines sociales de France in 2012. "Hommes et Femmes, la nouvelle donne").

77 On this subject see the analysis of Jean-François Braunstein, *La philosophie devenue folle Le genre, l'animal, la mort,* Paris, 2018, section entitled: "Le comble de la gnose: l'amputomanie."

78 The body, the prison of the soul, see *Phaedo,* 66b–66e.

79 See *Le Corps utopique* suivi de *Les Hétérotopies,* Paris, 2009, p. 10.

80 See Bruno Chaouat, *L'homme trans. Variations sur un préfixe,* Léo Scheer, Paris, 2019.

81 An allusion to certain psychotic states where the individual recognizes no limit to his physical and mental capacities.

82 *The Banquet,* 189e–190b.

83 This is the fundamental idea of existentialism applied to gender. Sartre sums it up thus in *L'existentialism est un humanism*: "What does it mean, that existence precedes essence? It means that first, man exists, takes account of himself, and wells up into the world; afterwards, he defines himself. Man, as the existentialist sees him, is undefinable for he starts as nothing. He comes to be only later and will be what he makes himself. Thus, there is no human nature for there is no God to conceive it. Man is not just what he conceives, but what he wants. As he conceives what he is after first existing, as he desires in his impetus to exist, man is nothing other than what he makes himself to be. This is the first principle of existentialism."

84 The rejection of science is a characteristic of postmodern thinking which includes gender theory. This sees science as a "narrative" composed by the dominant to affirm their dominance in the various fields to which it applies. See Marcel Kuntz, "Menaces "postmodernes" sur la science," *AFIS science,* 8 octobre 2013; "L'i idéologie postmoderne contre la science," *Contrepoints,* 29 aout 2015.

85 On the rejection of biological science—and by extension, of other sciences—by gender theory and woke thought in general see Jean-Francois Braunstein, *La religion woke,* Grasset, Paris, 2022, chapitre IV: "Une religion contre la science."

86 Lee Ellis, Scott Hershberger, Evelyn Field, Scott Wersinger, Sergio Pellis, David Geary, Craig Palmer, Katherine Hoyenga, Amir Hetsroni and Kazmer Karadi. *Sex differences: Summarizing more than a century of scientific research*, Psychology Press, New York, 2008, 990 pages, 1920 figures. The following sections are found in this book: (1) Basic biological factors; (2) The brain and biochemistry; (3) Health and illness factors; (4) Perceptual, motor, and emotional factors; (5) Intellectual, cognitive self-concept, and mental health/illness factors; (6); Preferences, interests, attitudes, beliefs and intentions; (7) Drug, therapeutic, and stress-related responses; (8) Personality and general behavior; (9) Social behavior; (10) Consuming and individual-institutional interactions; (11) Stratification and work-related behavior; (12) Attitudes and actions toward others in relation to their gender.

87 The man has a penis, testicles, a prostate, and seminal vesicles; the woman has a clitoris, a vagina, ovaries, fallopian tubes, a womb, and breasts.

88 The morphology and the skeleton differ. Men have a higher average height, a larger thorax, larger hands and feet, and thicker bones. Women have a lower average height, hips broader than their shoulders and a smaller ratio of waist to hips. Men have more hair on the torso, the abdomen, and the face. Women have hair which grows faster on the scalp, but much less on the face and body. Men have thicker and coarser skin. Women's skin has a finer texture. In men, fat accumulates most around the abdomen and the waist, whereas in women it accumulates on the buttocks, around the hips, and on the thighs. Man has stronger muscles, a pronounced Adam's apple and a deeper voice.

89 See, amongst others: D. Kimura, *Sex and cognition*, MIT Press Harvard, 2000; D. F. Swaab et al. "Structural and functional sex differences in the human hypothalamus," *Hormones and Behavior*, 40, 2001, pp. 93–98. S. Baron-Cohen, *The essential difference, men, women and the extreme male brain*, Allen Lane London, 2003. M. Hines, *Brain gender*, Oxford University Press, Oxford, 2004. L. Brizedine, *The female brain*, Morgan Road, New York, 2006. L. Eliot, *Pink brain, blue brain*, Houghton Mifflin Harcourt, Boston and New York, 2009; D. F. Halpern, *Sex differences in cognitive abilities*, ed. Lawrence Erlbaum, Malwah, 2009; L. Brizedine, *The male brain*, Broadway Book, New York, 2010. J.-A. Meynard, *Le sexe du cerveau. Hommes/femmes: les vraies différences*, L' Archipel, Paris, 2011. L. Wolpert, *Why can't a woman be more like a man? The evolution of sex and gender*, Faber and Faber, London, 2013. J. Baltharzart, *Quand le cerveau devient masculin*, humenSciences Éditions, Paris, 2019.

90 See, amongst others: J. Connellana et al., "Sex differences in human neonatal social perception," *Infant Behavior and Development,* 2, 2000, pp. 113–118. B. Macmillan, *Why boys are different,* Hamlyn, London, 2004. G. Einstein (ed.), *Sex and the brain,* M.I.T. Cambridge, 2007. L. Ellis et al., *Sex differences: Summarizing more than a century of scientific research,* Psychology Press, New York, 2008. L. ELIOT, *op. cit.*

91 *Sex aequo. Le quiproquo des sexes,* Albin Michel, Paris, 2011, pp. 26–27.

92 *See,* for example, the article of J. Connellana et al., "Sex differences in human neonatal perception." *Infant Behavior and Development,* 2, 2000, pp. 113–118. This shows that the biology of a new-born girl makes her more sociable than a new-born boy. This difference in sociability has been observed in many studies of adults.

93 See *ibid.*

94 S. Baron-Cohen, *The essential difference, male and female brains and the truth about autism,* Basic Books, New York, 2004.

95 See, amongst others: L. Ellis et al., *Sex differences: Summarizing more than a century of scientific research,* Psychology Press, New York, 2008. Ciofi (Philippe), "La différenciation sexuelle du cerveau: une synthèse récente," *Métabolismes Hormones Diabètes et Nutrition,* vol. 12, n° 6, 2008, pp. 199–204. J. Balthazart, *Quand le cerveau devient masculin,* humenSciences Éditions, Paris, 2019. See too the work of the same author: *Biologie de l'homosexualité,* Mardaga, Bruxelles, 2010, 2e éd. Revised and augmented as *On naît hétéro ou homosexuel, on ne choisit pas de l'être*, Mardaga, Bruxelles, 2021, which, before looking at homosexuality, looks at the subject in general and draws on a vast bibliography. See also his summary: "Sex differences in partner preferences in human and animals," *Philosophical Transactions of the Royal Society B: Biological Sciences,* vol. 371, n° 1688, 19 February 2016, pp. 1–11. There is also the well-informed work of popularization by A. and B. Pease, *Why men don't listen and women can't read maps,* Orion, London 2001.

96 Systemization is more marked in men than in women, whilst empathy is stronger in women. This led Baron-Cohen to postulate that Asperger's autism, which is characterized by an over-systematization of the world and a lack of empathy, could be due to an excessive level of testosterone during gestation leading to a hypermasculinization.

97 *Politique des sexes,* Seuil, Paris, 1998, p. 106.

98 See *Le deuxième sexe,* Gallimard, Paris, 1949.

99 See especially Elisabeth Badinter, *L'amour en plus. Histoire de l'amour maternel XVIIe–XXe siècle*, Flammarion, Paris, 1980. On the weaknesses of this work see the critical review of Dominique Julia dans *Histoire de l'éducation*, 9, 1980, pp. 46–52, and of Marcel Bernos, Catherine Fouquet and Yvonne Knibiehler, in the *Revue d'Histoire Moderne et Contemporaine*, 28–1, 1981, pp. 207–209.

100 Elisabeth Badinter, a leading advocate of the feminism of Simon de Beauvoir, stated with regret: "The ideology of maternity has become the intangible key to feminine life" (*Fausse route. Réflexions sur 30 années de féminisme*, Odile Jacob, Paris, 2003).

101 It is the "essentialist" or "differentialist" school which recognizes that men and women are different at birth, and which tries to value what is specific to women rather than denying it. The "universalist" school promotes the idea of a universal, undifferentiated human being. There is also the "androcentric" school which follows Simone de Beauvoir in recommending that women should adopt virile values as their own. Amongst those of the differentialist school who have promoted maternity as a feminine value are Luce Irigaray, Antoinette Fouque, Hélène Cixous, Julian Kristeva, and Sylviane Agakinski. Luce Irigaray and Antoinette Fouque are those who have most strongly emphasized the value of maternity for women. See Antoinette Fouque: *Il y a deux sexes. Essai de féminologie*, Gallimard, Paris, 1995, pp. 156–157 and on the thought of A. Fouque on this subject: Ursula Del Aguila, "Antoinette Fouque ou la dette infinie et féconde à la Mère," *Huffpost* du 24.02.2014. (See also Sylviane Agakinski, *Politique des sexes*, Éditions du Seuil, Paris, 1998 where one finds in the chapter entitled "Liberté et fécondité," pp. 59–80) a most pertinent criticism of the positions of Simone de Beauvoir and her followers and a positive evaluation of how the particular nature of woman expresses itself especially in the potential for motherhood.

102 Sarah Blaffer Hrdy emphasizes especially the role of maternal hormones in all mammals—prolactin and ocytocin. (*Les instincts maternels*, Payot, Genève, 2002.)

103 Amongst recent work, see: Michel Odent, *L'amour scientifié*, Jouvence, Genève, 2001; Sarah Blaffer Hrdy, *Les instincts maternels*, Payot, Genève, 2002; Nicole M. Else-Quest, Janet Shibley Hyde et Roseanne Clark, "Breastfeeding, Bonding, and the Mother-Infant Relationship," *Merrill-Palmer Quarterly*, vol. 49, no.) 4, 2003, pp. 495–517; Craig Kinsley and Kelly Lambert, "L'instinct maternel niche dans le cerveau," *Pour la science*, 340, 2006; Daniel D. Chiras, *Human biology*,

Jones & Bartlett Learning, Burlington (MA), 2012; Niv Scott, Matthias Prigge, Ofer Yizhar et Tali Kimchi, "A sexually dimorphic hypothalamic circuit controls maternal care and oxytocin secretion," *Nature*, 525, 2015, pp. 519–522; Marc H. Bornstein et al., "Neurobiology of culturally common maternal responses to infant cry," *Proceedings of the National Academy of Sciences*, 2017. See also the book of Edwige Antier, Éloge des mères. Faire confiance à l'instinct maternel et favoriser l'épanouissement, Robert Laffont, Paris, 2003, where she describes her experience as a pediatrician.

104 See Elisabeth Badinter, *L'amour en plus*, Flammarion, Paris, 1980.

105 See the work cited above of Sylvaine Agakinski and the balanced scientific studies of Sarah Blaffer Hrdy. *Les Instincts maternels*, Payot Geneva.

106 *Politique des sexes*, Seuil, Paris, 1998, p. 77.

107 Sylviane Agacinski observes this. Following Françoise Héritier (*Masculin/Féminin, La pensée de la différence*, Odile Jacob, Paris, 1996), she writes: "Based on its biological root, the difference between masculine and feminine is a model which structures all societies, though the value and content attributed to this difference vary between cultures." (*La politique des sexes*, Seuil, Paris, 1998, p. 20.)

108 On this subject see Esther Pivet *Enquête sur la théorie du genre. Comment les idéologues règnent encore sur l'école de nos enfants*, Artège, Paris, 2019.

109 See on this subject the work of G. M. Alexander et M. Hines, "Sex Differences in Response to Children's Toys in Non-human Primates," *Evolution and Human Behaviour*, 2002, pp. 467–479. See also the more general study of C.-M. Clozel, *Pourquoi les petits garçons ne sont pas des petites filles …: Un secret bien gardé*, Tryptique, Montréal, 2007.

110 Such moving objects are found in 92 percent of drawings by boys and only 5 percent of drawings by girls. People figure in 97 percent of girl's drawings but only 26 percent of boys'.

111 See the work of Lisa Littman, "Parent reports of adolescents and young adults perceived to show signs of a rapid onset of gender dysphoria," *PLoS One*, 16 August 2018. On the role of social media see also Abigail Shrier, *Irreversible damage: The transgender craze seducing our daughters*, Regnery Publishing, Washington, 2020, chapter 3: The Influencers.

112 Dr Kenneth Zucker, Professor of Psychiatry and Psychology at the University of Toronto recommends this approach, based on his observations of many cases. He is an international authority on identity troubles in children and adolescents.

113 Gender theorists used the iconic sex change case of David Reiner as a reference long before its tragic end was revealed. Reiner's parents agreed under the influence of Dr John Money. It is recounted in the book by J. Colapinto, *As nature made him: The boy who was raised as a girl,* Harper Perennial, New York 2001. A summary of the story is to be found in *Le Point* of January 31, 2014, "L'experience tragique du gourou de la théorie du genre."

114 See Ryan T. Anderson, *When Harry became Sally,* Enconter Books, New York, 2018. Celine Masson et al., "Changing the sex of children: 'We can no longer remain silent about this dangerous drift.' Fifty or so psychologists, doctors and intellectuals denounce an ideological grip on the bodies of children set forth as the emancipation of the 'transgender child.'" *L'Express* du 20 septembre 2021. Olivier Vial, *Détrans. Les Cassandre de la communauté trans,* Ceru, Paris, 2021. Claude HABIB, *La question trans,* Gallimard, Paris, 2021. Christian Flavigny, *"Aider les enfants transgenre": contre l'américanisation des soins,* Tequi, Paris, 2021. Caroline Eliacheff et Celine Masson, *La fabrique de l'enfant transgenre,* L'Observatoire, Paris, 2022. Abigail Shrier, *Irreversible damage: The transgender craze seducing our daughters,* Regnery Publishing, Washington, 2020; Pauline Quillon, *Enquête sur la dysphorie de genre,* Mame, Paris, 2022. Aude Mirkovic et Claire De Gattalier, *Questionnements de genre chez les enfants et les adolescents,* Artege, Paris, 2022. Helen Joyce, *Trans: When ideology meets reality,* Oneworld Publications, London, 2022. Matt Walsh, *What is a woman? One man's journey to answer the question of a generation,* DW Books, Nashville, 2022. See also the warning of the Académie de médecine published on its site le 25 février 2022: "La médecine face à la transidentité de genre chez les enfants et les adolescents."

115 See: K. J. Zucker and S. Bradley, *Gender identity disorder and psychosexual problems in children and adolescents,* Guilford, New York, 1995; N. M. Mukaddes, "Gender identity problems in autistic children," *Child: Care, Health and Development,* 28 (6), 2002, pp. 529–532; Annelou L. C. De Vries, Ilse L. J. Noens, Peggy T. Cohen-Kettenis, Ina A. van Berckelaer-Onnes and Theo A. Doreleijers, "Autism spectrum disorders in gender dysphoric children and adolescents," *Journal of autism and developmental disorders,* 40 (8), 2010, pp. 930–936; Anna Churcher Clarke and Anastassis Spiliadis, "Taking the lid off the box": The value of extended clinical assessment for adolescents presenting with gender identity difficulties," *Clinical Child Psychology and Psychiatry,* 24, 2019, pp. 338–352; Lena Herrmann, Carola Bindt, Katinka Schweizer, Jan Micheel, Timo Ole Nieder, Judith Haass, Daniel Schöttle, Inga Becker-Hebly, "Autism spectrum disorders and gender dysphoria among children and

adolescents: Systematic review on the co-occurrence," *Psychiatrische Praxis*, 47 (6), 2020, pp. 300–307; Jane Galloway, *Autism and gender identity*, Transgender Trend, 2022; M. Huys and K. Dhondt, "Gender variance or gender dysphoria and autism spectrum disorder in children and adolescents," *Tijdschrift voor psychiatrie*, 64 (1), 2022, pp. 25–31; Rachel K. Greene, Tara M. Rutter, Randy A. Phelps, Emily K. Olsen, Raquel Harmon, and Danielle N. Moyer, "Diagnostic assessment of autism spectrum disorder in transgender and gender diverse youth," *The Clinical Neuropsychologist*, 26, 2024, pp. 1–22. An extensive additional bibliography can be found at the end of these articles.

116 Some studies show that the same mental health disorders also affect a significant proportion of adults who experience gender dysphoria and are transgender or transsexual. See, among others: Vickie Pasterski, Liam Gilligan, and Richard Curtis, "Traits of autism spectrum disorders in adults with gender dysphoria," *Archives of Sexual Behavior*, 43, 2014, pp. 387–393; M. Urban-Kowalczyk, "Gender Dysphoria as a Clinical Manifestation of Schizophrenia—Case Series," *European Psychiatry*, 30, Supplement 1, 2015, p. 1773; Derek Glidden, Walter Pierre Bouman, Bethany A. Jones, and Jon Arcelus, "Gender dysphoria and autism spectrum disorder: A systematic review of the literature," *Sexual Medicine Reviews*, 4, 2016, pp. 3–14; Anna I. R. Van Der Miesen, Hannah HURLEY, Annelou L. C. de Vries, "Gender dysphoria and autism spectrum disorder: A narrative review," *International Review of Psychiatry*, 28 (1), 2016, pp. 70–80; Gunter Heylens, Lore Aspeslagh, Jesper Dierick, Kariann Baetens, Birgit Van Hoorde, Griet de Cuypere, Els Elaut, "The Cooccurrence of gender dysphoria and autism spectrum disorder in adults: An analysis of cross-sectional and clinical chart data," *Journal of Autism and Developmental Disorders*, 48 (6), 2018, pp. 2217–2223; J. Stusiński and M. Lew-Starowicz, "Gender dysphoria symptoms in schizophrenia," *Psychiatria Polska*, 52 (6), 2018, pp. 1053–1062; Varun Warrier, David M. Greenberg, Elizabeth Weir, Clara Buckingham, Paula Smith, Meng-Chuan Lai, Carrie Allison and Simon Baron-Cohen, "Elevated rates of autism, other neurodevelopmental and psychiatric diagnoses, and autistic traits in transgender and gender-diverse individuals," "The Co-occurrence of gender dysphoria and autism spectrum disorder in adults: An analysis of cross-sectional and clinical chart data," *Journal of Autism and Developmental Disorders*, 48 (6), 2018, pp. 2217–2223; J. Stusiński and M. Lew-Starowicz, "Gender dysphoria symptoms in schizophrenia," *Psychiatria Polska*, 52 (6), 2018, pp. 1053–1062; Varun Warrier, David M. Greenberg, Elizabeth Weir, Clara Buckingham, Paula Smith, Meng-Chuan Lai, Carrie Allison and Simon Baron-Cohen, "Elevated rates

of autism, other neurodevelopmental and psychiatric diagnoses, and autistic traits in transgender and gender-diverse individuals," *Nature Communications*, 11, Article n° 3959, 2020; Kristy A. Fisher, Samantha Scemla, Clara L. Alvarez Villalba, Jessica Kroin, "Gender dysphoria versus acute psychosis: Can one properly diagnose gender dysphoria solely during acute psychosis?," *HCA Healthcare Journal of Medicine*, 3 (3), 2022, pp. 167–173; Aimilia Kallitsounaki and David M. Williams, "Autism Spectrum Disorder and Gender Dysphoria/Incongruence. A systematic Literature Review and Meta-Analysis," *Journal of Autism and Developmental* Disorders, 53, 2023, pp. 3103–3117.

117 The testimony of the author of *Gosse des homos* (Max Milo, Paris, 2021) is an example of this. Without a father and lost between a biological mother and a social mother (s)he could call neither "maman." Born a boy, (s)he now identifies as transsexual. "At the end of 2019 my non-biological mother was able to adopt me and become officially my second mother. My sister and I were both born by artificial insemination in Holland from a Taiwanese Hong Konger. My mothers had been together for some time when they decided to have children. It proved difficult. To start with, my social mother tried to conceive but was unable. So, my other mother took over. At birth I was assigned as a boy, but now I identify as trans. My sister and I lived with two mothers for a few years until they separated. It was very hard as a child to accept two mothers. . . . Often people would say "Your mother" meaning my biological mother. I always found that very hard since for me there was no difference between them. This is why I and my sister never called them "maman." If I call one "maman" what should I call the other? For me it was a question of equality."

118 Examples are Judith Butler, Monique Wittig, Anne Fausto-Sterling, Adrienne Rich, Andrea Dworkin, and Christine Delphy.

119 They are listed in Chapter 1.

120 A psychoanalyst and author of *La confusion des sexes*, Flammarion, Paris, 2007.

121 In the show "Repliques" on France Culture broadcast on October 8, 2011 entitled "Gender theory, the difference of the sexes" hosted by Alain Finkelkraut. Since then, many books and articles have appeared which present heterosexuality as deficient and homosexuality as normal. See, for instance, the recent article by Maïa Mazaurette, "Comment peut-on être encore hétérosexuel?," *Le Monde* du 5 juin 2022.

122 Many of those in the feminist movement are inspired by the work of Simone de Beauvoir *Le deuxième sexe*, to reject femininity. They reject their physical appearance and even all that is involved in motherhood which they consider

as a construct of a masculine culture whose manliness they wish to make their own. This feminism which works to "rub out what is feminine" is pointedly criticized by Sylviane Agacinski in her work *Politique des sexes,* Seuil, Paris, 1998, p. 60, 85–86.

123 Colette Chiland is one of those who accompanies transsexuals "on their long and painful path." She is nonetheless obliged to admit: "We have entered a new era where surgery and hormonology have made possible a certain transformation of the body. However, this does not change a biological man into a biological woman or a biological woman into a biological man. It just changes the appearance and the identity card." (*Changer de sexe: illusion et réalité,* Odile Jacob, Paris, 2011.) See the testimony of transsexuals quoted in the work of Claude Habib, *La question trans,* Gallimard, Paris, 2021.

124 The title of the futuristic novel by Aldous Huxley in which children are conceived in test tubes in the laboratory.

125 From the show "Répliques" of France Culture broadcast on October 8, 2011, entitled "Théorie du genre, différence des sexes," hosted by Alain Finkielkraut.

126 There are certain currents in this movement which are regrettable as pointed out by Sabine Prokhoris, *Le Mirage #MeToo. Réflexions à partir du cas français,* Cherche-midi, Paris, 2021.

127 Amongst those feminist works which preach and justify such detestation and hatred are those of Alice Coffin, *Le Génie lesbien,* Grasset, Paris, 2020, and Pauline Harmange, *Moi les hommes, je les déteste,* Seuil, Paris, 2020. The first is a lesbian, co-president of the Association des Journalistes LGBT and the co-founder of la Conférence Européenne Lesbienne. She advocates boycotting masculine artists, writers, producers, and composers alleging that all men are "aggressors." "It is not enough that we help each other. We must eliminate them," she writes. The second recommends misandry which she defines as "a negative sentiment towards the masculine race as a whole …, which forms a spectrum from simple mistrust to outright hostility."

128 Logically, on the basis of the policies of feminist associations and the LGBTQI+ lobbies, androphobia should be punished by law just like homophobia, xenophobia, and racism. However, like ethnic groups, these groups also benefit from positive discrimination. It's fine to have a meeting of black people where whites are excluded, but the reverse is illegal.

129 Looking at how modern Western societies have evolved over the last fifty years, the feminists' concept of a "patriarchy," an enemy to be destroyed, may seem

rather irrelevant. See Emmanuel TODD, *Où en sont-elles? Une esquisse de l'histoire des femmes*, Seuil, Paris, 2022.

130 An example is the word of Caroline de Haas: "one man in every two or three is a sexual aggressor" ("'One man in every two or three is an aggressor'. La militante féministe Caroline de Haas balance des chiffres," 20minutes.fr, 15 février 2018). Another is the statement of Alice Coffin, a lesbian and LGBT militant: "Not having a husband means that I am not at risk of rape, murder, or beatings, and nor are my children." She makes the same generalization in her book *Le Génie lesbian*: "Men kill women. With no let up. They rape them. Without stopping. They attack them, bully them, sequester them, and exploit them. Going even further than Caroline de Haas she writes: "It's obvious. From the beginning of humanity, we're always far from the mark" *(ibid)*. This idea that all men are violent toward women comes from American radical feminists. They maintain that this marks every sexual relationship, even with no physical contact. They correctly condemned pornography and sexual harassment, but then, most improperly, generalized these cases to the whole male race. For them, the most normal of sexual relationships is rape, even within a married couple. Examples of this attitude may be found in: Kathleen Barry, *Female sexual slavery*, Prentice Hall, Hoboken, 1979; Andrea Dworkin, *Pornography: Men possessing women*, New York, Perigee Books, 1981; *Intercourse*, Free Press, New York, 1987, trad. fr. *Coïts*, Éd du Remue-ménage, Montréal et Éd. Syllepse, Paris, 2019; Catharine A. Mackinnon (for whom rape is the model of all heterosexuality): *Toward a feminist theory of the state*, Harvard University Press, Cambridge, 1989; *Feminism unmodified: Discourses on life and law*, Harvard University Press, Cambridge, 1998. However, though their denunciation of pornography is perfectly justified, it has aroused, paradoxically, some opposition from certain feminists. They say that a woman should be free to use her body as she likes, in pornography, as a prostitute, or as a surrogate mother, defending the social rights of sex workers. All this is quite at odds with the dignity of woman.

131 Aggressivity is undoubtedly stronger in men than in women due to both biological and cultural factors. However, this male aggression is usually directed toward other males, as in wars and brawls which are the affairs of men. Moreover, women can also be violent. They can be violent toward men, something that feminists hide, but which is very real though less frequent. See Elisabeth BADINTER in chapter 2 of her book *Fausse route* (Odile Jacob, Paris, 2003). The longest section is "Feminine violence." It has three subsections: "Historical violence," "Daily Violence," and "Conjugal Violence."

132 See Irene, *La terreur féministe: Petit éloge du féminisme extrémiste,* Divergences, Paris, 2022. Christiane Rochefort even wrote fifty years ago: "The time comes when one must draw the knife." ("Definition of the Oppressed" in Valeria Solanas (éd.), *SCUM Manifesto,* Olympia Press, New York, 1968, p. 3; This manifesto is seen as one of the founding texts of radical feminism.)

133 Élisabeth Badinter has criticized the exaggerations of this idea of victimization of women in *Fausse route,* Odile Jacob, Paris, 2003, in its Introduction and in the section entitled "La logique de l'amalgame" in chapter 1. This idea of victimization, which goes far beyond the feminist movement, is also criticized by Pascal Bruckner in his book *La tentation de l'innocence,* Grasset, Paris, 1995.

134 See Christina Hoff Sommers, *The War against boys: How misguided feminism is harming our young men,* Simon & Schuster, New York, 2001. Paul-François Paoli, *La tyrannie de la faiblesse. La féminisation du monde ou l'éclipse du guerrier,* Françoise Bourin, Paris, 2010. A. De Benoist, *L'idéologie du genre,* dans *Les démons du bien,* Paris, 2013, pp. 208–214.

135 Bérénice Levet uses this as a sub-title in her book, *La théorie du* genre "ou Le monde rêvé des anges" and includes a section named: "Gender, a new puritanism."

136 See, for instance Adrienne Rich, "La contrainte à l'hétérosexualité et l'existence lesbienne," *Nouvelles questions féministes,* 1, 1981, pp. 15–43.

137 See above.

138 Amongst "materialist feminists," or Marxists, such as Monique Wittig and Christine Delphy, an analogous intersectionality may be observed. They treat genders as unequal classes, obliged to struggle with each other.

139 Nathalie Heinich writes: "To deny differences between races, sexes or social classes rests on an implied logic: any difference is clearly discrimination. Here we have the classic confusion between equality and likeness which marks a large part of the modern feminist movement. It feels obliged to deny any difference between sexes so as to struggle against sexual inequality. But racism, contrary to what is often said, is not to say "that races are different." It means believing that race makes men unequal." ("Six naïvetés à propos du mot "race"," *Libération,* 25 juillet 2013.)

140 On this subject, see the works of the ethnologist, Françoise Heritier. According to her, the distinction between masculine and feminine is universal, and "everywhere, in every age and place, the masculine is considered as superior to the feminine"; she calls this the "differential valence of the sexes" (in Françoise

Héritier, Michelle Perrot, Sylviane Agacinski, Nicole Bacharan, *La plus belle histoire des femmes,* Seuil, Paris 2011, p. 21).

Chapter 4

139 Discrimination by the LGBTQI+ movement against heterosexuals and by radical feminism against men.

140 As can be seen in the slogans and publications of radical feminism.

141 Like the remarks of St Maximus, the Confessor in his *Letter 2 to John the Cubiculary on Love.*

142 See the proposal of Rod Dreher in his book which had great success in the United States *The benedict option: A strategy for Christians in a post-Christian nation,* Sentinel, New York, 2017.

143 This is also the case of virginity, which before the coming of monasticism was strongly promoted during the first centuries of Christianity. See P. Brown, *Men, women and sexual renunciation in early Christianity,* Faber and Faber, London and Boston, 1988.

144 See F. Quéré, *Les femmes de l'Évangile,* Seuil, Paris, 1982. D. LONG, *Jésus, l'homme qui aimait les femmes,* Francoise Bourin, Paris, 2014. C. Pedotti, *Jésus, l'homme qui préférait les femmes,* Albin Michel, Paris, 2018. C. Reynier, *Les femmes de saint Paul,* Cerf, Paris, 2020.

145 See below, Chapter 12.

146 See *ibid.*

147 Such descriptions are not appreciated by those who adopt these behaviors. Instead, they seek to promote them as normal. Yet they describe themselves as "queer," which means "strange," " bizarre," "uncommon," or "twisted."

148 The same goes for those who belong to racial or social minorities. This is summed up by St Paul "There is neither Jew nor Greek, there is neither slave nor free, there is neither male nor female: for you are all one in Christ Jesus." Gal 3:28.

Chapter 5

149 *On the origin of man* I, 18, SC 160, p. 212.

150 *The creation of man* XVI, PG 44, 185B.

151 Gregory does not make the distinction here between image and resemblance. For him, both indicate participation in Divine attributes (see J. Danielou, *Platonisme et théologie mystique*).
Doctrine spirituelle de saint Grégoire de Nysse, Paris, 1944, pp. 48–49.

152 See *The Creation of man* XVI, PG 44, 181A–B.

153 *Ibid.*, 181C.

154 Cf. *ibid.*, 189D; XXII, 205A–B.

155 See *ibid.*, XVI, 185A. And the commentary of J. DANIELOU, *op. cit.*, p. 52.

156 See La *création de l'homme*, 177C, 181B, 181C, 185A, 185D, 189C, 205A.

157 Voir *ibid.*, 188A, 188B, 189A, 189B.

158 St Gregory writes: "What we have taken from the skins of animals is sexual union ..." (*On the soul and the resurrection*, PG 46, J148C).

159 Gregory writes: "What we have taken from the skin of the animals is sexual union ..." *On the soul and the resurrection*, PG 46, 148C.

160 "Le sens de la "division des sexes" chez Grégoire de Nysse," *Revue des Sciences Religieuses*, XXVII, 2, 1953, p. 108.

161 *Ambigua to John*, 67, PG 91, 1401'AB.

162 See for example *Ambigua to John*, 7, PG 91, 1073C. On this triad, especially the first and third terms, see P. Sherwood, "Maximus and Origenism. ΑΡΧΗ ΚΑΙ ΤΕΛΟΣ," in *Berichte zum XI. internationalen Byzantinisten-Kongress München 1958*, III, 1, Munich, 1958, pp. 1–17.

163 On this triad, see *Ambigua to John*, 7, PG 91, 1069B, 1072A–C, 1073A–C, 1080A, 1081AB; 10, PG 91, 1176C, 1177A–1180D, 1181A–1188C; 15, PG 91, 1217A–1220C; 21, PG 91, 1245B–D; 35, PG 91, 1288D–1289A; 42, PG 91, 1328B; 67, PG 91, 1393A, 1397AB: for commentaries: P. Sherwood, *The earlier Ambigua of St Maximus the Confessor*, Rome, 1955, pp. 92–123, 181–204. ID., "Maximus and Origenism. ΑΡΧΗ ΚΑΙ ΤΕΛΟΣ," dans *Berichte zum XI. internationalen Byzantinisten-Kongress München 1958*, III, 1, Munich, 1958, pp. 1–17. H. U. Von Balthazar, *Kosmische Liturgie*, Einsiedeln, 19612, pp. 132–141. J.-C. Larchet, Introduction à Maxime le Confesseur, *Ambigua*, Paris-Suresnes, 1994, pp. 24–27, 50–54.

164 See my work *La divinisation de l'homme selon saint Maxime le Confesseur*, Paris, 1996, pp. 112–118.

165 The form of the Greek word ποιήσωμεν is a subjunctive with an imperative quality. (The imperative does not exist in the first person.) It can be translated as "let us make." In the Hebrew text, the verbal form used clearly indicates something unfinished, which is why some translations use the future tense: "We will make." Both versions indicate something yet to be done.

166 See *Centuries on love*, III, 25, ed. Ceresa-Gastaldo, p. 154; IV, 90, ed. Ceresa-Gastaldo, p. 234; *Questions et difficulties*, III/1, CCSG 10, p. 170; *Commentary on the Lord's Prayer*, CCSG 23, p. 50; *Ambigua to John*, 7, PG 91, 1092B; 10,

PG 91, 1140B; 42, PG 91, 1345D; 48, PG 91, 1361AB; *Questions to Thalassios*, 53, CCSG 7, p. 435; *Centuries on theology and economy*, I, 13, PG 90, 1088BC; *Letters*, 1, PG 91, 265C, 377B; 6, PG 91, 429B; *Theological and polemical works*, 1, scholie 2, PG 91, 37BC; *Disputation with Pyrrhus*, PG 91, 309B–312A, Doucet pp. 566–567.

167 See *Questions and difficulties*, 113, CCSG 10, pp. 83–84; I, 3, CCSG 10, p. 138; *Ambigua to John*, 41, PG 91, 1309A; 42, PG 91, 1341C.

168 See *Questions and difficulties*, I, 3, CCSG 10, p. 138; *Ambigua to John*, 41, PG 91, 1309A.

169 See Cf. *Questions to Thalassios*, 21, PG 90, 312C–313A, CCSG 7, p. 127; 61, CCSG 22, p. 87 et 97; *Questions and difficulties*, I, 3, CCSG 10, p. 138. For a more detailed commentary, see my article on "L'heredite adamique," in *Maxime le Confesseur, médiateur entre l'Orient et l'Occident*, 2e ed., 2017, pp. 82–91.

170 See *Qu. D.*, I, 3, CCSG 10, p. 138; *Ambigua to John*, 41, PG 91, 1309A; 42, PG 91, 1341C.

171 See Cf. *Questions to Thalassios*, 49, CCSG 7, pp. 367–369.

172 See The *creation of man* XVII, PG 44, 188A–192A.

173 We may remark that Tertullian, who considered that body and soul were created together, thought that both the soul, and the body had sexes. "The soul, sown in the womb at the same instant as the flesh, also receives its sex. Sown at the same instant, neither substance has priority as concerns the sex" (*Of the Soul*, 36).

174 See The *creation of man*, XVI, PG 44, 185A.

175 There is a passage in the *Ambigua to John*, directed against the Manicheans and Gnostics, where St Maximus sees in the "natural law of birth"—the sexual process of procreation—a gift of the Creator.

176 On this principle see P. Sherwood, "Maximus and Origenism. ΑΡΧΗ ΚΑΙ ΤΕΛΟΣ," in *Berichte zum XI. internationalen Byzantinisten-Kongress München 1958*, III, 1, Munich, 1958, pp. 1–17.

177 See C. Batsch, "Les deux récits de création de la femme dans la Genèse," *Semitica et Classica*, 2012, 5, pp. 184–187.

178 See A. Kayayan, "Le retour du gnosticisme," *Acta Theologica*, vol. 24, n° 2, 2004, Supplementum 5, pp. 232–233. The main Gnostic sect which thought that man was created androgyne is the Naassennesa, sometimes called Ophites. It is mentioned by: Irénée de Lyon, *Contre les hérésies*, I, 29–30; Hippolyte de Rome, *Philosophumena, ou Réfutation de toutes les hérésies*, V, 12–18; Epiphane de Salamine, *Panarion*, XXXVII, 5 et XXXIX–LXIV.

Chapter 6

179 *Démonstration de la prédication apostolique*, 14, SC 406, p. 102.

180 *Ambigua to John*, 41, PG 91, 1304D–1308C.

181 St Maximus mentions this where he writes of division according to science and ignorance.

182 *Ambigua to John*, 41, PG 91, 1304D–1305C.

183 *Ambigua to John*, 41, PG 91, 1305CD.

Chapter 7

184 The Masoretic Hebrew test reads: "whom You placed beside me."

185 As St Irenaeus of Lyon remarks, "All the curse fell on the serpent who had beguiled them" (*Contre les hérésies*, III, 23, 3, SC 211, p. 452).

186 The Septuagint reads: "Cursed is the ground in your labors."

187 As St Irenaeus of Lyon remarks, "God, as the Scripture recounts, does not curse Adam himself, but the ground he was to work" (*Contre les hérésies*, III, 23, 3, SC 211, p. 450).

188 As St Irenaeus of Lyon remarks, "God hated the one who beguiled man, but, little by little, He came to feel pity for the man beguiled" (*Contre les hérésies*, III, 23, 5, SC 211, p. 460).

189 In paradise, man collected the fruits of the earth with no effort. He lived by gathering.

190 The Septuagint has "in pain you will eat of it all the days of your life."

191 Here, and in what follows, "marriage" means sexual union.

192 As just stated, "to marry" implies sexual relations.

193 *La création de l'homme*, XVII, 188A–192A.

194 *Contre les hérésies*, III, 23, 5, SC 211, p. 458.

195 *Ibid.*, p. 460.

196 *On the soul and resurrection*, PG 46, 148C–149A.

197 Cf. *Questions and difficulties*, I, 3, CCSG 10, p. 138. *Ambigua to John*, 41, PG 91, 1309A.

198 Cf. *Questions and difficulties*, I, 3, CCSG 10, pp. 83–84. *Ambigua to John*, 41, PG 91, 1309A.

199 Cf. *Questions and difficulties*, I, 3, CCSG 10, p. 138. *Ambigua to John*, 41, PG 91, 1309A. Paradoxically, the effect of this union was to establish sexual difference which would become, through the passions, division and opposition. Yet God's plan was for a polarity which would be reconciled in Adam along with all the other polarities of creation.

200 Cf. *Questions to Thalassios*, 49, PG 90, 457D, CCSG 7, pp. 367–369.

201 Cf. *Questions and difficulties*, I, 3, CCSG 10, p. 138; *Questions to Thalassios*, 61, PG 90, 632B, CCSG 22, p. 91; PG 90, 632C, CCSG 22, p. 91; PG 90, 636B, CCSG 22, p. 97.

202 Cf. *Questions to Thalassios*, 21, PG 90, 312C–313A, CCSG 7, p. 127.

203 Cf. *Questions to Thalassios*, 61, PG 90, 628C, CCSG 22, p. 87; PG 90, 632B, CCSG 22, p. 91.

204 *Questions and difficulties*, I, 3, CCSG 10, p. 138; *Ambigua to John*, 42, PG 91, 1348C.

205 Cf. *Questions to Thalassios*, 61, PG 90, 628C, CCSG 22, p. 87; PG 90, 632B, CCSG 22, p. 91; PG 90, 632D, CCSG 22, p. 93; PG 90, 636B, CCSG 22, p. 97.

206 Cf. *Questions and difficulties*, I, 3, CCSG 10, p. 138: "This 'In sin did my mother concieve me'" (Ps 50[51], 7) "Our first mother, the mother of all, Eve, conceived in sin by her passionate desire of pleasure"; *Questions to Thalassios*, 21, PG 90, 312C–313A, CCSG 7, p. 127.

207 Cf. *Questions to Thalassios*, 61, PG 90, 628C, CCSG 22, p. 87; PG 90, 636B, CCSG 22, p. 97.

208 As for St Gregory of Nyssa, the word signifies sexual union.

209 *Questions and difficulties*, I, 3, CCSG 10, pp. 138–139. Some feminists have blamed Christian anthropology for sticking to the concepts of ancient philosophy and physiology. Aristotle, especially, minimized the role of woman (a passive recipient) and emphasized the role of man. This text shows that this idea is false. The responsibility of man and woman is shared. Adam's transgression is given first place. It is also implied that Adam, just as much as Eve, "passionately desired pleasure."

210 Cf. *Ambigua to John*, 42, PG 91, 1320D; 1348C; *Questions to Thalassios*, 21, PG 90, 312BC, CCSG 7, p. 127; 61, PG 90, 628C, CCSG 22, p. 87; PG 90, 633A, CCSG 22, p. 93.

211 *Ambigua to John*, 31, PG 91, 1276B. Cf. 42, PG 91, 1320D–1321A.

212 *Ambigua to John*, 31, PG 91, 1276C.

213 Cf. *Questions to Thalassios*, 49, PG 90, 457D, CCSG 7, p. 369. However, the law of sin is not restricted to this.

214 *Ambigua to John*, 31, PG 91, 1276AB; *Questions to Thalassios*, 21, PG 90, 313C, CCSG 7, p. 129. Note that the word "nature" has a positive sense in other passages where it no longer means "fallen nature" but "nature defined by its *logos*." It then refers to its spiritual sense, its beginning and end in God. We will return to this fundamental distinction later.

215 Cf. *Commentary on the Lord's Prayer*, PG 90, 897B, CCSG 23, p. 60; PG 90, 904C, CCSG 23, p. 67.714; *Questions to Thalassios*, 49, PG 90, 457D, CCSG 7, pp. 367–369.

216 Cf. *Questions to Thalassios*, 61, PG 90, 628CD, CCSG 22, p. 87; PG 90, 632B, CCSG 22, p.91; PG 90, 636BC, CCSG 22, p. 97.

217 In *The therapy of spiritual illnesses,* volume 1, Alexander Press, Montreal, 2012.

218 More precisely, the word used by St Maximus indicates the disposition of the will.

219 *Letter 2, to John the Cubiculary on love*, PG 91, 396D–397A.

220 This philosophy is clearly exposed by J.-P. SARTRE in his book, *L'existentialisme est un humanisme*, Paris, 1966, pp. 21–22: "Atheist existentialism, which I represent … declares that if God does not exist, there is at least one being where existence precedes essence, a being who exists before any concept can define him, and this being is man, or human reality as Heidegger puts it. What does it mean that existence precedes essence? It means that man first exists, becomes conscious of himself, erupts into the world, and then defines himself. The existentialist sees man as undefinable since to begin with he is nothing. He will only later come to be and will be what he makes of himself. So, there is no human nature since there is no God to conceive it. Man is not just what he sees himself to be but what he wants to be, and how he sees himself and how he wishes to be after his upsurge into existence. Man is nothing other than what he makes himself to be. This is the fundamental principle of existentialism."

Chapter 8

221 See my work *The Therapy of Spiritual Illnesses,* Alexander Press, Montreal, 2012.

222 See E. Mersch, "La doctrine de la récapitulation en saint Irénée," *Recherches de science religieuse*, 6, 1916, p. 185–211. B. Sesboue, *Tout récapituler dans le Christ: christologie et sotériologie d'Irénée de Lyon*, Paris, 2000. V. D. A. Wilson, *La récapitulation chez Irénée de Lyon: Le dessein absolu de Dieu pour l'homme*, Paris, 2019.

223 The dyad, male-female, is mentioned in the lines preceding this passage (1309D–1312A) quoted above.

224 *Ambigua to John*, 41, PG 91, 1312AB.

225 *Ambigua to John*, 41, PG 91, 1308D–1309B.

226 See *Ambigua to John*, 42, PG 91, 1317C; *Ambigua to Thomas*, 2, PG 91, 1037A, CCSG 48, pp. 8.7–8; 5, PG 91, 1052D–1053A, CCSG 48, pp. 26.140–149; *Letters*, 14, PG 91, 537A; *Letter 2 to Thomas*, 10, CCSG 48, pp. 43.25–26.

227 See *Questions to Thalassios*, 61, CCSG 22, pp. 87–89, 91; *Ambigua to John*, 31, PG 91, 1276A; *Fifteen chapters*, 14, PG 90, 1185A.

228 See *Ambigua to John*, 41, PG 91, 1305CD.

229 *Commentary on the Lord's Prayer*, CCSG 23, p. 54, 468–470.

230 *Ibid.*, p. 50, 397–402.

231 *Questions to Thalassios*, 48, CCSG 7, pp. 333.66–335.70.

232 *Commentary on the Lord's Prayer*, CCSG 23, p. 47, 341–343.

233 *Stromates*, III, 13, 93. Philo of Alexandria (*Of Agriculture*, 73) already related the two genders, male and female, to aggression and desire. The idea can be found in Plato who in *Phaedra* compares the soul to a chariot drawn by two horses, one male, the other female—aggression and desire. In reality these two passions are shared by the two genders and are not specific to either.

234 *Ambigua to John*, 67, PG 91, 1401AB.

235 *Ambigua to John*, 41, PG 91, 1309D–1312A.

Chapter 9

236 On these subjects see our book *La vie après la mort selon la Tradition orthodoxe*, Cerf, Paris, 2004, especially chapters 10 and 11.

237 "Where eternity reigns there is no need of marriage," says Origen (*Homélies sur Luc*, XXXIX, 2).

238 *To his wife*, 1, 4.

239 See, for example, Irénée de Lyon, *Contre les hérésies*, V, 31, 2; Athenogore, *Sur la résurrection des morts*, XXV, 3; Tertullien, *De la résurrection*, 62; Grégoire de Nysse, *Homélies pascales*, I, 8; Jean Chrysostome, *Homélies sur la première épître aux Corinthiens*, 41.

240 See Athenogore, *Sur la résurrection des morts*, II, 3; XV, 3; Tertullien, *De la résurrection*, 62; Macaire d'Egypte, *Homélies* (coll. II), XV, 10.

241 See our work *La vie après la mort selon la tradition orthodoxe*, Cerf, Paris, 2001, pp. 75–80.

242 See Tertullien, *De la résurrection*, 65; 67; Isaac le Syrien, *Discours ascétiques*, 85; and our work *La vie après la mort selon la tradition orthodoxe*, Cerf, Paris, 2001, pp. 253–259.

243 See Jérôme Alexandre, *L'anthropologie réaliste et mystique de Tertullien*, Beauchesne, Paris, 2001, pp. 486–511; "Tertullien et la différence sexuelle," in P. Delage (dir.), *Les Pères de l'Église et les femmes. Actes du colloque de La Rochelle, 6–7 septembre 2003*, Histoire et culture, Rochefort, 2003, pp. 79–99. Guillaume Bady and Laurence Mellerin, "A l'image de Dieu ... homme et femme. Regards

patristiques sur la différence des sexes," *Connaissance des Pères de l'Église,* 130, 2013, pp. 36–41.

244 *La résurrection des morts,* 63.

245 See *De l'âme,* 36.

246 See *De la résurrection,* 60–61.

247 See note 240 above, the text of the quotation from *To his wife,* I, 4.

248 *La toilette des femmes (The adornment of women),* I, 2.

249 For a detailed study, see Michelle Cutino, "La différenciation sexuelle et son accomplissement eschatologique chez Augustin," *Revue des Sciences Religieuses,* 91, 2017, pp. 565–588.

250 *The City of God,* XXII, 17.

Chapter 10

251 Or, more accurately, dispositions to will—*gnômai.*

252 On the nature of Christian love, which is spiritual and not just psychological, emotional, and sentimental, see my book *Variations sur la charité,* Paris, Cerf, 2007.

253 That is, of humanity.

254 That is, abandoning egoism.

255 Not personal but individual.

256 *Letter 2 to John the Cubiculary on love,* PG91, 397C–400B.

257 That is, to what defines nature in its original and normative state.

258 Reference to Gen 16: 1–33.

259 The objects of the created world.

260 *Letter 2 to John the Cubiculary on love,* PG91, 400C–401B.

261 [*Ascesis* is a spiritual struggle, an exercise in self-discipline. —Ed.]

262 Freudian psychoanalysis, using its own categories, emphasizes the deep roots of narcissism and how hard it is to overcome.

263 See my book *Variations sur la charité,* Cerf, Paris 2007.

264 See my book, *The Therapy of Spiritual Illnesses,* volume 1, Alexander Press, Montreal, 2012.

265 *Stromates,* III, 13.

266 The word πορνεία literally means prostitution; but the Greek Fathers grouped under this term all kinds of sexual passion. The word "lust" seems the best word to translate this idea. We have described this passion and its evil effects in detail in our work, *The Therapy of Spiritual Illnesses,* volume 1, Alexander Press, Montreal, 2012.

267 Remember that for Christians, marriage is always between a man and a woman.

268 For this reason, the Orthodox Church recommends abstention from sex during the four annual fasts, and on the weekly days of fasting, Wednesdays and Fridays, when the sufferings and crucifixion of Christ are remembered. Following the Apostle, St Gregory the Theologian teaches: "They should abstain with mutual consent to practice prayer, that most precious of works." He goes on: "It is not a law, but advice" (*Discourse* XL, 18). This shows how the Orthodox Tradition is not judicial in this respect. It places on the spouses the responsibility for examining their consciences to see what would be best for them spiritually. The same spirit is found in the teaching of St John Chrysostom (see, for instance, *Homilies on 1 Corinthians*, XIX, 2).

269 *The life of Moses* II, 289. Cf. *Treatise on virginity* VII, 2.

270 Cf. *ibid.* St Maximus the Confessor, *Centuries on love.* II, 17.

271 Cf. St Gregory of Nyssa, *Treatise on virginity* VII, 2.

272 *Conferences*, XII, 10.

273 *Treatise on virginity*, 38.

274 Cf. Clement of Alexandria, *Stromates*, III, 6.

275 *Treatise on virginity*, VII, 3.

276 *Ibid.*, VIII.

277 *Discourse* XXXVII, 9.

278 Cf. St Gregory of Nyssa *Treatise on virginity*, VIII.

279 *Ibid.*

280 *Ibid.*

281 *Ibid.*, IX, 1.

282 CF. St Basil of Caesarea, *Letters*, II. John Climacus, *The Ladder*, XV, 3.

283 *Conferences*, XII, 11.

284 Cf. Evagrios, *Practical treatise*, 89.

285 *The Ladder*, XV, 3.

286 *Ibid.*, 4.

287 *Ibid.*, 7.

288 *Ibid.*, 58.

289 Gregory the Great, *Morals on Job*, X, 6; Symeon the New Theologian, *Catechisms*, I, 60–62.

290 Cf. John Chrysostom, *Homily on perfect love*, 1; John of Gaza, *Letters*, 339.

291 Cf. Gregory the Great, *Morals on Job*, X, 6.

292 Cf. Dorotheos of Gaza, *Spiritual instructions*, III, 44; Maximus the Confessor, *Centuries on charity*, I, 41.

293 Cf. 1 Cor 13:4; Maximus the Confessor, *Centuries on charity,* I, 55.

294 John of Gaza, *Letters,* 342.

295 Cf. 1 Cor 13:5; Maximus the Confessor, *Centuries on charity,* I, 42; 57.

296 Cf. 1 Cor 13:6; Maximus the Confessor *Loc. Cit.,* I, 56.

297 Cf. Maximus the Confessor, *Loc. Cit.*

298 *Ibid.,* 55.

299 Cf. Maximus the Confessor, *Centuries on charity,* I, 26. Macarios of Egypt *Homilies* (Coll. II) XL, 6.

300 Cf. Maximus the Confessor, *Centuries on charity,* I, 26.

301 Cf. Matt 5:44.

302 Cf. John Chrysostom, *Homily on perfect charity,* 1; John Climacus, *The Ladder,* VI, 52; John of Gaza, *Letters,* 339.

303 Cf. John of Gaza, *Letters,* 339.

304 *Treatise on prayer.*

305 *Letters,* IV, 9.

306 *Centuries on charity* I, 71.

307 *Letters,* 2.

308 *Centuries on charity* II, 30.

309 *Commentary on Psalm 9,* 8.

310 *Variations sur la charité,* Cerf, Paris, 2007. *The therapy of spiritual illnesses,* volume 3, Alexander Press, Montreal, 2012 pp. 173–182.

311 See *Apothegms,* Arm II, 365 (33). Evagrios, *Practical treatise,* Prologue, 8; 81. John Climacus, *The Ladder,* XXX, 8–9. Diadocus of Photicé, *One hundred gnostic chapters,* 16. Maximus the Confessor, *Centuries on charity,* I, 2. Cf. II, 30; IV, 91. Nicetas Stethatos, *Centuries,* II, 1.

312 Cf. Maxime le Confesseur, *Centuries on charity,* II, 30; IV, 37. Isaac the Syrian, *Ascetical homilies,* 81.

313 Cf. Maximus the Confessor, *Centuries on charity* II, 9.

314 *Ibid.,* IV, 92.

Chapter 11

315 Note that all illegitimate unions are condemned, but not polygamy, provided it consists of several legitimate unions between man and woman.

316 Note that in these last two passages only the case of the husband who repudiates his wife is discussed. This was the general rule in the societies of Antiquity. In the earlier passage from St Mark the wife who repudiates her husband is also mentioned in parallel.

317 On this point see my work: "Amour conjugal et charité," dans *Variations sur la charité*, Cerf, Paris, 2007, pp. 107–129.

318 Elsewhere, the Church is defined by St Paul as the Body of Christ (1 Cor 12: 12–27).

319 The blessed person refers to David. (2 Kgs 2:26 LXX [2 Sam 1:26]).

320 The closest friend is Jonathan. See note 319.

321 *Commentary on the epistle to the Ephesians,* XX. 1.

322 See the prayer of St Ephraim the Syrian repeated many times throughout Great Lent: "O Lord and Master of my life, take from me the spirit .... of lust for power ... ."

323 *Commentary on the epistle to the Ephesians,* XX. 1.

324 *Commentary on the first epistle to the Corinthians,* XIX. 1. The emphasis is ours.

325 *Treatise on virginity,* 38.

326 See for example Cf. Clement of Alexandria *Le Pédagogue,* II, X, 83, 1; 92, 2; *Stromates,* II, 143, 3; 144; III, 72, 1. Tertullian *To his wife,* 2. Basil of Ankyra, *Treatise on virginity,* 38. Dorotheos of Gaza, *Spiritual instructions,* XV, 162. John Chrysostom, *Commentary on St Matthew,* XVII, 1; *Homilies on marriage,* I, 3; *Treatise on virginity,* 19. Augustine of Hippo, *The good of marriage,* 19; 22; 32. Isaac the Syrian, *Ascetical homilies,* 27. Maximus the Confessor, *Centuries on charity,* II, 17. See my work *Pour une éthique de la procréation. Éléments d'anthropologie patristique,* Editions du Cerf, Paris, 1998, pp. 32–45.

327 The question of sterility and sexuality in sterile couples is discussed in my work, *Pour une éthique de la procréation,* Cerf, Paris 1998, pp. 13–30. To support the idea that childbearing is not the sole end of marriage one may quote St Augustine: "Let us ask ourselves why marriage is good. It seems to me that childbearing is not the only reason. There is also the solidarity which nature seals between the two sexes. Without this, we could not say that old folks were married, especially if the children had died or if they had remained childless. Spouses burdened with many years find that though the fires of youth are quenched yet love still shines out in their hearts" (*The good of Marriage,* 3).

328 See Tertullian, *The veil of the virgins.* Gregory of Nyssa, *Treatise on virginity.* Methodios of Olympos, *The banquet of the ten virgins.* Basil of Ankyra, *Of true integrity in virginity.* John Chrysostom, *On virginity.* Jerome, *Letter 22, to Eustochium.* Ambrose of Milan, *Of virgins; of virginity; on the instruction of a virgin.* Augustine, *Of holy virginity.*

329 See, amongst others, John Chrysostom, *Treatise on virginity* 38; 53; 56–58; 56; *Exhortations to Theodore,* II, 5. Note that St Ambrose sees in virginity a way for

a woman to escape from the domination of a man: "The wife must submit to the domination of a man, but not the virgin" (*Des veuves*, 81).

330 See France Quéré (née Jaulmes), "Le mariage dans l'Eglise ancienne," dans *Le mariage dans l'Église ancienne*, Le Centurion et Grasset, Paris, 1969, p. 18.

331 The Encratites, the Gnostics, the Montanists and the Priscillianists. The Council of Gangres, in 340, condemned their hostility to marriage in Canons 1, 4, 9 and 10.

332 See, for example, Gregory of Nyssa, *Treatise on virginity*, VII. St Gregory the Theologian, *Discourses*, XXXVII, 9. John Chrysostom, *Treatise on virginity*, 8; 9; 10; 25; *Homilies on Hosea*, III, 3; *Homilies on Genesis*, XXI, 4; *Homilies on marriage*, I, 2; *Homilies on Priscilla and Aquila*, I, 3.

333 See John Chrysostom, *Commentary on the epistle to the Ephesians*, XX, 9: "… such a marriage [where the two spouses lead a common spiritual life] is hardly inferior to monastic life." P. Maraval writes of the position of St Basil of Caesarea: "Many have noticed that St Basil of Caesarea did not practice an exclusively monastic asceticism. He presents the ideal of the Christian life to all who have been baptized, with monastic life being its most perfect expression" (Introduction à Grégoire de Nysse, *Vie de sainte Macrine*, SC 178, p. 91).

334 See, for example, Tertullian *To his wife*, 3; John Chrysostom, *Treatise on virginity*. 11.13; Athanasius of Alexandria *Letter to the Monk Ammoun*, PG 25, 1173: ("There are two paths in life, one easier and common, the other superior and worthy of the angels: virginity. If the common life is chosen, marriage, no blame is incurred, but less grace is received."); John of Damascus, *An exact exposition of the Orthodox Faith*. IV, 24 ("Virginity is better than what is good, for there are degrees in virtue, higher or lower").

335 St John Chrysostom writes that the only reproach one can make to marriage is that it is restricted to more modest aims than virginity (Treatise *on Virginity*, 10). St John of Damascus says: "Marriage is good, … but better is virginity which enriches the fertility of the soul." *An exact exposition of the Orthodox Faith*. IV, 24. However, St Gregory of Nyssa in his treatise praising virginity considers it as a path which should be followed by those who cannot assume married life with the measure and virtues required. See especially *Treatise on virginity* VIII and the work of Mark D. Hart: *Marriage, celibacy and the life of virtue: An interpretation of Gregory of Nyssa's "De Virginitate."* Dissertation Boston College, 1987. "Reconciliation of Body and Soul: Gregory of Nyssa's Deeper Theology of Marriage," *Theological Studies*, 51, 1990, pp. 450–478; "Gregory of Nyssa's ironic praise of the celibate life," *Heythrop Journal*, 33, 1992, pp. 1–19.

Valerie A. Karras sees this in a slightly different light to Hart ("A re-evaluation of marriage, celibacy, and irony in Gregory of Nyssa's *On virginity*," *Journal of Early Christian Studies*, 13–1, 2005, pp. 111–121).

336 *Homilies on the epistle to the Ephesians*, XX, 6.

337 According to Clement of Alexandria and some other interpreters Philip the deacon is the same person as Philip the Apostle.

338 *To his wife* II, 9.

339 *Le Pédagogue*, I, IV, 1–3, SC 70, p. 128.

340 St Ephraim the Syrian calls it the spirit of domination, or lust for power.

Chapter 12

341 See St John Chrysostom, *Commentary on the first epistle to Timothy*, XI, 1.

342 See John Chrysostom, *Commentary on the first epistle to Timothy*, IX, 1–2. Cf. Tim. 2:13.

343 See John Chrysostom, *Consolations to Stagirios*, 1, 2, referring to 1 Cor. 2:9.

344 See Diodoros of Tarsus, *Fragments on Genesis*, PG 33, 1564D. The author refers to 1 Cor 11:7. See also Augustine, *On the Trinity* XII, 10. For a wider study of this theme see Hervé Legrand, "Les femmes sont-elles a l'image de Dieu de la même manière que les hommes?," *Nouvelle revue théologique*, 128, 2006, pp. 214–239.

345 See Tertullian, *The adornment of women*. I, 1, 2. Ambrose of Milan, *On Paradise*, IV, 24. St Paul says the same: "And Adam was not deceived, but the woman being deceived, fell into transgression" (I Tim. 2:14).

346 See Tertullian, *The adornment of women*, I, 1, 2. John Chrysostom, *Discourse on Genesis*, IV 1. Ambrose of Milan, *On Paradise*, IV, 24; XII, 56.

347 See Tertullian, *The adornment of women*, I, 1, 2. Jerome, *Commentary on Ecclesiastes*, VII, 26.

348 See Tertullian, *The adornment of women*, I, 1, 2. John Chrysostom, *Discourse on Genesis*, IV, 1.

349 John Chrysostom, *Discourse on Genesis*, IV, 1.

350 John Chrysostom, *Discourse on Genesis*, IV, 1.

351 See Tertullian, *The adornment of women*, II, 2.

352 See Tertullian, *The adornment of women*, II, 2.

353 See John Chrysostom, *Treatise on illicit cohabitation*, II, 6.

354 See Tertullian, *The adornment of women*, II, 2.

355 See Ambrose of Milan, *On Paradise* II, 11. AUGUSTINE, *On Genesis, against the Manichaeans*, II, 11, 15.

356 See Epiphanios of Salamis, *Panarion*, VII, 79, 1, 6.
357 See Cyril of Alexandria, *On the Gospel of John*, 2, 4, 16, PG 73, 301.
358 Ibid.
359 See Origen, *Fragments on the first epistle to the Corinthians*, 74.
360 See Epiphanios of Salamis, *Panarion*, VII, 79, 1, 6.
361 See Isidore of Seville, Étymologies, XI, 2, 17–19.
362 Ibid.
363 See John Chrysostom, *Commentary on the epistle to the Ephesians*, XX, 1.
364 See John Chrysostom, *Commentary on the epistle to the Ephesians*, XX, 6.
365 This argument is raised several times by John Chrysostom, as in his *Commentary on the epistle to the Ephesians* XX, 1, 4, 5. He writes: "If God gave authority to one and ordained submission for the other, it is that peace may reign. It is vain to seek peace where equality holds sway, for either there is no master of the family, or all are masters" (*ibid.*, 5). See also Augustin, *On Genesis, against the Manichaeans* II, 11, 15.
366 See Irenaeus of Lyon, *Fragmenta varia*, XXXI, ed. W. W. Harvey, *Sancti Irenaei episcopi Libros quinque adversus haereses*, vol. 2, Cambridge, 1857, p. 495: "Nature and law make woman subordinate to man."
367 See John Chrysostom, *Letters* 170, "It is accepted that the woman remains at home whilst the man takes care of the interests of the city"; *Treatise on illicit cohabitation*, II, 4.
368 See John Chrysostom, *Commentary on the first epistle to the Corinthians*, XXVI, 5.
369 See John Chrysostom, *Commentary on the epistle to Titus*, VI, 4; *Homilies on marriage*, III, 4; *Treatise on illicit cohabitation*, II, 5.
370 For example, this formula, attributed to Simons de Beauvoir: "Amongst all the wild beasts, there is none as harmful as woman." Some anthologies also attribute it to St John Chrysostom, even though it is not to be found in his writings. There is also the phrase, attributed inexactly to Tertullian: "Woman is a temple built over a cesspool."
371 See Rosine Lambin, "Paul et le voile des femmes," *Clio. Femme, Genre, Histoire*, 2, 1995, pp. 61–84. Marie de Merode, "Une théologie primitive de la femme?," *Revue théologique de Louvain*, 9, 1978, p. 177. Sophie Malick, "Le corps féminin et ses représentations poétiques dans la latinité tardive," Dissertation, Université de Paris IV—Sorbonne, 2008, p. 124.
372 This difference is clearly stated in the work of Hervé Legrand, "Les femmes sont-elles à l'image de Dieu de la même manière que les hommes?," *Nouvelle revue théologique*, 128, 2006, pp. 214–239.

373 See, amongst others: Nicholas D. Smith, "Plato and Aristotle on the nature of women," *Journal of the History of Philosophy*, 21, 1983, pp. 467–478. Dana Jalbert Stauffer, "Aristotle's account of the subjection of women," *The Journal of Politics*, 70, 2008, pp. 929–941. Diagne Ramatoulaye, "Philosophie et représentation de la femme: la longévité du modèle aristotélicien," in: Fatou Sow (ed.), *La recherche féministe francophone. Langue, identités et enjeux*, Karthala, Paris, 2009, pp. 101–107. Jean-Baptiste Bonnar, Lillian E. Doherty et Violaine Sebillotte Cuchet, "Male and female bodies according to ancient Greek physicians," *Clio. Women, Gender, History*, 37, 2013, pp. 19–37. Katherine Helen Barker, "The perception of women in late antiquity and the impact it had on female asceticism," Dissertation, University of Wales Trinity Saint David, 2014. Hannelie Wood, "Feminists and their perspectives on the Church Fathers' beliefs regarding Women: An inquiry," *Verbum et Ecclesia*, 38, 2017, pp. 2–3. Alain Galonnier, "Stercoris saccus: la représentation de la femme comme corps adjuvant et transgressif dans la pensée chrétienne à la basse Antiquité et au Moyen Age," *HAL Archives ouvertes*, 2018 (en ligne), pp. 5–7.

374 See Jean-Marie Van Gangh, "La femme dans l'Evangile de Luc. Comparaison des passages narratifs propres à Luc avec la situation de la femme dans le judaïsme," *Revue théologique de Louvain*, 24, 1993, pp. 299–306. Berthe Rantz, "Aperçu sur la situation de la femme à Rome," *Les études classiques*, 56, 1988, pp. 285–293. Chantal Reynier, *Les femmes de saint Paul*, Cerf, 2021. Rosine Lambin, "Paul et le voile des femmes," *Clio. Femme, Genre, Histoire*, 2, 1995, pp. 61–84.

375 See France Quéré, *La femme et les Pères de l'Église*, Desclée de Brouwer, Paris, 1997, pp. 49–50.

376 On the status of woman throughout history, see Georges Duby et Michelle Perrot (dir.), *Histoire des femmes en Occident*, 5 volumes, Perrin, Paris, 1992; Michelle Perrot, *Mon histoire des femmes*, Seuil, Paris, 2008.

377 See France Quéré-Jaulmes, "Le mariage dans l'Eglise ancienne," dans *Le mariage dans l'Église ancienne*, Le Centurion et Grasset, Paris, 1969, pp. 38–39. Alain Galonnier, "Stercoris saccus: la représentation de la femme comme corps adjuvant et transgressif dans la pensée chrétienne a la basse Antiquité et au Moyen Age," *HAL Archives ouvertes*, 2018 (en ligne), pp. 2–24. Graham Gould, "Women in the Writings of the Fathers: Language, Belief, and Reality," *Studies in Church History*, 27, 1990, pp. 1–13. Claude Rambaux, "Le jugement de Tertullien sur les femmes," *Vita Latina*, 122, 1991, pp. 2–20.

378 See Angeline Rais, "Le regard de Paul de Tarse sur les femmes," Expose au séminaire de sciences bibliques du Prof. Martin Rose, Université de Neuchâtel,

aout 2009. See also the excellent analysis of France Quéré, "Codes et mentalités des sociétés antiques," *Croire aujourd'hui*, Octobre 1980, repris dans ID., *La femme et les Pères de l'Église*, Desclée de Brouwer, Paris, 1997, pp. 37–46.

379 It should be added that for the Christians of the early centuries, the end of the world was imminent.

380 France Quéré writes on this subject: "The Fathers started no revolution in society as we understand the term nowadays. They did not cast deep doubt on things as do the teachings of modern nihilism. These belong to modern politics, unknown in Antiquity, at least in a systematic way. What they sought was conversion. They did not seek to change customs but mankind's relationship to them. They aimed to bring perfection to the conduct of life." (*La femme et les Pères de l'Église*, Desclée de Brouwer, Paris, 1997, p. 66.)

381 *Thérapeutique des maladies spirituelles*, 6e ed., Cerf, Paris, 2013, pp. 277–284. *Maxime le Confesseur, médiateur entre l'Orient et l'Occident*, 2e ed., Cerf, Paris, 2017, chapitre 2: "La question de l'hérédité adamique," pp. 79–126. See also Rom 5, 12.14–15. [English translation: *Therapy of Spiritual Illness* (Alexander Press: Montreal) 2012.]

382 The parallel between the two Adams was especially developed by Cyril of Alexandria. See *Thérapeutique des maladies spirituelles*, 6e ed., Cerf, Paris, 2013, pp. 277–284. *Maxime le Confesseur, médiateur entre l'Orient et l'Occident*, 2e ed., Cerf, Paris, 2017, chapitre 2: "La question de l'hérédité adamique," pp. 79–126. See also Rom 5, 12.14–15.

383 She who brought forth God in the flesh.

384 The parallel between Eve and the new Eve is taught, for example by St Irenaeus of Lyon: *Contre les hérésies*, III, 22, 4, SC 211, pp. 438–444.

385 *Homilies*, 5, PG 65, 720B.

386 *Discourses on Genesis* IV, 1.

387 *Commentary on the epistle to the Ephesians.* XX, 3.

388 *Ibid.* 4.

389 *Discours*, XXXVII, 6–7, SC 318, pp. 284–286.

390 *Thérapeutique des maladies helléniques*, V, 56–57, SC 57, pp. 244–245.

391 *Commentary on the epistle to the Ephesians.* XX, 1.

392 *Homily 5 on Matthew*, 19:3.

393 *Commentary on the epistle to the Ephesians.* XX, 4.

394 *Commentary on the first epistle to the Corinthians*, XXVI, 5.

395 *On the Trinity*, XII. 12.

396 *Sur la Genèse*, 62, SC 233, p. 158.

397 *Le Pédagogue*, I, IV, 1–3, SC 70, p. 128.

398 *Homily 1 on Psalm 1*, 3, PG29, 216D–217A. Note that this position differs from that of Plato, who, in *Timaeos*, affirms that woman is morally inferior to man. (*Timée*, 42, collections des Universités de France, p. 158.)

399 *Homélies sur l'origine de l'homme*, I, 18, SC 160, pp. 212–215.

400 *Discourses*, XVIII, 7.

401 *Homily on the martyrdom of Julitte*, PG 37, 240D–241A.

402 See Gregoire Nazianzus, *Discours*, XXXVII, 6–7, SC 318, pp. 282–284, quoted above.

403 *Discours*, XXXVII, 6.

404 *Homilies*, XCIX.

405 From the Greek, *ethos*, which means way of life.

406 *La femme et les Pères de l'Église*, Desclée de Brouwer, Paris, 2005, pp. 117–118.

407 In other words, males.

408 Grégoire de Nazinaze, *Discours*, XXXVII, 6–7, SC 318, pp. 282–286.

409 Canon 9.

410 *Letters* LXXVII, 3.

411 See Angeliki E. Laiou, "Sex, consent and coercion in Byzantium," dans ID., (ed.), *Consent and coercion to sex and marriage in ancient and medieval societies*, Dumbarton Oaks, Washington D. C., 1993, pp. 109–221.

412 St John Chrysostom writes to the husband in this way: "Should you die for your wife? Do not hesitate. If the Lord loved His servant to the point of sacrifice, even more should you show the same love to your companion in slavery" (*Homilies on marriage*, III, 2).

413 The Greek word *kenosis* is the act of emptying. It refers here to Christ voluntarily humbling himself regarding His incarnation. He is fully God and at the same time fully man.

414 *Commentary on the first epistle to the Corinthians*, XIX, 1.

415 *Homilies on marriage*, I, 3.

416 John Chrysostom, *Homilies on the epistle to the Ephesians*, XX, 9.

417 *La femme et les Pères de l'Église*, Desclée de Brouwer, Paris, 2005, p. 90.

418 *Discourses* XVIII, 7.

419 *On the virtue of marriage*, 3.

420 The Fathers of old, just as those of our day, link mother and father closely in the raising of children. St John Chrysostom, *Sur la vaine gloire et comment les parents doivent élever leurs enfants*, "Sources chrétiennes" n° 188, Cerf, Paris, 1972; J. C. Larchet, "Le rôle de l'amour dans l'éducation des enfants selon l'Ancien

Porphyre," dans Id., *Variations sur la charité*, Cerf, Paris, 2007. Sister Magdalen, *Reflections on children in the Orthodox Church today,* Stavropegical Monastery of St John the Baptist, Tolleshunt Knights, 2020.

421 *Letters,* CLX, 4.

422 *Homilies,* I, 17–18, PG 30, 25–28; II, 2, PG 30, 44.

423 *The demonstration of the Gospel,* I, 9, PG 22, 77–81.

424 See, for example, Basil of Ankyra, *Of the true integrity of virginity,* 54–55; John Chrysostom *Treatise on virginity,* 19.

425 Ibid., "When the world was covered on all sides by its own fruits, and the Earth was sown with a multitude of men so numerous that there was no more space for the arrival of future generations."

426 Cf. Éveline Patlagean, "Sur la limitation de la fécondité dans la haute époque byzantine," *Annales ESC,* 24, 1969, pp. 1356–1357. Th. Camelot, "Les Traités "De Virginitate" au ive siècle," dans *Mystique et continence,* Études carmélitaines, 13, 1952, p. 279.

427 As Éveline Patlagean, writes: "The praise of the large family as such is nowhere to be found in the preaching. . . . On the contrary, the idea of descendance is kept to a minimum" (op. cit. p. 1366). Having two children was considered the optimum (see *ibid.,* p. 1358). It is significant that the first Christian Emperor, Constantine, repealed the laws of Augustus which punished the lack of children.

428 Cf. Pierre Thomas Camelot, *op.cit.* pp. 273–292.

429 See Derwas Chitty, *The Desert a City,* St Vladimir's Seminary Press, Crestwood, 2020.

430 John T. Noonan, *Contraception: A history of its treatment by Catholic theologians and canonists,* 2nd ed., Cambridge, 1986, pp. 83–84.

431 Cf. *Homilies on marriage,* 1,3; *Treatise on Virginity,* 19.

432 Cf. *Treatise on Virginity* 15; 16; 19.

433 Cf. *ibid.,* 13–14.

434 Cf. *Homilies on marriage,* I, 3. *Treatise on Virginity* 19.

435 *Homilies on marriage,* I, 3.

436 Cf. *Homilies on marriage,* I, 3: "If you wish to have children, there are better ways, far more desirable which only depend on you as father, now that there are spiritual conceptions and childbearing of a higher order."

437 Cf. *Homilies on marriage,* I, 3. *Treatise on virginity* 15.

438 *Homilies on marriage,* I, 3, repeated in *Treatise on virginity* 15.

439 See *Le Pédagogue,* II, X, 96–97.

440 *Poems*, II, II, 6.

441 See our work *La vie liturgique*, Cerf, Paris, 2016, chap. 3: "Les périodes de jeune et d'abstinence," pp. 111–151.

442 As an aside to the thoughts expressed in this section it is worth noting that in Epirus during the XIII century the mean number of children per family was 1.6. Some families had 7 children, but most of them had just one. This is quite at odds with the idea that the ideal for Christian families is to have many children. See Angeliki Laiou, "Contribution a l'étude de l'institution familiale en Epire au XIIIe siècle," *Fontes Minores* (*Forschungen zur byzantinischen Rechtsgeschichte*), 6, 1984, p. 281.

443 *Of widows*, XVII, 81.

444 *Exhortation to virginity*, 21 and 24.

445 *Données à Dieu. Figures féminines dans les premiers siècles chrétiens*, Ed. de Bellefontaine, Begrolles-en-Mauges, 2001, p. 249.

446 This is denounced many times by Clement of Alexandria.

447 France Quéré remarks that chastity, along with the indissolubility of marriage, are the two rules promoted by the Fathers to protect woman from the constant abuse of men (*La femme et les Pères de l'Église*, Desclée de Brouwer, Paris, 2005, p. 83).

448 See John Chrysostom, *Homilies on the first epistle to Timothy*, IX, 2. See also St Gregory the Theologian who wrote these fine words of his sister Gorgonia: "The fruit of her body, that is her children and grandchildren, she transformed to become fruits of the spirit" (*Discourses*, VIII, 8).

449 These are abortions for which there is no pressing reason, such as a medical reason. See our work: *Pour une éthique de la procréation. Éléments d'anthropologie patristique*, Cerf, Paris, 1998, chap. 3: "L'avortement," where we present the Orthodox position which is more subtle in this respect than the Catholic position.

450 For more details see our work *Pour une éthique de la procréation. Éléments d'anthropologie patristique*, Cerf, Paris, 1998, pp. 31–64.

451 Another form of radical feminism has recently appeared which values maternity while continuing to exclude men from conception, from accompanying gestation and from education. It has become possible thanks to methods of medically assisted procreation which were originally developed as a therapy for sterile couples which militant feminists have managed to have enshrined in common law as a way of procreation for single women and lesbians. This abuse of medicine to promote maternity with no father has the evil effect of

depriving the child of the normal conditions for psychological development. It also betrays its own egotistical idea of existence, so careless for the well-being and growth of the child. It has received much criticism which is easy to find.

452 *La femme et les Pères de l'Église,* Desclée de Brouwer, Paris, 2005, p. 38.

453 France Quéré writes: "That woman belongs to the private sphere is a basic fact. It is found in all Mediterranean societies and has such ancient roots that it is never seen as a 'problem', even by women" (*ibid.,* p. 40).

454 *Commentaries on St John,* LXI, 3.

455 This includes menservants and maidservants in well to do families.

456 "De l'annonce du royaume a l'Eglise. Rôles, ministères, pouvoirs des femmes," dans G. Duby and M. Perrot, *Histoire des femmes,* t. 1, Plon, Paris, 1991, p. 470.

457 See Jean Delumeau (dir.), *La religion de ma mère. Le rôle des femmes dans la transmission de la foi,* Cerf, Paris, 1992.

458 *Commentary on St John,* LXI, 3.

459 *La femme et les Pères de l'Église,* Desclée de Brouwer, Paris, 2005, p. 67.

460 *Vie de sainte Macrine,* 7 et 11, SC 178, p. 164 et 174–180.

461 *Homilies on the epistle to the Ephesians,* XX, 6.

462 *Letter,* 170.

463 As indicated in the following paragraph John Chrysostom has in mind: "the deserts of Egypt, which shine with an infinity of monasteries and holy houses."

464 *Commentary on St Matthew,* VIII, 4.

465 *Commentary on St John,* LXI, 3.

466 *Commentary on St John,* LXI, 3–4.

467 *Discourses,* XVIII, 8.

468 *La femme et les Pères de l'Église,* Desclée de Brouwer, Paris, 2005, p. 66.

469 See André Dumas, Introduction à *Le mariage dans l'Église ancienne,* Le Centurion et Grasset, Paris, 1969, pp. 10–17; France Quéré-Jaulmes, "Le mariage dans l'Église ancienne," in *Le mariage dans l'Église ancienne,* Le Centurion et Grasset, Paris, 1969, p. 18.

470 See Régine Pernoud, *Pour en finir avec le Moyen Âge,* Seuil, Paris, 1977, pp. 86–100.

471 Cf. P. Brown, *Le renoncement à la chair, op. cit.* p. 338.

472 *Ibid.,* p. 196.

473 See Monique Alexandre, "De l'annonce du Royaume à l'Église. Rôles, ministères, pouvoirs des femmes," dans G. Duby and M. Perrot (dir.), *Histoire des femmes en Occident,* t. 1, Plon, Paris, pp. 439–471.

474 "Le corps féminin et ses représentations poétiques dans la latinité tardive," Dissertation, Université de Paris IV—Sorbonne, 2008, p. 165.

475 Descriptions of women who were eminent as martyrs, ascetics, deaconesses, teachers, patrons, theologians, or political leaders during the first centuries can be found in the works of Mariella Carpinello, *Données à Dieu. Figures féminines dans les premiers siècles chrétiens,* Bellefontaine, Bégrolles-en-Mauges, 2001. Patricia Cox Miller, *Women in early Christianity,* The Catholic University of America, Washington, 2005. Lynn H. Cohick and Amy Brown Hughes, *Christian women in the patristic world,* Baker Academic, Grand Rapids, 2017.

476 See Elisabeth Schüssler Forenza, *In memory of her: A feminist theological reconstruction of Christian origins, he Crossroad Publishing Company,* New York, 1994; trad. fr. *En mémoire d'elle. Essai de reconstruction des origines chrétiennes selon la théologie féministe,* "Cogitatio fidei" n° 136, Cerf, Paris, 1986. Jean-Marie Van Cangh, "La femme dans l'Évangile de Luc. Comparaison des passages narratifs propres à Luc avec la situation de la femme dans le judaïsme," *théologique de Louvain,* 24, 1993, pp. 306–324.

477 Cf. John 4:9: "Then the woman of Samaria said to Him, "How is it that You, being a Jew, ask a drink from me, a Samaritan woman?" For Jews have no dealings with Samaritans.

478 As I explain in my book livre *L'Église, corps du Christ, tome 1, Nature et structure,* Cerf, Paris, 2012, pp. 186–201, the bishop and his delegate, the priest, are icons of Christ during the liturgy so they must be of the masculine sex because that was the sex of Christ. It is for this symbolic reason and not because of sexist discrimination that women cannot exercise the priestly role.

479 France Quéré writes: "In Matthew 10, Jesus explains their mission to His disciples, a completely outward-looking mission. It involves travel from town to town, brief stays with unknown hosts with all the risks attached to such adventurous endeavors. Christ respected the taboo. If He had broken it, it is likely that the mission of women would have been impossible. Society could not have imagined such a thing or accepted it, and still less would have tolerated it in practice" (*La femme et les Pères de l'Église,* Desclée de Brouwer, Paris, 1997, pp. 41–42).

480 France Quéré, *Les femmes de l'Évangile,* Seuil, Paris, 1982. Monique Alexandre, "De l'annonce du Royaume l'Église. Rôles, ministères, et pouvoirs des femmes," dans G. Duby et M. Perrot, *Histoire des femmes en Occident,* tome 1, Plon, Paris, 1990, pp. 439–471. Pierre Mourlon Beernaert, *Marthe, Marie et les autres,* Lumen Vitae, Bruxelles, 1992.

481 As shown in the works of Chantal Reynier, *Les femmes de saint Paul*, Cerf, 2021 et Michel Quesnel, *Paul et les femmes. Ce qu'il a écrit, ce qu'on lui a fait dire*, Mediaspaul, Paris, 2021.

482 Like Priscilla, mentioned in Rom 16:3.

483 Like Junia, mentioned in Rom 16:7.

484 Like Phoebe mentioned in Rom 16:1.

485 This was what Priscilla did when, with her husband Aquila she catechized the newly converted Apollos (Acts 18:26).

486 Such a one was Lydia, mentioned in Acts 16:15, as was Nympha, mentioned in Col 4:15 and Priscilla with her husband Aquila (1 Cor 16:19).

487 *Actes de Paul*, III–IV, in F. Bovon et P. Geoltrain (éd.), Écrits apocryphes chrétiens, tome 1, Gallimard, Paris, 1997, pp. 1131–1142.

488 See *Lettre des Églises d Lyon et de Vienne aux Églises d'Asie et de Phrygie*, in P. Maraval (ed.), *Actes et passions des martyrs chrétiens*, 17–55, Cerf, Paris, 2010, pp. 74–85. This account is partially reproduced in Eusebios of Caesarea, *Ecclesiastical History*, V, I, 17–19, 37, 41–42, 53–56.

489 *Passion de Perpétue et Félicité*, dans P. Maraval (ed.), *Actes et passions des martyrs chrétiens*, Cerf, Paris, 2010, pp. 117–144.

490 Amongst the early sources see Ambrose of Milan, *Of the Virgins*, 1, 2, 5–9; *Hymns* 8.

491 See Basil of Caesarea, *Panegyric of St Julitte, martyr*, PG 31, col. 237–251.

492 Quoted by St John Chrysostom, *To a young widow*, 2.

493 Found under their names in the alphabetical collection.

494 In chapter 41, he mentions Paula of Rome, her daughter Eustochium, Vebernia, Theodora, Hosia, Adolia, Basianilla, Photina, Sabiniana, and Asella; in chapter 34, a fool for Christ, a great ascetic; in chapter 57, the blessed Candida and her daughter Gelasia; in chapter 59, Amma Talis and her disciple, Taor. In Chapter 61, he praises the ascetic qualities of Melania the younger and her mother, Albina. [An English edition: Palladius of Aspuna, The Lausiac History (trans. John Wortley, Cistercian Publications: Kalamazoo, MI, 2015).]

495 Gregory of Nyssa, *Vie de sainte Macrine*, SC 178, Cerf, Paris, 1971.

496 *Vie de sainte Synclétique*, Éd. de Bellefontaine, Bégroles-en-Mauges, 1972.

497 Arnaud d'Andilly, *Les vies des saints Péres des désert et de quelques saintes écrites par des Péres de l'Église et autres anciens auteurs ecclésiastiques grecs et latins* (Paris: Chez George & Louis Josse, 1736).

498 John Chrysostom, *Homily 30 on the epistle to the Romans*; Theodoret of Cyrus, *Commentary on the epistle to the Romans*, PG82, 217D, 220A.

499 Cf. *Didascalia*, 16; *Apostolic Constitutions*, III, 16, 2; VIII, 28, 6. Nowadays the anointing is usually restricted. But if the ancient ritual is used, as in Greece or on Mount Athos, the anointing of the chest, the back, the ears, the hands and the feet is followed by the anointing of the whole body like the wrestlers of Antiquity. This is a sign that the newly baptized will have to struggle spiritually throughout this earthly life against the spirits of evil and will receive strength for the fight from baptism.

500 Cf. *Didascalia*, 16.

501 Cf. *ibid.*

502 Cf. E. Theodorou, Ἡ "χειροτονία" ἤ "χειροθεσία" τῶν διακονισσῶν, Athens, 1954, pp. 91–92.

503 Cf. *Apostolic Constitutions*, III, 16, 1.

504 Cf. *ibid.*, II, 57, 10; VIII, 20, 1; 28, 6.

505 K. K. Fitzgerald, "The Nature and Characteristics of the Order of the Deaconess," in Thomas Hopko (ed.), *Women and Priesthood*, Crestwood, 1999, p. 102.

506 Cf. *Apostolic Constitutions*, VIII, 28, 6.

507 Cf. *ibid.*, II, 26, 6.

508 Cf. Canon 19. See also Mgr Hiéronymo Kotsonis, "A Contribution to the Interpretation of the 19th Canon of the First Ecumenical Council," *Revue des Études Byzantines*, 19, 1961, pp. 189–197.

509 Cf. Canon 15 de Chalcedon. The great protagonist of this idea is J. Karamis, Ἡ Θέσις καὶ ἡ Διακονία τῶν Γυναικῶν ἐν τῇ Ὀρθοδόξῳ Ἐκκλησίᾳ, Athens, 1978.

510 See E. Theodorou, Ἡ "χειροτονία" ἤ "χειροθεσία" τῶν διακονισσῶν, Athens, 1954; G. Trembelas, *Dogmatique de l'*Église catholique orthodoxe, vol. 3, Chevetogne, 1968, p. 309.

511 Cf. *Apostolic Constitutions*, VIII, 20, 1–2; G. Limouris (ed.), *The Place of the Woman in the Orthodox Church and the Question of the Ordination of Women*, Katerini, 1992, pp. 229–238.

512 See E. Theodorou, Ἡ "χειροτονία" ἤ "χειροθεσία" τῶν διακονισσῶν, Athens, 1954, p. 56, 60–63.

513 *Apostolic Constitutions*, VIII, 12, 42; 19.

514 Cf. *ibid.*, III, 16, 1.

515 Cf. E. Theodorou, Ἡ "χειροτονία" ἤ "χειροθεσία" τῶν διακονισσῶν, Athens, 1954, p. 36; J. Karimis, Ἡ Θέσις καὶ ἡ Διακονία τῶν Γυναικῶν ἐν τῇ Ὀρθοδόξῳ Ἐκκλησίᾳ, Athens, 1978, p. 50.

516 Cf. J. Davis, "Deacons, deaconesses and the minor orders in the patristic period," *Journal of Ecclesiastical History*, 14, 1969, pp. 1–12.

517 See, for the early centuries, Catherine Kroeger, "The neglected history of women in the early Church," *Christian History*, 17, 1988.

518 See Gregory of Nyssa, *Vie sainte Macrine*, SC 178, Paris, 1971, *passim*. In his introduction, Pierre Maravel writes: "Throughout the work Gregory presents her as a guide, a counsellor who teaches. . . . Macrina is presented as the teacher of her mother, of Basil [of Caesarea], of Gregory [of Nyssa], of Peter, of the virgins and the widows both in word and deed" (p. 102).

519 See Abbé Petit, *Histoire de sainteMonique, mère de saint Augustin*, 2e éd., Lefort, Lille, 1947.

520 The collection of the lives of the saints.

521 See the work of John Chryssavgis, *In the heart of the desert. The spirituality of the desert Fathers and Mothers*, World Wisdom Books, Bloomington (Indiana), 2005.

522 See *Apothegms*, alphabetical collection, Theodora.

523 See *Apothegms*, alphabetical collection, Sarra.

524 See *Apothegms*, alphabetical collection, Syncletica.

525 Respectively in PG 65, 1487–1558 and PG 28, 251–282, There is a French translation: *Vie de sainte Synclétique et Discours de salut à une vierge*, Bellefontaine, Bégroles-en-Mauges, 1972. For further details on Syncletica see, in addition to the introduction to this work, Mariella Carpinello, *Données à Dieu. Figures féminines dans les premiers siècles chrétiens*, Éd. de Bellefontaine, Bégroll-es-en-Mauges, 2001, chapitre 3, pp. 99–131.

526 *Lausaic History*, 56.

527 A French translation of the Life of St Mary of Egypt was published in 1644 by Arnaud d'Andilly. There is a recent re-edition of this work in *Vie de Sainte Marie Égyptienne pénitente*, Jérôme Million, Montbonnot-St Martin, 1985. Further information on St Mary of Egypt can be found in: Mariella Carpinello, *Vouées à Dieu. Figures féminines dans les premiers siècles chrétiens*, Éd. de Bellefontaine, Bégrolles-en-Mauges, 2001, chapitre 5, pp. 159–188.

528 There are several examples in the collection of Hieromonk Euthymios *Ascètes au milieu du monde*, Éditions des Syrtes, Geneva, 2021.

529 The monks and nuns lived in separate buildings in close proximity and participated together in the Liturgy. They were forbidden by Justinian in the VI century and by the 20th canon of the second Council of Nicea in 787, which nonetheless permitted them to persist under certain conditions, and they continued to exist. Examples in the XIII century are the monastery of Nea Moni in Ganos and another monastery also founded by the monk Anastasios. There

are also the monasteries of the Savior, lover of mankind and the Virgin full of Grace in Constantinople. They were restored by the Princess Irene, widow of the son of the Emperor Andronicus II. She was a spiritual daughter of St Theoleptus of Philadelphia and became a nun with the name Eulogia. Such a monastery still exists today in the Orthodox Church: The Monastery of St John the Baptist at Tolleshunt Knights in Great Britain, founded by St Sophrony (Sakharov).

530 See Jules Pargoire, "Les monastères doubles chez les Byzantins," *Revue des études byzantines*, 56, 1906, pp. 21–25.

531 See Régine Pernoud, *Pour en finir avec le Moyen Âge*, Seuil, Paris, 1977, p. 95.

532 See Gregory of Nyssa, *Life of St Macrina*, 7; 11.

533 See Palladius *Lausaic History*, 46, 54.

534 See Jerome *Letters*, CXXVII, 5.

535 See Gregory of Nyssa, *Life of St Macrina*, 12 and 26.

536 See Jerome *Letters*, LXXVII. Fernand Vicari, "Sainte Fabiola († 399). Patronne des infirmières et des femmes battues," *Hegel*, 1, 2014, pp. 112–113.

537 See Palladius *Lausaic History*, 54. For further details on St Melania the elder see Mariella Carpinello, *Vouées à Dieu. Figures féminines dans les premiers siècles chrétiens*, Éd. de Bellefontaine-en-Mauges, 2001, chapitre 9, pp. 301–339.

538 Palladius *Lausaic History*, 61.

539 *Vie de sainte Mélanie*, SC 90, Cerf, Paris, 1962.

540 *Vie anonyme d'Oympias*, 5–7, SC 13bis, Cerf, Paris, 1968, pp. 415–421.

541 *Ibid.*, 6, pp. 419–421. For further details of St Olympias, not found in her life, see Mariella Carpinello, *Vouées à Dieu. Figures féminines dans les premiers siècles chrétiens*, Éd. de Bellefontaine, Bégrolles-en-Mauges, 2001, chapitre 2, pp. 55–98.

542 *Lausaic History*, LXIV.

543 See *Homélies sur la Cantique es cantiques*, SC 613, Cerf, Paris, 2021, Prologue.

544 See Marie Turcan, "Saint Jérôme et les femmes," *Bulletin de l'Association Guillaume Budé*, 4e série, 2–3, 1968, pp. 259–272. Patrick Laurence, *Jérôme et le nouveau modèle féminin. La conversion à la vie parfaite*, Brepols, Turnhout, 1997.

545 *Letters*, 59. Subsequent passages give examples of the problems she raised.

546 Mariella Carpinello, *Vouées à Dieu. Figures féminines dans les premiers siècles chrétiens*, Bellefontaine, Bégrolles-en-Mauges, 2001, p. 225.

547 *Letters*, CXXVII, 7.

548 Jerome himself recognized that Marcella played a key role in the condemnation of the Origenists with her theology.

549 For more details of Marcella, see Mariella Carpinello, *Vouées à Dieu. Figures féminines dans les premiers siècles chrétiens*, Éd. de Bellefontaine, Bégrolles-en-Mauges, 2001, chapitre 7, pp. 209–246.

550 On Paula, apart from her life, see Mariella Carpinello, *op. ci.t*, chapitre 8, pp. 247–300.

551 See Palladius, *Lausaic History*, XLVI, 3–4 and 6.

552 *Vie de sainte Mélanie*, LIV, SC 90, pp. 233–235. On Melania the younger, see also Mariella Carpinello, *Vouées à Dieu. Figures féminines dans les premiers siècles chrétiens*, Éd. de Bellefontaine, Bégrolles-en-Mauges, 2001, pp. 305–339.

553 See Patrick Laurence, "Proba, Juliana et Démétrias. Le christianisme des femmes de la *gens Anicia* dans la première moitié du ve siècle," *Revue des Études Augustiniennes*, 48, 2002, pp. 131–163.

554 On the Theodosian Empresses see Kenneth G. Holum, *Theodosian Empresses: Women and Imperial Dominion in Late Antiquity*, University of California Press, Berkeley, 1989, chap. III, 5–6.

555 See Angeliki E. Laiou, "The role of women in Byzantine society," *Jahrbuch der österreichischen Byzantinitik*, 31, 1981, p. 251.

556 Ibid., pp. 253–257.

557 See Régine Pernoud, *La femme au temps des cathédrales*, Stock, Paris, 1980, pp. 71–75.

558 See Angeliki E. Laiou, "The role of women in Byzantine society," *Jahrbuch der österreichischen Byzantinitik*, 31, 1981, pp. 249–250.

559 For the West and the Middle Ages see Regine Pernoud, *La femme au temps des cathédrales*, Stock, Paris, 1980.

560 See Voir France Quéré, *La femme et les Pères de l'Église*, Desclée de Brouwer, Paris, 1997, p. 37. The Abbey of Fontevraud is an example; see Régine Pernoud, *La femme au temps des cathédrales*, Stock, Paris, 1980, pp. 131–132.

561 Acts 18: 2–3, "And he found a certain Jew named Aquila, born in Pontus, who had recently come from Italy with his wife Priscilla (because Claudius had commanded all the Jews to depart from Rome); and he came to them. So, because he was of the same trade, he stayed with them and worked; for by occupation they were tentmakers."

562 The opposite is also true.

563 For the Byzantine world see, Angeliki E. Laiou, "The role of women in Byzantine society," *Jahrbuch der Österreichischen Byzantinitik*, 31, 1981, pp. 241–249; and, for the Medieval West, Régine Pernoud, *La femme au temps des cathédrales*, Stock, Paris, 1980, pp. 193–196, 206–208.

564 An example is Hersent, the lady doctor whom the King, St Louis and his wife, Margaret of Provence took with them on their Crusade.

565 On the trades of women during the Middle Ages, see: Régine Pernoud, *La femme au temps des cathédrales*, Stock, Paris, 1980, pp. 71–75, 202–207; Simone Roux, "Les femmes dans les métiers parisiens: xiiie-xve siècles," *Clio. Histoire, femmes et société*, 3, 1996, pp. 13–30. In the Byzantine world at the same period women are also to be found exercising various professions, often independently: agriculture, commerce, and crafts, but also in medicine as doctors and midwives. See Angeliki E. Laiou *loc. cit.*

566 See Régine Pernoud, *Pour en finir avec le Moyen Âge*, Seuil, 1977, pp. 86–100; *La femme au temps des cathédrales*, Stock, Paris, 1980.

567 Such as the confusion between difference and inequality.

568 This is the condition of most women today, something of which most feminists are unaware since they are journalists or teach in universities.

569 See the thoughts of Christopher Lasch on this subject: *Women and the common life. love, marriage, and feminism*, W. W. Norton & Company, New York, 1997; trad. fr. *Les Femmes et la vie ordinaire: Amour, mariage et féminisme*, Climats, Paris, 2006.

Chapter 13

570 They even justify prostitution and pornography, saying that a woman is free to dispose of her own body as she wishes. This is strange, since in both cases the woman's body is exploited for commercial profit as a pure object of pleasure for men.

571 The distinction between these two kinds of feminism is clearly described by Elisabeth Badinter, *Fausse route*, Hachette, Paris, 2003, chapter 3: "Contradiction."

572 *Le Monde* March 8, 2014.

573 *La théorie du genre ou Le monde rêvé des anges*, Grasset, Paris, 2014, pp. 113–115.

574 "La théorie du genre: ce nouveau puritanisme," *Le Point*, 2 novembre 2014 et *BibliObs*, 21 décembre 2014.

575 *An exact exposition of the Orthodox Faith*, IV, 20. Cf. II 12: 20.

576 *Homilies on Genesis*, XVIII, 4. Cf. *Treatise on virginity*, 14. The same teaching can be found in: Irenaeus of Lyon *Demonstration of the apostolic faith*, 14: 17; Gregory of Nyssa, *The creation of man*, XVII. *Cyril of Jerusalem*, Catechisms, *XII*, 5. Athanasius of Alexandria, *Commentary on Psalm 50*, 7. Diadachos of Photiki, *A Hundred gnostic chapters*, 56. John of Damascus, *An exact exposition of the Orthodox Faith*, II, 12:20, IV 20. Symeon the New Theologian, *Catechisms*, XXV, 92–108.

577 Cf. Origen, *Homilies on Genesis,* III, 6; *Homilies on the Song of Songs,* 2; *Treatise on prayer,* XXV, 3. Gregory of Nyssa, *Treatise on virginity,* XII, 4.

578 Cf. John Chrysostom, *Treatise on virginity,* 11–12. John of Damascus, *An exact exposition of the Orthodox Faith,* IV 24. Gregory of Nyssa, *Treatise on virginity,* II, 3; IV, 8. Basil of Ankyra, *Treatise on virginity,* 51. Basil of Caesarea, *Letters,* XLVI, 2; *Vie de sainte Macrine,* 11; 12; 15, SC 178, pp. 179–181, 184, 192. Voir l'étude de Frank Suso, Ἀγγελικὸς βίος. Begriffnalytische und Begriffsgeschichtlische Untersuchung zum "Engelgleichen Leben" im frühen Mönchtum, Münster, 1964.

579 *Discourses,* XXXVII, 11.

580 Origen, *Fragments on the epistle to the Romans,* 29.

581 *Treatise on virginity,* 4.

582 Cf. Ibid. 1; 8.

583 Ibid., 8.

584 *Treatise against second marriages,* II, 3.

585 *Of holy virginity,* 56.

586 John Chryssavgis, *In the heart of the desert. The spirituality of the Desert Fathers and Mothers,* World Wisdom Books, Bloomington (Indiana), 2005, p. 90.

Chapter 14

587 Voir Henri Crouzel, *Mariage et virginité chez Origène,* Paris et Bruges, 1963, pp. 135–139. Karl Vogt, "Devenir mâle: aspects d'une anthropologie chrétienne primitive," *Concilium,* 202, 1985, pp. 95–107. Sylviane Agacinskii, *Métaphysique des sexes. Masculin/Féminin aux sources du christianisme,* Seuil, Paris, 2005, pp. 143–153. Nathalie Delierneux, "Virilité physique et sainteté féminine dans l'hagiographie orientale du ive au viie siècle," *Byzantion,* 67, 1997, pp. 179–243. Raphaëlle Ziade, *Les martyrs Maccabées: de l'histoire juive au culte chrétien. Les homélies de Grégoire de Nazianze et Jean Chrysostome,* Brill, Leiden, 2007, pp. 246–253. Sophie Malick-Prunier, "Le corps féminin et ses représentations poétiques dans la latinité tardive," Dissertation, Université de Paris IV-Sorbonne, 2008, pp. 160–164.

588 One of the most radical and extensive criticisms of female adornment is in the work Tertullian, *The adornment of women.* See also Clement of Alexandria, *Le Pédagogue,* III, 1–2. John Chrysostom, *Homilies on the word of the Prophet David: "Fear not…" (Ps 48:7)* and *On,* Hospitality, I, 5–6; *Commentary on St Matthew,* XXX, 5–6; *Commentary on the epistle to the Colossians,* X, 5; *Commentary on the first epistle to Timothy,* V, 3; *Commentary on St John,* LXI, 4. See also Gregory the

Theologian, *Poems,* I, II, 29; *Discourses,* VIII, 10. St Peter taught inner adornment rather than external adornment (1 Pet 3:5–6). And the Fathers emphasized that true beauty is inward and rather than outward. It is an expression of the image of God, which make-up and other devices blur and hide.

589 *La virginité,* XLVII, 1, SC 125, pp. 262–263.

590 *Homily on the martyrdom of Julitta,* PG. 37, 237B.

591 *Discourses,* XV, PG 35, 916.

592 *Lausaic history,* 41.

593 *Vie de sainte Mélanie,* SC 90, p. 203.

594 *Apophtegmes,* alphabetical collection, Sarra 4.

595 *Apophtegmes,* alphabetical collection, Sarra Supplement 1.

596 *Histoire des moines de Syrie,* XXIX, "Marana et Cyra," 1, SC 257, p. 232.

597 See Alain Corbin, Jean-Jacques Courntine et Georges Vigarello (dir.), *Histoire de la virilité,* 3 vol., Seuil, Paris, 2011.

598 This is clear from St Gregory of Nyssa's description of how his mother was supported by his sister, Macrina, after the accidental death of her son, Naucratios: "By her strong and unshakeable attitude she was a teacher of courage to the soul of my mother. So, my mother was not overcome with grief. Nor did she give way to anything unworthy or feminine such as railing against evil, tearing her clothes, bemoaning her sorrow or intoning odes of mourning and chants with groans" (*Vie de sainte Macrine,* 10, SC 178, p. 173). See also 4 Macc 14:11 where it is said: "The intelligence of a woman despised the most varied torments."

599 Rome, 1980, p. 25 s. Sophie Malick Prunier, "Le corps féminin et ses représentations poétiques dans la latinité tardive," Dissertation, Université de Paris IV—Sorbonne, 2008, p. 160. *Passion de Perpétue et Félicité,* X, 7. *Homily on the martyrdom of St Julittae,* PG 31, 240D–241A. He uses here the word *aner* (εἰς ἄνδρα τέλειον, εἰς μέτρον ἡλικίας τοῦ πληρώματος τοῦ Χριστοῦ), but in a sense which clearly corresponds to *Anthropos,* a term used in Eph 4:24 to signify "the new man which was created according to God." See, for example, St John Chrysostom who remarks that some women "reach, as far as that is possible, the impassibility of angels" (*De studio praesentium* 5, PG 63, 488).

600 It has been noticed that the expression *militia Christi* is close to the expression *mulier virilis,* just as for *mulier virilis* the metaphor of combat unites martyrdom and ascesis. See Elena Giannarelli, *La tipologia femminile nella biografia e nell'autobiografia cristiana del 4. secolo,* Istituto storico italiano per il Medio Evo, Rome, 1980, p. 25 s. Sophie Malick Prunier, "Le corps féminin et ses

représentations poétiques dans la latinité tardive," Dissertation, Université de Paris IV-Sorbonne, 2008, p. 160.

601 *Passion de Perpétue et Félicité*, X, 7.

602 *Homily on the martyrdom of St Julitta,* PG 31, 240D–241A.

603 He uses here the word *aner* (εἰς ἄνδρα τέλειον, εἰς μέτρον ἡλικίας τοῦ πληρώματος τοῦ Χριστοῦ), but in a sense which clearly corresponds to *Anthropos,* a term used in Eph 4:24 to signify "the new man which was created according to God."

604 *On the epistle to the Ephesians,* V, 28, PL 26, 533.

605 John Chrysostom, *De studio praesentum* 5, PG 63, 488.

606 "Playing the Man—the Courage of Christian Martyrs, Translated and Transposed," in R. N. Swanson (ed.), *Gender and Christian Religion,* The Boydell Press, Suffolk, 1998, pp. 1–11. See also Elena Martin, *Iconic women: Martyrdom and the female body in early Christianity,* Dissertation, University of Durham, 2006, pp. 14–97.

607 *Stromates,* VI, 12, 100, 3 SC 446, pp. 260–263.

608 *Discourse on salvation to a virgin,* 10.

609 John Chryssavgis, *In the heart of the desert. The spirituality of the Desert Fathers and Mothers,* World Wisdom Books, Bloomington (Indiana), 2005, p. 91.

610 *Vie de sainte Macrine,* 1, SC 178, p. 140.

611 *Vie de sainte Mélanie,* 39, SC 90, pp. 200–202.

612 In ancient usage, this word indicates the way of life.

613 The organizer of the contest.

614 *History of the monks of Syria, XXX,* 5, p. 246.

615 *The passion of Sts Perpetua and Felicity,* XV, 6.

616 *Letter of the Churches of Lyon and Vienne to the Churches of Asia and Phrygia,* 42.

617 *Sermon 280, for the feast of the holy Martyrs Perpetua and Felicity,* 1.

618 See Verna E. F. Harrison, "A gender reversal in Gregory of Nyssa's *First Homily on the Song of Songs," Studia Patristica,* 27, 1993, pp. 34–38.

619 "A gender reversal in Gregory of Nyssa's *First Homily on the Song of Songs," Studia Patristica,* 27, 1993, p. 38.

620 See Patrick Laurence, "La faiblesse féminine chez les Pères de l'Église," in B. Pouderon and V. Boudon-Millot (ed.) *Les Pères de l'Église face à la science médicale de leur temps,* Beauchesne, Paris, 2005, pp. 351–378.

621 See Myrrha Lot-Borodine, "Le mystère du "don des larmes" dans la spiritualité de l'Orient chrétien," *Supplément à La Vie spirituelle,* 1er septembre 1936, pp. 65–110. Piroska Nagy, *Le don des larmes au Moyen Age. Un instrument spirituel en quête d'institution (v[e]-xiiie siècle),* Albin Michel, Paris, 2000. Francis

Conte, "Кончаете правило, паки начах молитися Христу и богородице со слезами …" Les larmes dans la spiritualité russe," *Cahiers slaves*, 9, 2008, pp. 137–151.

622 See Isaac the Syrian, *Ascetical homilies*, 81.

623 *What rich man can be saved?* 37.

624 *Spiritual homilies* XLVI, 3.

Bibliography

FIRST PART

Gender Studies and Radical Feminism

Butler (Judith), *Gender Trouble and the Subversion of Identity*, Routledge, New York, 1991; trad. fr. *Trouble dans le genre*, 2e éd., La Découverte, Paris, 2006.

Id., *Bodies That Matter: On the Discursive Limits of " Sex,"* Routledge, New York, 1993; trad. fr. *Ces corps qui comptent: de la matérialité et des limites discursives du sexe*, Amsterdam, Paris, 2009.

Id., *Undoing Gender*, Routledge, 2004; trad. fr. *Défaire le genre*, 2e éd., Amsterdam, Paris, 2012.

Coffin (Alice), *Le Génie lesbien*, Grasset, Paris, 2020.

Delphy (Christine), *L'ennemi principal*, tome 1: Économie politique du patriarcat, Syllepse, Paris, 1998; *L'ennemi principal*, tome 2: *Penser le genre*, Syllepse, Paris, 2001.

Fassin (Éric), "Le genre aux États-Unis et en France," Agora débats/jeunesses, 41, 2006, pp. 12–21.

Id., Preface to Judith Butler, *Trouble dans le genre*, 2e éd., La Découverte, Paris, 2006.

Id., "L'empire du genre. L'histoire ambiguë d'un outil conceptuel," *L'homme. Miroirs transatlantiques*, 187–188, 2008, pp. 375–392.

Fassin (Éric) et Margron (Véronique), *Homme, femme, quelle différence?*, Salvator, Paris, 2011 (Position d'É. Fassin).

Fausto-Sterling (Anne), *Myths of Gender: Biological Theories about Women and Men*, Basic Books, New York, 1992.

Id., "The Five Sexes: Why Male and Female Are Not Enough," *The Sciences*, Avril-Mai 1993, pp. 20–24.

Id., "The Five Sexes, Revisited," *The Sciences*, vol. 40, n° 4, 2000, pp. 18–23.

Id., *Sexing the Body: Gender Politics and the Construction of Sexuality*, Basic Books, New York, 2000, trad. fr. *Corps en tous genres: la dualité des sexes à l'épreuve de la science*, Paris, La Découverte, 2012.

Id., *Sex/Gender: Biology in a Social World*, Routledge, New York, 2012

Id., *Les cinq sexes: Pourquoi mâle et femelle ne suffisent pas*, Payot, Paris, 2013.

Id., "Why Sex Is Not Binary," *The New York Times*, October 25, 2018.

Haraway (Donna), *Simians, Cyborgs and Women: The Reinvention of Nature*, Free Association Books, 1991; trad. fr. *Des singes, des cyborgs et des femmes*: La *réinvention de la nature*, Actes Sud, Arles, 2009.

Harmange (Pauline), *Moi les hommes, je les déteste*, Seuil, Paris, 2020.

Hoff Sommers (Christina), *Who Stole Feminism? How Women Have Betrayed Women*, Simon & Schuster, New York, 1965.

Id., *The War against Boys: How Misguided Policies Are Harming Our Young Men*, Simon & Schuster, New York, 2000.

Irene, *La terreur féministe: Petit éloge du féminisme extrémiste*, Divergences, Paris, 2022.

MacKinnon (Catharine A.), *Toward a Feminist Theory of the State*, Harvard University Press, Cambridge, 1989

Id., *Feminism Unmodified: Discourses on Life and Law*, Harvard University Press, Cambridge, 1998.

Mazaurette (Maïa), "Comment peut-on être encore hétérosexuel?," *Le Monde*, 5 juin 2022.

Money (John), *Venuses Penuses. Sexology, Sexosophy and Exigence Theory*, Amherst, 1986.

Id., *Man & Woman, Boy & Girl: Gender Identity from Conception to Maturity*, Northvale, 1996.

Poo vey (Mary), "Feminism and Deconstruction," *Feminist Studies*, 14, 1988, pp. 51–65.

Rich (Adrienne), *Compulsory Heterosexuality and Lesbian Existence*, Antelope Publications, Trumansburg, NY, 1980.

Id., "La contrainte à l'hétérosexualité et l'existence lesbienne," *Nouvelles questions féministes*, 1, 1981, pp. 15–43.

Solanas (Valeria) [éd.], *SCUM Manifesto*, Olympia Press, New York, 1968.

Stoller (Robert), *Sex and Gender I: On the Development of Masculinity and Femininity*, New York City, 1968.

Id., *Sex and Gender II: The Transsexual Experiment*, London, 1968; trad fr. *Recherches sur l'identité sexuelle à partir du transsexualisme*, Paris, 1978.

Wittig (Monique), "On ne naît pas femme," *Questions féministes*, 8, mai 1980, pp. 75–84.

Critical Works

Id., *The Straight Mind*, Beacon Press, Boston (MA), 1992; trad. fr. *La Pensée straight*, Balland, Paris, 2001.

Agacinski (Sylviane), *Politique des sexes*, Seuil, Paris, 1998.

Id., "L'homoparentalité en question," *Le Monde*, 21 juin 2007.

Id., *Femmes entre sexe et genre*, Paris, Seuil, 2012.

Id., "Métamorphose de la différence sexuelle." Conférence donnée au cours de la session 2012 des Semaines sociales de France "Hommes et femmes, la nouvelle donne."

Id., *L'homme désincarné*, Gallimard, Paris, 2019.

Anatrella (Tony), *La différence interdite*, Flammarion, Paris, 1998.

Id., *Le Règne de Narcisse*, Presses de la Renaissance, Paris, 2005

Id., *La Tentation de Capoue*, éditions Cujas, 2008

Id., *Gender, la controverse*, éditions Pierre Téqui, Paris, 2011

Id., "*Gender*: les origines et les enjeux," dans Geffroy (Christophe) et Arduin (Pierre-Olivier) [éd.], *L'imposture du gender*, La Nef, Paris, 2011, pp. 11–23.

Id., *Mariage en tous genre. Chronique d'une régression culturelle annoncée*, L'échelle de Jacob, 2014.

Anatrella (Tony), Aumonier (Nicolas), Brague (Rémi), Balmary (Marie), *Homme et femme, Il les créa*, François-Xavier de Guibert, Paris, 2008.

Anderson (Ryan T.), *When Harry Became Sally*, Encounter Books, New York, 2018.

Arduin (Pierre-Olivier), "La science invalide la théorie du *gender*," on line on the site libertépolitique.com, 2011

Id., "Le mépris du corps sexué," dans Geffroy (Christophe) et (Arduin Pierre-Olivier) [éd.], *L'imposture du gender*, La Nef, Paris, 2011, pp. 35–39.

Id., "Le *gender* à Sciences-Po," dans Geffroy (Christophe) et Arduin (Pierre-Olivier) [éd.], *L'imposture du gender*, La Nef, Paris, 2011, pp. 51–54.

Id., "Le lycée frappé par le *gender*," dans Geffroy (Christophe) et Arduin (Pierre-Olivier) [éd.], *L'imposture du gender*, La Nef, Paris, 2011, pp. 55–62.

Arènes (Jacques), "La problématique du 'genre'," *Documents Épiscopat*, 12, 2006, pp. 1–18.

Arrighi (Pauline), *Les ravages du genre*, Cerf, Paris, 2023.

Badinter (Elisabeth), *Fausse route: Réflexions sur 30 années de féminisme* Paris, Odile Jacob, 2003.

Id., *L'un est l'autre: Des relations entre hommes et femmes*, Paris, Odile Jacob, 2004.

Bastié (Eugénie), *Adieu Mademoiselle. La défaite des femmes*, Éditions du Cerf, Paris, 2016.

Id., *Sauver la différence des sexes*, Gallimard, Paris, 2023.

Benglia (Jean-Paul), *La théorie du genre: Un délire philosophique imposé aux enfants et adolescents!*, Tatamis Editions, Blois, 2015.

Benoist (Alain de), *Les démons du bien. Du nouvel ordre moral à la théorie du genre*, Pierre Guillaume de Roux, Paris, 2013.

Id., *Non à la théorie du genre!*, Mordicus, 2014.

Berger (Anne-Emmanuelle), Le *grand théâtre du genre: identités, sexualités et féminisme en Amérique*, Belin, Paris, 2013; trad. angl. *The Queer Turn in Feminism: Identities, Sexualities, and the Theater of Gender*, Fordham University Press, New York, 2014.

Bergeret (Jean), *L'érotisme narcissique. Homosexualité et homoérotisme*, Dunod, Paris, 1999.

Bernos (Marcel), Fouquet (Catherine) et Knibiehler (Yvonne), Recension de E. Badinter, *L'amour en plus*, dans la *Revue d'Histoire Moderne et Contemporaine*, 28–1, 1981, pp. 207–209.

Bourges (Beatrice), Mirkovic (Aude), Montfort (Elisabeth), *De la théorie du genre au mariage de même sexe …*, Peuple Libre, Valence, 2013.

Braunstein (Jean-François), *La philosophie devenue folle: Le genre, l'animal, la mort*, Paris, Grasset, 2018.

Id., *La religion woke*, Grasset, Paris, 2022.

Chaouat (Bruno), *L'homme trans. Variations sur un préfixe*, Léo Scheer, Paris, 2019.

Chiland (Colette), *Changer de sexe: illusion et réalité*, Odile Jacob, Paris, 2011.

Clozel (Claire-Marie), *Pourquoi les petits garçons ne sont pas des petites filles …: Un secret bien gardé*, Tryptique, Montréal, 2007.

Colapinto (John), *As Nature Made Him: The Boy Who Was Raised as a Girl*, Harper Perennial, New York, 2001.

De Benoist (Alain), *Les démons du bien*, Paris, 2013, chapitre intitulé "L'idéologie du genre."

Eliacheff (Caroline) et Masson (Céline), *La fabrique de l'enfant transgenre*, L'Observatoire, Paris, 2022.

Fahs (Breanne) et Karger (Michael), " Women's Studies as Virus: Institutional Feminism and the Projection of Danger," *GÉNEROS—Multidisciplinary Journal of Gender Studies*, vol. 5, n° 1, 2016, pp. 929–957

Flavigny (Christian), *La querelle du genre. Faut-il enseigner le "gender" au lycée?*, Presses Universitaire de France, Paris, 2012.

Id., *"Aider les enfants transgenre": contre l'américanisation des soins*, Pierre Téqui, Paris, 2021.

Id., *Aider les enfants "transgenre,"* Pierre Téqui, Paris, 2021.

Geffroy (Christophe), "L'imposture du *gender*," dans Geffroy (Christophe) et Arduin (Pierre-Olivier) [éd.], *L'imposture du gender*, La Nef, Paris, 2011, pp. 5–9.

Geffroy (Christophe) et Arduin (Pierre-Olivier) [éd.], *L'imposture du gender*, La Nef, Paris, 2011.

Godefridi (Drieu), *La loi du genre*, Les Belles Lettres, Paris, 2015.

Habib (Claude), *La question trans*, Gallimard, Paris, 2021.

Halioua (Noémie), *La terreur jusque sous nos draps*, Plon, Paris, 2024.

Hamon (Clotilde), "Les psys contre le gender," *Famille chrétienne*, 1757, 2011.

Hargot (Thérèse), *Qu'est-ce qui pourrait sauver l'amour?*, Albin Michel, Paris, 2020.

Heinich (Nathalie), *Le wokisme serait-il un totalitarisme?*, Albin Michel, Paris, 2023.

Hoff-Sommers (Chrstina), *Who Stole Feminism How Women Have Betrayed Women*, New York and London, 1994.

Id., *The War against Boys. How Misguided Policies Are Harming Our Young Men*, Simon & Schuster, New York and London, 2015.

Joel (Daphna) et Viknaski (Luba), *Le cerveau a-t-il un sexe?*, Albin Michel, Paris, 2020.

Joyce (Helen), *Trans: When Ideology Meets Reality*, Oneworld Publications, London, 2022; trad. fr.: *Trans: Quand l'idéologie rencontre la réalité*, M éditeur, Montréal, 2022.

Julia (Dominique), Recension de E. Badinter, *L'amour en plus*, dans *Histoire de l'éducation*, 9, 1980, pp. 46–52.

Lacroix (Xavier), *La confusion des genres. Réponses à certaines demandes homosexuelles sur le mariage et l'adoption*, Bayard, Paris, 2005.

Lanez (Émile), "L'expérience tragique du gourou de 'la théorie du genre'," *Le Point*, du 31 janvier 2014.

Lasch (Christopher), *Women and the Common Life. Love, Marriage, and Feminism*, W. W. Norton & Company, New York, 1997; trad. fr. *Les Femmes et la vie ordinaire: Amour, mariage et fémnisme*, Climats, Paris, 2006.

Levet (Bérénice), *La théorie du genre ou Le monde rêvé des anges: L'identité sexuée comme malédiction*, Éditions Grasset & Fasquelle, Paris, 2014.

Id., *Libérons-nous du féminisme*, Éditions de l'Observatoire, Paris, 2018.

Id., "Pourquoi le féminisme n'est aujourd'hui plus une question de femmes, mais celle de l'imposition d'un nouveau modèle de société," *Atlantico*, septembre 16, 2018.

Masson (Céline) et al., "Changement de sexe chez les enfants: 'Nous ne pouvons plus nous taire face à une grave dérive'. Une cinquantaine de psys, médecins et intellectuels dénoncent une 'emprise idéologique sur le corps des enfants' faite au nom de l'émancipation de 'l'enfant-transgenre'," *L'Express* du 20 septembre 2021.

Mialet (Jean-Paul), *Sex æquo*, Albin Michel, Paris, 2011.

Montfort (Élizabeth), *Le genre démasqué: homme ou femme? Le choix impossible*, Peuple Libre, Valence, 2011.

Id., "Le tournant de Pékin," dans Geffroy (Christophe) et Arduin (Pierre-Olivier) [éd.], *L'imposture du gender*, La Nef, Paris, 2011, pp. 31–34.

Paoli (François), *La tyrannie de la faiblesse. La féminisation du monde ou l'éclipse du guerrier*, Françoise Bourin, Paris, 2010.

Peeters (Marguerite), *Le Gender, une norme mondiale? Pour un discernement*, Mame, Paris, 2013.

Perez (Sylvie), *En finir avec le wokisme*, Cerf, Paris, 2023.

Pivet (Esther), *Enquête sur la théorie du genre*, Artège, Paris, 2019.

Pluckrose (Helen) et Lindsay (James), *Cynical Theories: How Activist Scholarship Made Everything about Race, Gender, and Identity – And Why This Harms Everybody*, Pitchstone Publishing, Durham (NC), 2020; trad. fr. *Le triomphe des impostures intellectuelles: comment les théories sur l'identité, la race, le genre gangrènent l'université et nuisent à la société*, H&o, Béziers, 2021.

Pouliquen (Tanguy-Marie), *Consentir à la différence sexuelle: Théorie du genre, homosexualité, mariage pour tous, autosuffisance de la conscience comme fermetures à l'altérité*, Parole et Silence, Plans-sur-Bex, 2015.

Prokhoris (Sabine), *Le Mirage #MeToo. Réflexions à partir du cas français*, Cherche-midi, Paris, 2021.

Puppinck (Grégor), "Liberté, égalité, *gender*," dans Geffroy (Christophe) et Arduin (Pierre-Olivier) [éd.], *L'imposture du gender*, La Nef, Paris, 2011, pp. 45–49.

Quillon (Pauline), *Enquête sur la dysphorie de genre*, Mame, Paris, 2022.

Schneider (Michel), *La confusion des genres*, Flammarion, Paris, 2007.

Shrier (Abigail), *Dommages irréversibles. Comment le phénomène transgenre séduit les adolescents*, Cherche Midi, Paris, 2022.

Stock (Kathleen), *Material Girls: Why Reality Matters for Feminism*, Little, Brown and Company, Boston, 2021.

Szasz (Thomas), "Male and Female Created He Them," *The New York Times*, June 10, 1979.

Todd (Emmanuel), *Où en sont-elles? Une esquisse de l'histoire des femmes*, Seuil, Paris, 2022.

Valentin (Pierre), *L'idéologie woke*, vol. 1 et 2, Fondapol, Paris, 2021.

Id., *Comprendre la révolution woke*, Gallimard, Paris, 2023.

Vaquin (Monette) et Winter (Jean-Pierre), "Non à un monde sans sexes," *Le Monde*, December 4, 2012.

Verlinde (Jean-Marie), *L'idéologie du gender. Identité reçue ou choisie?*, Livre ouvert, Mesnil-Saint-Loup, 2012.

Vial (Olivier), *Détrans. Les Cassandre de la communauté trans*, CERU, Paris, 2021.

Vlahos (Michel), "Church of Woke: The Next American Religion?," *Humanitas*, vol. 34, n°s 1–2, 2021, pp. 113–122.

Walsh (Matt), *What Is a Woman?: One Man's Journey to Answer the Question of a Generation*, DW Books, Nashville, 2022.

Winter (Jean-Pierre), *Homoparenté*, Albin Michel, Paris, 2010.

Scientific and Popular Studies

Alexander (Gerianne M.) et M. Hines (Melissa), "Sex Differences in Response to Children's Toys in Non-human Primates," *Evolution and Human Behaviour*, 2002, pp. 467–479.

Balthazart (Jacques), *Biologie de l'homosexualité*, Mardaga, Bruxelles, 2010.

Id., "Sex Differences in Partner Preferences in Human and Animals," *Philosophical Transactions of the Royal Society B: Biological Sciences*, vol. 371, n° 1688, 2016, pp. 1–11.

Id., *Quand le cerveau devient masculin*, humen Sciences, Paris, 2019; 2e éd. revue et augmentée sous le titre *On naît hétéro ou homosexuel, on ne choisit pas de l'être*, Mardaga, Bruxelles, 2021.

Baron-Cohen (Simon), *The Essential Difference. Men, Women and the Extreme Male Brain*, Allen Lane, London, 2003.

Becker (Jill B.) et al. (éd.) *Sex Differences in the Brain from Genes to Behavior*, Oxford University Press, Oxford, 2008.

Blaffer Hrdy (Sarah), *Les instincts maternels*, Payot, Genève, 2002.

Blum (Deborah), *Sex on the Brain. The Biological Differences between Men and Women*, Penguin Books, New York, 1998.

Bornstein (Marc H.) et al., "Neurobiology of Culturally Common Maternal Responses to Infant Cry," *Proceedings of the National Academy of Sciences*, 2017.

Brizendine (Louann), *The Female Brain*, Broadway Books, New York, 2006; trad. fr. *Les Secrets du cerveau féminin*, Grasset, Paris, 2006.

Id., *The Male Brain*, Broadway Books, New York, 2010.

Chiras (Daniel D.), *Human Biology*, Jones & Bartlett Learning, Burlington (MA), 2012.

Ciofi (Philippe), "La différenciation sexuelle du cerveau: une synthèse récente," *Métabolismes Hormones Diabètes et Nutrition*, vol. 12, n° 6, 2008, pp. 199–204.

Connellana (Jennifer) et al., " Sex Differences in Human Neonatal Social Perception," *Infant Behavior & Development*, 23, 2000, pp. 113–118.

Einstein (Gillian) [éd.], *Sex and the Brain*, The MIT Press, Cambridge (MA) and London, 2007.

Eliot (Lise), *Pink Brain, Blue Brain*, Houghton Mifflin Harcourt, Boston (MA), and New York, 2009; trad. fr. *Cerveau bleu, cerveau rose. Les neurones ont-ils un sexe?*, Robert Laffont, Paris, 2011.

Ellis (Lee) et al., *Sex Differences. Summarizing More Than a Century of Scientific Research*, Psychology Press, New York, 2008.

Else-Quest (Nicole M.), Hyde (Janet Shibley) et Clark (Roseanne), "Breastfeeding, Bonding, and the Mother-Infant Relationship," *Merrill-Palmer Quarterly*, vol. 49, n° 4, 2003, pp. 495–517

Geary (David C.), *Male, Female. The Evolution of Human Sex Differences*, 3ᵉ éd., American Psychological Association, Washington, 2021.

Halpern (Diane F.), *Sex Differences in Cognitive Abilities*, 3ᵉ éd., Lawrence Erlbaum, Mahwah, 2009.

Hines (Melissa), *Brain Gender*, Oxford University Press, Oxford, 2004.

Ingalhalikar (Madhura) et al., "Sex Differences in the Structural Connectome of the Human Brain," Proceedings of the National Academy of Sciences, vol. 111, January 2014, pp. 823–828.

Kimura (Dorin), *Sex and Cognition*, MIT Press, Harvard, 2000; trad. fr. *Cerveau d'homme et cerveau de femme*, Odile Jacob, Paris, 2001.

Kinsley (Craig) et Lambert (Kelly), "L'instinct maternel niché dans le cerveau," *Pour la science*, 340, 2006.

Macmillan (Bonnie), *Why Boys Are Different*, Hamlyn, London, 2004; trad. fr. *Pourquoi les garçons sont différents*, Hachette, Paris, 2005.

Meynard (Jean-Albert), *Le sexe du cerveau. Hommes/femmes: les vraies différences*, L'Archipel, Paris, 2011.

Mialet (Jean-Paul), *Sex aequo. Le quiproquo des sexes*, Albin Michel, Paris, 2011.

Mirkovic (Aude) et de Gattalier (Claire), *Questionnements de genre chez les enfants et les adolescents*, Artège, Paris, 2022.

Odent (Michel), *L'amour scientifié*, Jouvence, Genève, 2001.

Pease (Allan et Barbara), *Pourquoi les hommes n'écoutent jamais rien et les femmes ne savent pas lire les cartes routières*, First, Paris, 1999 (ouvrage de vulgarisation).

Quillon (Pauline), *Enquête sur la dysphorie de genre*, Mame, Paris, 2022.

Scott (Niv), rigge (Matthias P), Yizhar (Ofer) et Kimchi (Tali), "A Sexually Dimorphic Hypothalamic Circuit Controls Maternal Care and Oxytocin Secretion," *Nature*, vol. 525, 2015, pp. 519–522.

Shrier (Abigail), *Irreversible Damage: The Transgender Craze Seducing Our Daughters*, Regnery Publishing, Washington, 2020; trad. fr.: *Dommages irréversibles. Comment le phénomène transgenre séduit les adolescents*, Cherche Midi, Paris, 2022.

Soh (Debra), *The End of Gender: Debunking the Myths about Sex and Identity in Our Society*, Threshold Editions, Simon & Schuster, New York, 2021.

Swaab (Dick Franz) et al., "Structural and Functional Sex Differences in the Human Hypothalamus," *Hormones and Behavior*, vol. 40, 2001, pp. 93–98.

Testard-Vaillant (Philippe), "Combien y a-t-il de sexes?," *CNRS LE JOURNAL*, 2 août 2016.

Wolpert (Lewis), *Why Can't a Woman Be More like a Man? The Evolution of Sex and Gender*, Faber & Faber, London, 2013.

SECOND PART

History

Alexandre (Monique), "De l'annonce du royaume à l'Église. Rôles, ministères, pouvoirs des femmes," dans G. Duby et M. Perrot, *Histoire des femmes*, t. 1, Plon, Paris, 1991, pp. 439–471.

Id., "La place des femmes dans le christianisme ancien. Bilan des études récentes," dans P. Delage (éd.), *Les Pères de l'Église et les femmes*, Actes du colloque de La Rochelle, 6–7 septembre 2003 "Histoire et culture," Rochefort, 2003, pp. 24–78.

Beaucamp (Joëlle), "La faiblesse féminine dans les textes postbyzantins," Cahiers du Centre Gustave Glotz, 5, 1994, pp. 199–220.

Brown (Peter), *Men, Women and Sexual Renunciation in Early Christianity*, Faber and Faber, London et Boston, 1988; trad. fr. *Le renoncement à la chair. Virginité, célibat et continence dans le christianisme primitif*, Gallimard, Paris, 1995.

Casey (Damien), "The Spiritual Valency of Gender in Byzantine Society," dans B. Neil et Lynda Garland (éd.), *Questions of Gender in Byzantine Society*, Farnham, 2013, pp. 167–181

Chryssavgis (John), "The Desert and Gender," dans Id., *In the Heart of the Desert. The Spirituality of the Desert Fathers and Mothers* World Wisdom Books, Bloomington (IN), 2005, ch. 15, pp. 89–91.

Clark (Elisabeth-Ann), *Ascetic Piety and Women's Faith: Essays on Late Ancient Christianity*, "Studies in Women and Religion" n° 20, The Edwin Mellon Press, Lewiston, 1986.

Clark (Gillian), *Women in Late Antiquity, Pagan and Christian Lifestyles*, Clarendon Press, Oxford, 1993.

Coakley (Sarah), "Questions of Gender in Byzantine Society," *Theology*, 16–1, 2000, pp. 61–73.

Id., *Powers and Submissioins: Spirituality, Philosophy and Gender (Challenges in Contemporary Theology)*, Wiley-Blackwell, Oxford, 2002, pp. 55–68.

Cobb (L. Stephanie), *Dying to Be Men: Gender and Language in Early Christian Martyr Texts*, Columbia University Press, New York, 2012.

Conway (Colleen M.), *Behold the Man. Jesus and Greco-Roman Masculinity*, Oxford University Press, Oxford, 2008.

Corbin (Alain), Courntine (Jean-Jacques) et Vigarello (Georges) [dir.], *Histoire de la virilité*, vol. 3, Seuil, Paris, 2011.

Cox Miller (Patricia), *Women in Early Christianity*, The Catholic University of America, Washington, 2005.

Delumeau (Jean) [dir.], *La religion de ma mère. Le rôle des femmes dans la transmission de la foi*, Cerf, Paris, 1992.

Dubesset (Mathilde), "Femmes et religions, entre soumission et espace pour s'exprimer et agir, un regard d'historienne," Communication au colloque "Les relations de genre dans le monde hispanique. Journée d'Études ILCEA/CERHIUS Université de Grenoble III 25 janvier 2008.

Duby (Georges) et Perrot (Michelle) (dir.), *Histoire des femmes en Occident*, vol. 5, Plon, Paris, 1991–1992.

Giannarelli (Elena), *La tipologia femminile nella biografia e nell'autobiografia cristiana del 4. secolo*, Istituto storico italiano per il Medio Evo, Rome, 1980.

Héritier (Françoise), Perrot (Michelle), Agacinski (Sylviane), et Bacharan (Nicole), *La plus belle histoire des femmes*, Seuil, Paris 2011.

Holum (Kenneth G.), *Theodosian Empresses: Women and Imperial Dominion in Late Antiquity*, University of California Press, Berkeley (CA), 1989, ch. III, pp. 5–6.

Houziaux (Alain), "L'idéal de chasteté dans les débuts du christianisme, pourquoi?," *L'esprit du temps*, 2008–4, pp. 17–45.

James (Liz), *Women, Men and Eunuchs. Gender in Byzantium*, Routledge, London and New York, 1997.

Jensen (Anne), *Gottes selbstbewusste Töchter. Selbstverständnis und Rolle der Frauen im frühen Christentum*, Herder, Fribourg-Bâme-Vienne, 1992.

Kraemer (Ross S.) et D'Angelo (Mary Rose) (éd.), *Women and Christian Origins*. Oxford University Press, New York, 1999.

Kroeger (Catherine), "The Neglected History of Women in the Early Church," *Christian History*, vol. 17, 1988.

Laiou (Angeliki E.), "The Role of Women in Byzantine Society," *Jahrbuch der Österreichischen Byzantinitik*, vol. 31, 1981, pp. 233–260.

Id., "Contribution à l'étude de l'institution familiale en Épire au xiiie siècle," *Fontes Minores (Forschungen zur byzantinischen Rechtsgeschichte)*, vol. 6, 1984, pp. 275–323.

Id., *Gender, Society, and Economic Life in Byzantium*, Ashgate, Hampshire, 1992.

Id., "Sex, Consent and Coercion in Byzantium," dans Angeliki E. Laiou (éd.), *Consent and Coercion to Sex and Marriage in Ancient and Medieval Societies*, Dumbarton Oaks, Washington (DC), 1993, pp. 109–221.

Lamy (Marielle) et Shimahara (Sumi), *Le pouvoir au féminin. Modèles et anti-modèles bibliques, du ive au xviie siècle*, Beauchesne, Paris, 2022.

Lebecq (Stéphane), Dierkens (Alain), Le Jean (Régine), Sansterre (Jean-Marie) (dir.), *Femmes et pouvoirs des femmes à Byzance et en Occident* (vi[e]-xe siècles), Publications de l'Institut de recherches historiques du Septentrion, Lille, 2018.

Lett (Didier), *Hommes et femmes au Moyen-Âge. Histoire du genre xiie-xve s.*, Armand Colin, Paris, 2013.

L'Hermite-Leclercq (Paulette), *L'Église et les femmes dans l'Occident chrétien des origines à la fin du Moyen Age*, Brepols, Turnhout, 1997.

Id., "Les femmes dans la vie religieuse au Moyen Âge. Un bref bilan bibliographique," *Clio. Histoire, femmes et sociétés*, vol. 8, 1998.

Lorenzato (Bernard) et Pety (Olivier), *Promenade au jardin des Mères de l'Église. Figures de femmes des premiers temps de l'Église - iie-ive siècle*, Mediaspaul, Paris, 2014.

Malick-Prunier (Sophie), "Le corps féminin et ses représentations poétiques dans la latinité tardive," Dissertation, Université de Paris IV - Sorbonne, 2008.

Id., *Le corps féminin dans la poésie latine tardive*, Les Belles Lettres, Paris, 2011 (version abrégée du précédent).

Masterson (Mark), Sorkin Rabinowitz (Nancy) and Robson (James) [éd.], *Sex in Antiquity. Exploring Gender and Sexuality in the Ancient World*, Routledge, London and New York, 2015.

Pargoire (Jules), "Les monastères doubles chez les Byzantins," Échos d'Orient, t. 9, n° 56, 1906, pp. 21–25.

Pelletier (Anne-Marie), *Le christianisme et les femmes. Vingt siècles d'histoire*, Cerf, Paris, 2001.

Penner (Todd C.) et Vander Stichele (Caroline) (éd.), *Mapping Gender in Ancient Religious Discourses*, Brill, Leiden, 2007.

Pernoud (Régine), *Pour en finir avec le Moyen Âge*, Seuil, Paris, 1977.

Id., *La femme au temps des cathédrales*, Stock, Paris, 1984.

Perrot (Michelle), *Mon histoire des femmes*, Seuil, Paris, 2008.

Riot-Sarcey (Michèle), *Histoire du féminisme*, La Découverte, Paris, 2002.

Schaus (Margaret) [éd.], *Women and Gender in Medieval Europe: An Encyclopedia*, Routledge, New York and London, 2006.

Siekel (Lou), "Masculin et féminin au haut Moyen-Âge," Mémoire de Master, Université de Poitiers, 2018.

Stewart (Eric), "Masculinity in the New Testament and Early Christianity," *Biblical Theology Bulletin*, 46, 2016, pp. 91–102.

Christian Anthropolgy

1. Bible and Apocrypha

Agacinski (Sylviane), *Métaphysique des sexes. Masculin/Féminin aux sources du christianisme*, Seuil, Paris, 2005.

Anderson (Janice Capel) et Moore (Stephen <unstruct>D.), "Matthew and Masculinity," dans in S. D. Moore et J. C. Anderson éd.), *New Testament Masculinities*, Society of Biblical Literature. Atlanta (GA), 2003, pp. 67–91.

Atlan (Gabrielle), "Le statut de la femme dans le judaïsme," *Société, droit et religion*, 4, 2014/1, pp. 33–46.

Bartchy (S. Scott), "'When I'm Weak, I'm Strong': A Pauline Paradox in Cultural Context," dans Christian Strecker (ed.), *Kontexte Der Schrift, Band I, Kultur, Politik, Religion, Sprache. Wolfgang Stegemann Zum 60. Geburtstag*, Kohlhammer, Stuttgart, 2005, pp. 49–60.

De Merode (Marie), "Une théologie primitive de la femme?," *Revue théologique de Louvain*, vol. 9, 1978. pp. 176–189.

Dubarle (André Marie), "Paul et l'antiféminisme," *Revue des Sciences Philosophiques et Théologiques*, vol. 60, 1976, pp. 261–280.

Feuillet (André), "La dignité et le rôle de la femme d'après quelques textes pauliniens: comparaison avec l'Ancien Testament," *New Testament Studies*, vol. 21, 1975, pp. 157–191.

Lambin (Rosine), "Paul et le voile des femmes," *Clio. Genre, femmes, histoire*, vol. 2, 1995, pp. 61–84.

Lemontzis (Archimandrite Theophilos), " Non-gender and One-gender in the Gnostic Gospels," *Pemptousia*, mai 12, 2018.

Long (Didier), *Jésus, l'homme qui aimait les femmes*, François Bourin, Paris, 2014.

Matzarioti-Kostara (Sophia), "The Theology of Gender," *Pemtousia*, 2017.

Mourlon Beernaert (Pierre), *Marthe, Marie et les autres*, Lumen Vitae, Bruxelles, 1992.

Payne (Philip B.), "Dans la Bible, l'homme et la femme ont le même statut," *Priscilla Papers*, January 30, 2015.

Pedotti (Christine), *Jésus, l'homme qui préférait les femmes*, Albin Michel, Paris, 2018.

Quéré (France), *Les femmes de l'Évangile*, Seuil, Paris, 1982.

Quesnel (Michel), *Paul et les femmes. Ce qu'il a écrit, ce qu'on lui a fait dire*, Mediaspaul, Paris, 2021.

Rais (Angéline), "Le regard de Paul de Tarse sur les femmes," Exposé au séminaire de sciences bibliques du Prof. Martin Rose, Université de Neuchâtel, août 2009.

Reynier (Chantal), *Les femmes de saint Paul*, Éditions du Cerf, Paris, 2020.

Schüssler Forenza (Elisabeth), *In Memory of Her: A Feminist Theological Reconstruction of Christian Origins*, The Crossroad Publishing Company, New York, 1994; trad. fr. *En mémoire d'elle. Essai de reconstruction des origines chrétiennes selon la théologie féministe*, Cerf, Paris, 1986.

Stewart (Eric), "Masculinity in the New Testament and Early Christianity," *Biblical Theology Bulletin*, vol. 46, 2016, pp. 91–102.

Van Cangh (Jean-Marie), "La femme dans l'Évangile de Luc. Comparaison des passages narratifs propres à Luc avec la situation de la femme dans le judaïsme," *Revue théologique de Louvain*, vol. 24, 1993, pp. 297–324.

2. Fathers and Mothers of the Church

Alexandre (Jérôme), *L'anthropologie réaliste et mystique de Tertullien*, Beauchesne, Paris, 2001.

Id., "Tertullien et la différence sexuelle," dans P. Delage (éd.), *Les Pères de l'Église et les femmes. Actes du colloque de La Rochelle, 6 et 7 septembre 2003* "Histoire et culture," Rochefort, 2003, pp. 79–99.

Alexandre (Monique), "De l'annonce du Royaume à l'Église. Rôles, ministères, pouvoirs des femmes," dans G. Duby et M. Perrot (dir.), *Histoire des femmes en Occident*, t. 1, Plon, Paris, pp. 439–471.

Aspegren (Kerstin), *The Male Woman: A Feminine Ideal in the Early Church*, René Kieffer, Uppsala, 1990.

Bady (Guillaume) et Mellerin (Laurence), "À l'image de Dieu … homme et femme. Regards patristiques sur la différence des sexes," *Connaissance des Pères de l'Église*, 130, 2013, pp. 31–42.

Barker (Katherine Helen), "The Perception of Women in Late Antiquity and the Impact It Had on Female Asceticism," Dissertation, University of Wales Trinity Saint David, 2014.

Baschet (Jérôme), "Distinction des sexes et dualité de la personne dans les conceptions anthropologiques de l'Occident médiéval," dans Irène Théry et Pascale Bonnemère (dir.), *Ce que le genre fait aux personnes*, Éditions de l'EHESS, Paris, 2008, pp. 175–195.

Behr (John), "The Rational Animal: A Rereading of Gregory of Nyssa's 'De hominis opificio'," *Journal of Early Christian Studies*, vol. 7, 1999, pp. 219–247.

Boersma (Hans), *Embodiment and Virtue in Gregory of Nyssa. An Analogical Approach*, Oxford University Press, Oxford, 2013.

Id., "Putting on Clothes: Body, Sex, and Gender in Gregory of Nyssa," *Crux*, vol. 54, n° 2, 2018, pp. 27–34.

Bonnard (Jean-Baptiste), Doherty (Lillian E.) et Sebillotte Cuchet (Violaine), "Male and Female Bodies according to Ancient Greek Physicians," *Clio. Women, Gender, History*, vol. 37, 2013, pp. 19–37.

Børresen (Kari Elisabeth), "In defense of Augustine: How *femina is homo*?," dans B. Bruning, M. Lamberrigts, J. van Houtem (éd.), *Collectanea augustiniana, Mélanges T. J. van Bavel*, Peters, Louvain, 1990, pp. 411–428.

Id., *Subordination et Equivalence. Nature et rôle de la femme d'après Augustin et Thomas d'Aquin*, KOK Pharos, Kampen, 1995.

Broc-Schmezer (Catherine), *Les figures féminines du Nouveau Testament dans l'œuvre de Jean Chrysostome. Exégèse et pastorale*, Brepols, Turnhout, 2010.

Broudehoux (Jean-Paul), *Mariage et famille chez Clément d'Alexandrie*, Beauchesne, Paris, 1970.

Camelot (Thomas), "Les Traités "De Virginitate" au ive siècle," dans *Mystique et continence*, Études carmélitaines, vol. 13, 1952, p. 279.

Carpinello (Mariella), *Données à Dieu. Figures féminines dans les premiers siècles chrétiens*, Éditions de Bellefontaine, Bégrolles-en-Mauges, 2001.

Casey (Damien), " Maximus and Irigaray: Metaphysics and Difference," dans W. Mayer, P. Allen et L. Cross (éd.), *Prayer and Spirituality in the Early Church*, Sidney, 2006, pp. 189–198.

Chitty (Derwas J.), *Et le désert devint une cité*, Éd. de Bellefontaine, Bégrolles-en-Mauges, 1980.

Chryssavgis (John), *In the Heart of the Desert. The Spirituality of the Desert Fathers and Mothers*, World Wisdom Books, Bloomington (IN), 2005.

Clark (Elisabeth-Ann), *Women in the Early Church*, Liturgical Press, Collegeville, Minn., 1990 (recueil de textes).

Coakley (Sarah), "The Eschatological Body: Gender, Transformation and God," *Modern Theology*, vol. 16, 2000, pp. 61–73.

Cohick (Lynn H.) et Brown Hughes (Amy), *Christian Women in the Patristic World*, Baker Academic, Grand Rapids, 2017.

Cooper (A. G.), *The Body in St Maximus the Confessor. Holy Flesh, Wholly Deified*, Oxford, 2005, pp. 208–227.

Id., "St Maximus on the Mystery of Marriage and the Body: a Reconsideration," dans Maksim Vasiljević (éd.), *"Knowing the Purpose of Creation through the Power of the Resurrection." Proceedings of the Symposium on St Maximus the Confessor, Belgrade, October 18–21, 2012*, Alhambra (CA) and Belgrade, 2013, pp. 195–121.

Costache (Doru), "Living above Gender: Insights from St Maximus the Confessor," *Journal of Early Christian Studies*, 21, 2013, pp. 261–290.

Id., "Gender, Marriage and Holiness in *Amb.Io.* 10 and 41," dans W. Mayer et I. J. Elmer (éd.), *Men and Women in the Early Christian Centuries*, Strathfield, 2014, pp. 351–371.

Id, "Mapping Reality within the Experience of Holiness," dans Pauline Allen et Bronwen Neil (éd.), *The Oxford Handbook of Maximus the Confessor*, Oxford, 2015, pp. 378–396.

Crouzel (Henri), *Théologie de l'image de Dieu chez Origène*, Aubier, Paris, 1956, pp. 148–153: "Les deux créations de l'homme".

Cutino (Michelle), "La différenciation sexuelle et son accomplissement eschatologique chez Augustin," *Revue des Sciences Religieuses*, vol. 91, 2017, pp. 565–588.

D'Alverny (Marie-Thérèse), "Comment les théologiens et les philosophes voient la femme," *Cahiers de civilisation médiévale*, vol. 10, n°78–79, 1977, pp. 105–129.

Delage (Pascal) (éd.), *Les Pères de l'Église et les femmes. Actes du colloque de La Rochelle, 6 et 7 septembre 2003* "Histoire et culture," Rochefort, 2003.

Delierneux (Nathalie), "Virilité physique et sainteté féminine dans l'hagiographie orientale du ive au viie siècle," *Byzantion*, vol. 67, 1997, pp. 179–243.

Dellopoulos (Achilleas P.), "'Weibliche und männliche Vernunft'. Die Geschlechterdifferenzierung nach der Theologie von Cyrill von Alexandrien," *Teologia*, 4, 2012, pp. 90–107.

De Merode (Marie), "Une théologie primitive de la femme?," *Revue théologique de Louvain*, 9, 1978, pp. 176–189.

Dominick (Judy Wu), "How Some of the Early Church Fathers' Views on Women Affect Us Today," *Life Reconsidered*, online: February 12, 2020 (publication en ligne).

Do Vale (Fellipe), "Cappadocian or Augustinian? Adjudicating Debates on Gender in the Resurrection," *International Journal of Systematic Theology*, vol. 21–2, 2019, pp. 182–198.

Duclow (Donald F.), "The Sleep of Adam, the Making of Eve: Sin and Creation in Eriugena," dans Willemien Otten et Michael I. Allen (éd.), *Eriugena and Creation, Proceedings of the 11th International Conference on Eriugeni Studies, Chicago, 2–12 November 2011*, Turnhout, 2014, pp. 235–261.

Dula-Gravier (Aude-Sophie), "Différenciation sexuelle et anthropologie dans la pensée d'Ambroise de Milan," *Revue des Sciences Religieuses*, vol. 91–4, 2017, pp. 543–564.

Dumas (André), Introduction à *Le mariage dans l'Église ancienne*, Le Centurion et Grasset, Paris, 1969, pp. 10–17.

Dupriez (Flore), *La condition féminine et les Pères de l'Église latine*, Éditions Paulines, Montréal, et Apostolat des Éditions, Paris, 1982.

Faivre (Alexandre), "Dieu a-t-il créé la femme voilée? Du voile des vierges en particulier et de toutes les femmes en général: quelle histoire? ….," *Revue des Sciences Religieuses*, vol. 77, 2003, pp. 85–96.

Floeri (Fernand), "Le sens de la 'division des sexes' chez Grégoire de Nysse," *Revue des Sciences Religieuses*, vol. 27–2, 1953, pp. 105–111.

Gain (Benoît), "Saint Basile, misogyne?," dans P. Delage, *Les Pères de l'Église et les femmes. Actes du colloque de La Rochelle, 6 et 7 septembre 2003*, Histoire et Culture, Rochefort, 2003, pp. 277–294.

Galonnier (Alain), "Stercoris saccus: la représentation de la femme comme corps adjuvant et transgressif dans la pensée chrétienne à la basse Antiquité et au Moyen Âge," *HAL Archives ouvertes*, 2018 (en ligne), pp. 11–24.

Gautier (Francis), "Le dépassement des genres chez les Cappadociens et chez Grégoire de Nazianze en particulier. À propos de la *Métaphysique des sexes* de Sylviane Agacinski," *Revue d'études augustiniennes et patristiques*, vol. 55, 2009, pp. 113–139.

Giannarelli (Elena), *La tipologia femminile nella biografia* e *nell'autobiografia cristiana del 4. secolo*, Istituto storico italiano per il Medio Evo, Rome, 1980.

Gould (Graham), "Women in the Writings of the Fathers: Language, Belief, and Reality," *Studies in Church History*, vol. 27, 1990, pp. 1–13.

Harrison (Verna E. F.), "Male and Female in Cappadocian Theology," *Journal of Theological Studies*, vol. 4–2, 1990, pp. 441–471.

Id., "A Gender Reversal in Gregory of Nyssa's *First Homily on the Song of Songs*," *Studia Patristica*, vol. 27, 1993, pp. 34–38.

Id., "Women in the Philokalia?," dans B. Bingaman et B. Nassif (éd.), *The Philokalia. A Classic Text of Orthodox Spirituality*, Oxford et New York, 2012, pp. 252–261.

Hart (Mark D.), Marriage, Celibacy and the Life of Virtue: An Interpretation of Gregory of Nyssa's "De virginitate," Dissertation, Boston College, 1987.

Id., "Reconciliation of Body and Soul: Gregory of Nysa's Deeper Theology of Marriage," *Theological Studies*, vol. 51, 1990, pp. 450–478.

Id., "Gregory of Nyssa's Ironic Praise of the Celibate Life," *Heythrop Journal*, vol. 33, 1992, pp. 1–19.

Karras (Valerie A.), "A Re-evaluation of Marriage, Celibacy, and Irony in Gregory of Nyssa's On Virginity," *Journal of Early Christian Studies*, vol. 13–1, 2005, pp. 111–121.

Id., "Sex/Gender in Gregory of Nyssa's Eschatology: Irrelevant or Inexistent?," *Studia Patristica*, vol. 41, 2006, pp. 363–368.

Kochańczyk-Bonińska (Karolina), "The Philosophical Basis of Maximus' Concept of Sexes: The Reasons and Purposes of the Distinction between Man and Woman," dans Sotiris Mitralexis, Georgios Steiris, Marcin Podbileski et Sebastian Lalla, *Maximus the Confessor as a European Philosopher*, Eugene (OR), 2016, pp. 229–238.

Ladner (Gerhart B.), "The Philosophical Anthropology of St Gregory of Nyssa," *Dumbarton Oaks Papers*, vol. 12, 1954, pp. 59–94.

Lambin (Rosine), *Le voile des femmes: un inventaire historique, social et psychologique*, Peter Lang, Bern, 1999.

Lamirande (Émilien), "Tertullien misogyne? Pour une relecture du 'De cultu feminarum'," *Science et. Esprit*, vol. 39, 1987, pp. 5–25.

Lancel, "Augustin et la société féminine de son temps," dans S. Lancel, S. Guédon, L. Maurin, *Saint Augustin. La Numidie et la société de son temps*, Ausonius Éditions, Bordeaux, 2005, pp. 45–54.

Larchet (Jean-Claude), *Pour une éthique de la procréation*, Cerf, Paris 1998.

Id., *Variations sur la charité*, Cerf, Paris, 2007.

Id., *Thérapeutique des maladies spirituelles*, 6e éd., Cerf, Paris, 2013.

Laurence (Patrick), *Jérôme et le nouveau modèle féminin. La conversion à la vie parfaite*, Brepols, Turnhout, 1997.

Id., "La faiblesse féminine chez les Pères de l'Église," dans B. Pouderon et V. Boudon-Millot (éd.), *Les Pères de l'Église face à la science médicale de leur temps*, Beauchesne, Paris, 2005, pp. 351–378.

Legrand (Hervé), "Les femmes sont-elles à l'image de Dieu de la même manière que les hommes? Sondage dans les énoncés de quelques Pères grecs," *Nouvelle Revue Théologique*, 128, 2006, pp. 214–239.

Maloney (M.), " The Arguments for Women's Difference in Classical Philosophy and Early Christianty," dans Anne Carr et Elizabeth Schüssler Fiorenza, The Special Nature of Women?, SCM Press, London, 1991, pp. 41–49.

Martin (Elena), *Iconic Women: Martyrdom and the Female Body in Early Christianity*, Dissertation, University of Durham, 2006.

Mattioli (Umberto), Ἀσθένεια e Ἀνδρεία. Aspetti della femminilità nella letteratura classica, biblica e cristiana antica, Bulzoni, Rome, 1983.

Matzarioti-Kostara (Sophia), "The Theology of Gender," *Pemtousia*, 2017.

Milkov (K), "Maximus and the Healing of the Sexual, Division of Creation," dans Maksim Vasiljević (éd.), "*Knowing the Purpose of Creation Through the Power of the Resurrection." Proceedings of the Symposium on St Maximus the Confessor, Belgrade, October 18–21, 2012*, Alhambra (CA) et Belgrade, 2013, pp. 427–436.

Mitralexis (Sotiris), "Rethinking the Problem of Sexual Difference in Ambiguum 41," *Analogia*, vol. 2, n°1, 2017, pp. 139–144.

Moriarty (Rachel), "Playing the Man—the Courage of Christian Martyrs, Translated and Transposed," dans R. N. Swanson (éd.), Gender and Christian Religion, The Boydell Press, Suffolk and Rochester (NY), 1998, pp. 1–11.

Moulard (Anatole), *Saint Jean Chrysostome, le défenseur du mariage et l'apôtre de la virginité*, Gabalda, Paris, 1923.

Munier (Charles) "'Ianua' chez Tertullien," *Revue des Sciences Religieuses*, vol. 65, 1991, pp. 197–21.

Nausner (Michael), "Gregory's Nyssa Transgendering," *Theology & Sexuality*, vol. 16, 2002, pp. 55–65.

Noonan (John T.), *Contraception: A History of Its Treatment by Catholic Theologians and Canonists*, 2e éd., Cambridge, 1986, pp. 83–84.

Partridge (Cameron Elliott), *Transfiguring Sexual Difference in Maximus the Confessor*, Dissertation, Harvard, 2008.

Patlagean (Éveline), "Sur la limitation de la fécondité dans la haute époque byzantine," *Annales ESC*, vol. 24, 1969, pp. 1356–1357.

Prinzivalli (Emanuela), "Valeurs de la différenciation sexuelle chez Origène et dans sa tradition," *Revue des Sciences Religieuses*, vol. 91–4, 2017, pp. 507–523.

Quéré (France), "Le mariage dans l'Église ancienne," dans *Le mariage dans l'Église ancienne*, Le Centurion et Grasset, Paris, 1969, pp. 7–48.

Id., “Codes et mentalités des sociétés antiques,” *Croire aujourd’hui*, Octobre 1980, repris dans Id., *La femme et les Pères de l’Église*, Desclée de Brouwer, Paris, 1997, pp. 37–46.

Id., La *femme et les Pères de l’Église*, Desclée de Brouwer, Paris, 1997.

Radford Ruether (Rosemary). “Misogynism and Virginal Feminism in the Fathers of the Church,” dans Id. (éd.), *Religion and Sexism; Images of Woman in the Jewish and Christian Traditions*, Simon and Schuster, New York, 1974, pp. 150–183.

Ramatoulaye (Diagne), “Philosophie et représentation de la femme: la longévité du modèle aristotélicien,” dans: Fatou Sow (éd.), *La recherche féministe francophone. Langue, identités et enjeux*, Karthala, Paris, 2009, pp. 101–107.

Rambaux (Claude), “Le jugement de Tertullien sur les femmes,” *Vita Latina*, 122, 1991, pp. 2–20.

Reydams-Schils (Gretchen J.), “Clement of Alexandria on Woman and Marriage in the Light of the New Testament Household Codes,” dans D. E. Aune et F. E. Brenk (éd.), *Greco-Roman Culture and the New Testament Studies Commemorating the Centennial of the Pontifical Biblical Institute*, Brill, Leiden, 2012, pp. 113–133.

Rich (Bryce E.), “The Origin of Gender in Eriugena’s Periphyseon,” *Fides quaerens intellectus*, 17 novembre 2011.

Savon (Hervé), “Saint Ambroise et les femmes,” dans P. Delage, *Les Pères de l’Église et les femmes. Actes du colloque de La Rochelle, 6 et 7 septembre 2003* “Histoire et Culture,” Rochefort, 2003, pp. 262–276.

Skliris (Dionysios), “The Ontology of Mode in the Thought of Maximus the Confessor and Its Consequences for a Theory of Gender,” dans Sotiris Mitralexis (éd.), *Mustard Seeds in the Public Square*, Wilmington, 2017, pp. 50–59.

Smith (J. Warren), “Gender and Angelic Life in Gregory of Nyssa,” *Harvard Theological Review*, vol. 99–2, 2006, pp. 207–228.

Suso (Frank), Ἀγγελικὸς βίος. Begriffnalytische und Begriffsgeschichtlische Untersuchung zum “Engelgleichen Leben” im frühen Mönchtum, Münster, 1964.

Szczur (Przemyslaw), “Les objectifs du mariage chrétien chez Jean Chrysostome,” *Vox Patrum*, vol. 53, 2009, pp. 95–111.

Tazdaït (Fawzia), “L’idéal de virginité d’après les Pères de l’Église latine,” *L’Esprit du temps*, vol. 134, 2016, pp. 49–62.

Turcan (Marie), “Saint Jérôme et les femmes,” *Bulletin de l’Association Guillaume Budé*, 4e série, vol. 2–3, 1968, pp. 259–272.

Id., “Être femme selon Tertullien,” *Vita Latina*, vol. 119, 1990, pp. 15–21.

Van Sickle (Jakob N.), *The Meaning of “Male and Female” in St Maximus the Confessor*, Dissertation, Saint Louis University, 2017.

Vasiljević (Maksim), “A Prolegomenon on a Study of Gender,” *Philotheos*, vol. 11, 2011, pp. 261–269.

Vogt (Karl), “Devenir mâle: aspects d’une anthropologie chrétienne primitive,” *Concilium*, vol. 202, 1985, pp. 95–107.

Id., “’Becoming Male’: A Gnostic and Early Christian Metaphor,” dans K. E. Børresen (éd.), *Image of God and Gender Models in Judaeo-Christian Tradition*, Oslo, 1991, pp. 172–187.

Id., "'Becoming Male': a Gnostic, Early Christian and Islamic Metaphor," dans K. E. Børresen et K. Vogt (éd.), *Women's Studies of the Christian and Islamic Traditions*, Springer, New York, 1993, pp. 217–242.

Id., "The Desert Mothers: Female Asceticism in Egypt from the 4th to the 6th Century," dans K. E. Børresen et K. Vogt (éd.), *Women's Studies of the Christian and Islamic Traditions*, Springer, New York, 1993, pp. 193–216.

Wachowicz (Andrzej), "La notion de Parthenia chez Jean Chrysostome," *Revue d'éthique et de théologie morale*, vol. 244, 2007, pp. 9–30.

Wood (Hannelie), "Feminists and Their Perspectives on the Church Fathers' Beliefs regarding Women: An inquiry," *Verbum et Ecclesia*, vol. 38, 2017, pp. 1–10.

Ziadé (Raphaëlle), *Les martyrs Maccabées: de l'histoire juive au culte chrétien. Les homélies de Grégoire de Nazianze et Jean Chrysostome*, Brill, Leiden, 2007, pp. 246–253, "La virilité".

3. Canons of the Church

Matzarioti-Kostara (Sofia), *Gender Distinction and Canonical Tradition*, Dissertation, Holy Cross Greek Orthodox School of Theology, Brookline (MA), 2010, repris dans *The Theology of Gender*, Pemptousia, 2017.

Regule (Teva) "Canons of the Church and Women: A Tough Relationship." Communication au colloque international "Orthodox Canonical Tradition and contemporary challenges," Académie de Volos (Grèce), May 8–11, 2014.

Index

HOLY TRINITY PUBLICATIONS
JORDANVILLE, NEW YORK

PSJP PRINTSHOP OF SAINT JOB OF POCHAEV

HTSP HOLY TRINITY SEMINARY PRESS

The New Media Epidemic

The Undermining of Society, Family, and Our Own Soul

By Jean-Claude Larchet
Translated by Archibald Andrew Torrance

If we realize how gravely sick is our civilization, we may gain strength to resist. Philosopher and patrologist Dr Jean-Claude Larchet, renowned for his examinations of patristic writings on the causes and consequences of spiritual and physical illness, here tackles the pressing question of the societal and personal effects of our use of new media. His meticulous diagnosis concludes with a discussion of the ways individuals might limit and counteract the deleterious consequences of this new epidemic.

ISBN: 9780884654711

The Spiritual Roots of the Ecological Crisis

By Jean-Claude Larchet
Translated by Archibald Andrew Torrance

In this text, noted theologian and scholar Jean-Claude Larchet finds the roots of the global ecological crisis in a rejection of a truly Christian cosmology and proposes principles and actions deeply rooted in an Orthodox Christian ethos that would allow mankind to restore and reinvigorate its relationship with nature.

ISBN: 9780884654810